NON SANZ DROICT.

THE TRAGEDIE OF
MACBETH.

Decorative headband and title from the earliest publication of *Macbeth*, in the First Folio, 1623

William Shakespeare

The Tragedy of Macbeth

With New and Updated
Critical Essays
and a Revised Bibliography

Edited by Sylvan Barnet

THE SIGNET CLASSIC SHAKESPEARE
General Editor: Sylvan Barnet

A SIGNET CLASSIC

SIGNET CLASSIC
Published by New American Library, a division of
Penguin Group (USA) Inc., 375 Hudson Street,
New York, New York 10014, U.S.A.
Penguin Books Ltd, 80 Strand,
London WC2R 0RL, England
Penguin Books Australia Ltd, 250 Camberwell Road,
Camberwell, Victoria 3124, Australia
Penguin Books Canada Ltd, 10 Alcorn Avenue,
Toronto, Ontario, Canada M4V 3B2
Penguin Books (N.Z.) Ltd, Cnr Rosedale and Airborne Roads,
Albany, Auckland 1310, New Zealand

Penguin Books Ltd, Registered Offices:
80 Strand, London WC2R 0RL, England

Published by Signet Classic, an imprint of New American Library, a division of
Penguin Group (USA) Inc. The Signet Classic edition of *The Tragedy of Macbeth*
was first published in 1963, and an updated edition was published in 1986.

First Signet Classic Printing (Second Revised Edition), April 1998
40 39 38 37

Afterword copyright © Sylvan Barnet, 1963, 1986, 1987, 1998
All rights reserved

Library of Congress Catalog Card Number: 97-69248

Printed in the United States of America

Contents

Shakespeare: An Overview

Biographical Sketch

Between the record of his baptism in Stratford on 26 April 1564 and the record of his burial in Stratford on 25 April 1616, some forty official documents name Shakespeare, and many others name his parents, his children, and his grandchildren. Further, there are at least fifty literary references to him in the works of his contemporaries. More facts are known about William Shakespeare than about any other playwright of the period except Ben Jonson. The facts should, however, be distinguished from the legends. The latter, inevitably more engaging and better known, tell us that the Stratford boy killed a calf in high style, poached deer and rabbits, and was forced to flee to London, where he held horses outside a playhouse. These traditions are only traditions; they may be true, but no evidence supports them, and it is well to stick to the facts.

Mary Arden, the dramatist's mother, was the daughter of a substantial landowner; about 1557 she married John Shakespeare, a tanner, glove-maker, and trader in wool, grain, and other farm commodities. In 1557 John Shakespeare was a member of the council (the governing body of Stratford), in 1558 a constable of the borough, in 1561 one of the two town chamberlains, in 1565 an alderman (entitling him to the appellation of "Mr."), in 1568 high bailiff—the town's highest political office, equivalent to mayor. After 1577, for an unknown reason he drops out of local politics. What *is* known is that he had to mortgage his wife's property, and that he was involved in serious litigation.

The birthday of William Shakespeare, the third child and the eldest son of this locally prominent man, is unrecorded, but the Stratford parish register records that the infant was baptized on 26 April 1564. (It is quite possible that he was born on 23 April, but this date has probably been assigned by tradition because it is the date on which, fifty-two years later, he died, and perhaps because it is the feast day of St. George, patron saint of England.) The attendance records of the Stratford grammar school of the period are not extant, but it is reasonable to assume that the son of a prominent local official attended the free school—it had been established for the purpose of educating males precisely of his class—and received substantial training in Latin. The masters of the school from Shakespeare's seventh to fifteenth years held Oxford degrees; the Elizabethan curriculum excluded mathematics and the natural sciences but taught a good deal of Latin rhetoric, logic, and literature, including plays by Plautus, Terence, and Seneca.

On 27 November 1582 a marriage license was issued for the marriage of Shakespeare and Anne Hathaway, eight years his senior. The couple had a daughter, Susanna, in May 1583. Perhaps the marriage was necessary, but perhaps the couple had earlier engaged, in the presence of witnesses, in a formal "troth plight" which would render their children legitimate even if no further ceremony were performed. In February 1585, Anne Hathaway bore Shakespeare twins, Hamnet and Judith.

That Shakespeare was born is excellent; that he married and had children is pleasant; but that we know nothing about his departure from Stratford to London or about the beginning of his theatrical career is lamentable and must be admitted. We would gladly sacrifice details about his children's baptism for details about his earliest days in the theater. Perhaps the poaching episode is true (but it is first reported almost a century after Shakespeare's death), or perhaps he left Stratford to be a schoolmaster, as another tradition holds; perhaps he was moved (like Petruchio in *The Taming of the Shrew*) by

> Such wind as scatters young men through the world,
> To seek their fortunes farther than at home
> Where small experience grows.   (1.2.49–51)

In 1592, thanks to the cantankerousness of Robert Greene, we have our first reference, a snarling one, to Shakespeare as an actor and playwright. Greene, a graduate of St. John's College, Cambridge, had become a playwright and a pamphleteer in London, and in one of his pamphlets he warns three university-educated playwrights against an actor who has presumed to turn playwright:

> There is an upstart crow, beautified with our feathers, that with his *tiger's heart wrapped in a player's hide* supposes he is as well able to bombast out a blank verse as the best of you, and being an absolute Johannes-factotum [i.e., jack-of-all-trades] is in his own conceit the only Shake-scene in a country.

The reference to the player, as well as the allusion to Aesop's crow (who strutted in borrowed plumage, as an actor struts in fine words not his own), makes it clear that by this date Shakespeare had both acted and written. That Shakespeare is meant is indicated not only by *Shake-scene* but also by the parody of a line from one of Shakespeare's plays, *3 Henry VI*: "O, tiger's heart wrapped in a woman's hide" (1.4.137). If in 1592 Shakespeare was prominent enough to be attacked by an envious dramatist, he probably had served an apprenticeship in the theater for at least a few years.

In any case, although there are no extant references to Shakespeare between the record of the baptism of his twins in 1585 and Greene's hostile comment about "Shake-scene" in 1592, it is evident that during some of these "dark years" or "lost years" Shakespeare had acted and written. There are a number of subsequent references to him as an actor. Documents indicate that in 1598 he is a "principal comedian," in 1603 a "principal tragedian," in 1608 he is one of the "men players." (We do not have, however, any solid information about which roles he may have played; later traditions say he played Adam in *As You Like It* and the ghost in *Hamlet*, but nothing supports the assertions. Probably his role as dramatist came to supersede his role as actor.) The profession of actor was not for a gentleman, and it occasionally drew the scorn of university men like Greene who resented writing speeches for persons less educated than themselves, but it was respectable enough; players, if prosperous, were in effect members of the bourgeoisie, and there is nothing to suggest that Stratford considered William Shakespeare less than a solid citizen. When, in 1596, the Shakespeares were granted a coat of arms—i.e., the right to be considered gentlemen—the grant was made to Shakespeare's father, but probably William Shakespeare had arranged the matter on his own behalf. In subsequent transactions he is occasionally styled a gentleman.

Although in 1593 and 1594 Shakespeare published two narrative poems dedicated to the Earl of Southampton, *Venus and Adonis* and *The Rape of Lucrece*, and may well have written most or all of his sonnets in the middle nineties, Shakespeare's literary activity seems to have been almost entirely devoted to the theater. (It may be significant that the two narrative poems were written in years when the plague closed the theaters for several months.) In 1594 he was a charter member of a theatrical company called the Chamberlain's Men, which in 1603 became the royal company, the King's Men, making Shakespeare the king's playwright. Until he retired to Stratford (about 1611, apparently), he was with this remarkably stable company. From 1599 the company acted primarily at the Globe theater, in which Shakespeare held a one-tenth interest. Other Elizabethan dramatists are known to have acted, but no other is known also to have been entitled to a share of the profits.

Shakespeare's first eight published plays did not have his name on them, but this is not remarkable; the most popular play of the period, Thomas Kyd's *The Spanish Tragedy*, went through many editions without naming Kyd, and Kyd's authorship is known only because a book on the profession of acting happens to quote (and attribute to Kyd) some lines on the interest of Roman emperors in the drama. What is remarkable is that after 1598 Shakespeare's name commonly appears on printed plays—some of which are not his. Presumably his name was a drawing card, and publishers used it to attract potential buyers. Another indication of his popularity comes from Francis Meres, author of *Palladis Tamia: Wit's Treasury* (1598). In this anthology of snippets accompanied by an essay on literature, many playwrights are mentioned, but Shakespeare's name occurs more often than any other, and Shakespeare is the only play-wright whose plays are listed.

From his acting, his play writing, and his share in a playhouse, Shakespeare seems to have made considerable money. He put it to work, making substantial investments in Stratford real estate. As early as 1597 he bought New Place, the second-largest house in Stratford. His family moved in soon afterward, and the house remained in the family until a granddaughter died in 1670. When Shakespeare made his will in 1616, less than a month before he died, he sought to leave his property intact to his descendants. Of small bequests to relatives and to friends (including three actors, Richard Burbage, John Heminges, and Henry Condell), that to his wife of the second-best bed has provoked the most comment. It has sometimes been taken as a sign of an unhappy marriage (other supposed signs are the apparently hasty marriage, his wife's seniority of eight years, and his residence in London without his family). Perhaps the second-best bed was the bed the couple had slept in, the best bed being reserved for visitors. In any case, had Shakespeare not excepted it, the bed would have gone (with the rest of his household possessions) to his daughter and her husband.

On 25 April 1616 Shakespeare was buried within the chancel of the church at Stratford. An unattractive monument to his memory, placed on a wall near the grave, says that he died on 23 April. Over the grave itself are the lines, perhaps by Shakespeare, that (more than his literary fame) have kept his bones undisturbed in the crowded burial ground where old bones were often dislodged to make way for new:

> Good friend, for Jesus' sake forbear
> To dig the dust enclosed here.
> Blessed be the man that spares these stones
> And cursed be he that moves my bones.

A Note on the Anti-Stratfordians, Especially Baconians and Oxfordians

Not until 1769—more than a hundred and fifty years after Shakespeare's death—is there any record of anyone expressing doubt about Shakespeare's authorship of the plays and poems. In 1769, however, Herbert Lawrence nominated Francis Bacon (1561–1626) in *The Life and Adventures of Common Sense*. Since then, at least two dozen other nominees have been offered, including Christopher Marlowe, Sir Walter Raleigh, Queen Elizabeth I, and Edward de Vere, 17th earl of Oxford. The impulse behind all anti-Stratfordian movements is the scarcely concealed snobbish opinion that "the man from Stratford" simply could not have written the plays because he was a country fellow without a university education and without access to high society. Anyone, the argument goes, who used so many legal terms, medical terms, nautical terms, and so forth, and who showed some familiarity with classical writing, must have attended a university, and anyone who knew so much about courtly elegance and courtly deceit must himself have moved among courtiers. The plays do indeed reveal an author whose interests were exceptionally broad, but specialists in any given field—law, medicine, arms and armor, and so on—soon find that the plays do not reveal deep knowledge in specialized matters; indeed, the playwright often gets technical details wrong.

The claim on behalf of Bacon, forgotten almost as soon as it was put forth in 1769, was independently reasserted by Joseph C. Hart in 1848. In 1856 it was reaffirmed by W. H. Smith in a book, and also by Delia Bacon in an article; in 1857 Delia Bacon published a book, arguing that Francis Bacon had directed a group of intellectuals who wrote the plays.

Francis Bacon's claim has largely faded, perhaps because it was advanced with such evident craziness by Ignatius Donnelly, who in *The Great Cryptogram* (1888) claimed to break a code in the plays that proved Bacon had written not only the plays attributed to Shakespeare but also other Renaissance works, for instance the plays of Christopher Marlowe and the essays of Montaigne.

Consider the last two lines of the Epilogue in *The Tempest*:

As you from crimes would pardoned be,
Let your indulgence set me free.

What was Shakespeare—sorry, Francis Bacon, Baron Verulam—*really* saying in these two lines? According to Baconians, the lines are an anagram reading, "Tempest of Francis Bacon, Lord Verulam; do ye ne'er divulge me, ye words." Ingenious, and it is a pity that in the quotation the letter *a* appears only twice in the cryptogram, whereas in the deciphered message it appears three times. Oh, no problem; just alter "Verulam" to "Verul'm" and it works out very nicely.

Most people understand that with sufficient ingenuity one can torture any text and find in it what one wishes. For instance: Did Shakespeare have a hand in the King James Version of the Bible? It was nearing completion in 1610, when Shakespeare was forty-six years old. If you look at the 46th Psalm and count forward for forty-six words, you will find the word *shake*. Now if you go to the end of the psalm and count backward forty-six words, you will find the word *spear*. Clear evidence, according to some, that Shakespeare slyly left his mark in the book.

Bacon's candidacy has largely been replaced in the twentieth century by the candidacy of Edward de Vere (1550–1604), 17th earl of Oxford. The basic ideas behind the Oxford theory, advanced at greatest length by Dorothy and Charlton Ogburn in *This Star of England* (1952, rev. 1955), a book of 1297 pages, and by Charlton Ogburn in *The Mysterious William Shakespeare* (1984), a book of 892 pages, are these: (1) The man from Stratford could not possibly have had the mental equipment and the experience to have written the plays—only a courtier could have written them; (2) Oxford had the requisite background (social position, education, years at Queen Elizabeth's court); (3) Oxford did not wish his authorship to be known for two basic reasons: writing for the public theater was a vulgar pursuit, and the plays show so much courtly and royal disreputable behavior that they would have compromised Oxford's position at court. Oxfordians offer countless details to support the claim. For example, Hamlet's phrase "that ever I was born to set it right" (1.5.89) barely conceals "E. Ver, I was born to set it right," an unambiguous announcement of de Vere's authorship, according to *This Star of England* (p. 654). A second example: Consider Ben

Jonson's poem entitled "To the Memory of My Beloved Master William Shakespeare," prefixed to the first collected edition of Shakespeare's plays in 1623. According to Oxfordians, when Jonson in this poem speaks of the author of the plays as the "swan of Avon," he is alluding not to William Shakespeare, who was born and died in Stratford-on-Avon and who throughout his adult life owned property there; rather, he is alluding to Oxford, who, the Ogburns say, used "William Shakespeare" as his pen name, and whose manor at Bilton was on the Avon River. Oxfordians do not offer any evidence that Oxford took a pen name, and they do not mention that Oxford had sold the manor in 1581, forty-two years before Jonson wrote his poem. Surely a reference to the Shakespeare who was born in Stratford, who had returned to Stratford, and who had died there only seven years before Jonson wrote the poem is more plausible. And exactly why Jonson, who elsewhere also spoke of Shakespeare as a playwright, and why Heminges and Condell, who had acted with Shakespeare for about twenty years, should speak of Shakespeare as the author in their dedication in the 1623 volume of collected plays is never adequately explained by Oxfordians. Either Jonson, Heminges and Condell, and numerous others were in on the conspiracy, or they were all duped—equally unlikely alternatives. Another difficulty in the Oxford theory is that Oxford died in 1604, and some of the plays are clearly indebted to works and events later than 1604. Among the Oxfordian responses are: At his death Oxford left some plays, and in later years these were touched up by hacks, who added the material that points to later dates. *The Tempest*, almost universally regarded as one of Shakespeare's greatest plays and pretty clearly dated to 1611, does indeed date from a period after the death of Oxford, but it is a crude piece of work that should not be included in the canon of works by Oxford.

The anti-Stratfordians, in addition to assuming that the author must have been a man of rank and a university man, usually assume two conspiracies: (1) a conspiracy in Elizabethan and Jacobean times, in which a surprisingly large number of persons connected with the theater knew that the actor Shakespeare did not write the plays attributed to him but for some reason or other pretended that he did; (2) a conspiracy of today's Stratfordians, the professors who teach Shakespeare in the colleges and universities, who are said to have a vested interest in preserving Shakespeare as the author of the plays they teach. In fact, (1) it is inconceivable that the secret of Shakespeare's non-authorship could have been preserved by all of the people who supposedly were in on the conspiracy, and (2) academic fame awaits any scholar today who can disprove Shakespeare's authorship.

The Stratfordian case is convincing not only because hundreds or even thousands of anti-Stratford arguments—of the sort that say "ever I was born" has the secret double meaning "E. Ver, I was born"—add up to nothing at all but also because irrefutable evidence connects the man from Stratford with the London theater and with the authorship of particular plays. The anti-Stratfordians do not seem to understand that it is not enough to dismiss the Stratford case by saying that a fellow from the provinces simply couldn't have written the plays. Nor do they understand that it is not enough to dismiss all of the evidence connecting Shakespeare with the plays by asserting that it is perjured.

The Shakespeare Canon

We return to William Shakespeare. Thirty-seven plays as well as some nondramatic poems are generally held to constitute the Shakespeare canon, the body of authentic works. The exact dates of composition of most of the works are highly uncertain, but evidence of a starting point and/or of a final limiting point often provides a framework for informed guessing. For example, *Richard II* cannot be earlier than 1595, the publication date of some material to which it is indebted; *The Merchant of Venice* cannot be later than 1598, the year Francis Meres mentioned it. Sometimes arguments for a date hang on an alleged topical allusion, such as the lines about the unseasonable weather in *A Midsummer Night's Dream*, 2.1.81–117, but such an allusion, if indeed it is an allusion to an event in the real world, can be variously interpreted, and in any case there is always the possibility that a topical allusion was inserted years later, to bring the play up to date. (The issue of alterations in a text between the time that Shakespeare drafted it and the time that it was printed—alterations due to censorship or playhouse practice or Shakespeare's own second thoughts—will be discussed in "The Play Text as a Collaboration" later in this overview.) Dates are often attributed on the basis of style, and although conjectures about style usually rest on other conjectures (such as Shakespeare's development as a playwright, or the appropriateness of lines to character), sooner or later one must rely on one's literary sense. There is no documentary proof, for example, that *Othello* is not as early as *Romeo and Juliet*, but one feels that *Othello* is a later, more mature work, and because the first record of its performance is 1604, one is glad enough to set its composition at that date and not push it back into Shakespeare's early years. (*Romeo and Juliet* was first published in 1597, but evidence suggests that it was written a little earlier.) The following chronology, then, is indebted not only to facts but also to informed guesswork and sensitivity. The dates, necessarily imprecise for some works, indicate something like a scholarly consensus concerning the time of original composition. Some plays show evidence of later revision.

Plays. The first collected edition of Shakespeare, published in 1623, included thirty-six plays. These are all accepted as Shakespeare's, though for one of them, *Henry VIII*, he is thought to have had a collaborator. A thirty-seventh play, *Pericles*, published in 1609 and attributed to Shakespeare on the title page, is also widely accepted as being partly by Shakespeare even though it is not included in the 1623 volume. Still another play not in the 1623 volume, *The Two Noble Kinsmen*, was first published in 1634, with a title page attributing it to John Fletcher and Shakespeare. Probably most students of the subject now believe that Shakespeare did indeed have a hand in it. Of the remaining plays attributed at one time or another to Shakespeare, only one, *Edward III*, anonymously published in 1596, is now regarded by some scholars as a serious candidate. The prevailing opinion, however, is that this rather simpleminded play is not Shakespeare's; at most he may have revised some passages, chiefly scenes with the Countess of

Salisbury. We include *The Two Noble Kinsmen* but do not include *Edward III* in the following list.

1588–94	*The Comedy of Errors*
1588–94	*Love's Labor's Lost*
1589–91	*2 Henry VI*
1590–91	*3 Henry VI*
1589–92	*1 Henry VI*
1592–93	*Richard III*
1589–94	*Titus Andronicus*
1593–94	*The Taming of the Shrew*
1592–94	*The Two Gentlemen of Verona*
1594–96	*Romeo and Juliet*
1595	*Richard II*
1595–96	*A Midsummer Night's Dream*
1596–97	*King John*
1594–96	*The Merchant of Venice*
1596–97	*1 Henry IV*
1597	*The Merry Wives of Windsor*
1597–98	*2 Henry IV*
1598–99	*Much Ado About Nothing*
1598–99	*Henry V*
1599	*Julius Caesar*
1599–1600	*As You Like It*
1599–1600	*Twelfth Night*
1600–1601	*Hamlet*
1601–1602	*Troilus and Cressida*
1602–1604	*All's Well That Ends Well*
1603–1604	*Othello*
1604	*Measure for Measure*
1605–1606	*King Lear*
1605–1606	*Macbeth*
1606–1607	*Antony and Cleopatra*
1605–1608	*Timon of Athens*
1607–1608	*Coriolanus*
1607–1608	*Pericles*
1609–10	*Cymbeline*
1610–11	*The Winter's Tale*
1611	*The Tempest*

1612–13	*Henry VIII*
1613	*The Two Noble Kinsmen*

Poems. In 1989 Donald W. Foster published a book in which he argued that "A Funeral Elegy for Master William Peter," published in 1612, ascribed only to the initials W.S., *may* be by Shakespeare. Foster later published an article in a scholarly journal, *PMLA* 111 (1996), in which he asserted the claim more positively. The evidence begins with the initials, and includes the fact that the publisher and the printer of the elegy had published Shakespeare's *Sonnets* in 1609. But such facts add up to rather little, especially because no one has found any connection between Shakespeare and William Peter (an Oxford graduate about whom little is known, who was murdered at the age of twenty-nine). The argument is based chiefly on statistical examinations of word patterns, which are said to correlate with Shakespeare's known work. Despite such correlations, however, many readers feel that the poem does not sound like Shakespeare. True, Shakespeare has a great range of styles, but his work is consistently imaginative and interesting. Many readers find neither of these qualities in "A Funeral Elegy."

1592–93	*Venus and Adonis*
1593–94	*The Rape of Lucrece*
1593–1600	*Sonnets*
1600–1601	*The Phoenix and the Turtle*

Shakespeare's English

1. Spelling and Pronunciation. From the philologist's point of view, Shakespeare's English is modern English. It requires footnotes, but the inexperienced reader can comprehend substantial passages with very little help, whereas for the same reader Chaucer's Middle English is a foreign language. By the beginning of the fifteenth century the chief grammatical changes in English had taken place, and the final unaccented *-e* of Middle English had been lost (though it survives even today in spelling, as in *name*); during the fifteenth century the dialect of London, the commercial and political center, gradually displaced the provincial dialects, at least in writing; by the end of the century, printing had helped to regularize and stabilize the language, especially spelling. Elizabethan spelling may seem erratic to us (there were dozens of spellings of *Shakespeare*, and a simple word like *been* was also spelled *beene* and *bin*), but it had much in common with our spelling. Elizabethan spelling was conservative in that for the most part it reflected an older pronunciation (Middle English) rather than the sound of the language as it was then spoken, just as our spelling continues to reflect medieval pronunciation—most obviously in the now silent but formerly pronounced letters in a word such as *knight*. Elizabethan pronunciation, though not identical with ours, was much closer to ours than to that of the Middle Ages. Incidentally, though no one can be certain about what Elizabethan English sounded like, specialists tend to believe it was rather like the speech of a modern stage Irishman (*time* apparently was pronounced *toime*, *old* pronounced *awld*, *day* pronounced *die*, and *join* pronounced *jine*) and not at all like the Oxford speech that most of us think it was.

An awareness of the difference between our pronunciation and Shakespeare's is crucial in three areas—in accent, or number of syllables (many metrically regular lines may look irregular to us); in rhymes (which may not look like rhymes); and in puns (which may not look like puns). Examples will be useful. Some words that were at least on occasion stressed differently from today are *aspèct*, *còmplete*, *fòrlorn*, *revènue*, and *sepùlcher*. Words that sometimes had an additional syllable are *emp[e]ress*, *Hen[e]ry*, *mon[e]th*, and *villain* (three syllables, *vil-lay-in*). An additional syllable is often found in possessives, like *moon's* (pronounced *moones*) and in words ending in *-tion* or *-sion*. Words that had one less syllable than they now have are *needle* (pronounced *neel*) and *violet* (pronounced *vilet*). Among rhymes now lost are *one* with *loan*, *love* with *prove*, *beast* with *jest*, *eat* with *great*. (In reading, trust your sense of metrics and your ear, more than your eye.) An example of a pun that has become obliterated by a change in pronunciation is Falstaff's reply to Prince Hal's "Come, tell us your

reason" in *1 Henry IV*: "Give you a reason on compulsion?
If reasons were as plentiful as blackberries, I would give no
man a reason upon compulsion, I" (2.4.237–40). The *ea* in
reason was pronounced rather like a long *a*, like the *ai* in
raisin, hence the comparison with blackberries.

Puns are not merely attempts to be funny; like metaphors
they often involve bringing into a meaningful relationship
areas of experience normally seen as remote. In *2 Henry IV*,
when Feeble is conscripted, he stoically says, "I care not. A
man can die but once. We owe God a death" (3.2.242–43),
punning on *debt*, which was the way *death* was pronounced.
Here an enormously significant fact of life is put into simple
commercial imagery, suggesting its commonplace quality.
Shakespeare used the same pun earlier in *1 Henry IV*, when
Prince Hal says to Falstaff, "Why, thou owest God a death,"
and Falstaff replies, " 'Tis not due yet: I would be loath
to pay him before his day. What need I be so forward with
him that calls not on me?" (5.1.126–29).

Sometimes the puns reveal a delightful playfulness;
sometimes they reveal aggressiveness, as when, replying to
Claudius's "But now, my cousin Hamlet, and my son,"
Hamlet says, "A little more than kin, and less than kind!"
(1.2.64–65). These are Hamlet's first words in the play, and
we already hear him warring verbally against Claudius.
Hamlet's "less than kind" probably means (1) Hamlet is not
of Claudius's family or nature, *kind* having the sense it still
has in our word *mankind*; (2) Hamlet is not kindly (affec-
tionately) disposed toward Claudius; (3) Claudius is not
naturally (but rather unnaturally, in a legal sense incestu-
ously) Hamlet's father. The puns evidently were not put in
as sops to the groundlings; they are an important way of
communicating a complex meaning.

2. *Vocabulary.* A conspicuous difficulty in reading Shakespeare is rooted in the fact that some of his words are no
longer in common use—for example, words concerned with
armor, astrology, clothing, coinage, hawking, horsemanship, law, medicine, sailing, and war. Shakespeare had a
large vocabulary—something near thirty thousand words—
but it was not so much a vocabulary of big words as a
vocabulary drawn from a wide range of life, and it is partly

his ability to call upon a great body of concrete language that gives his plays the sense of being in close contact with life. When the right word did not already exist, he made it up. Among words thought to be his coinages are *accommodation, all-knowing, amazement, bare-faced, countless, dexterously, dislocate, dwindle, fancy-free, frugal, indistinguishable, lackluster, laughable, overawe, premeditated, sea change, star-crossed.* Among those that have not survived are the verb *convive,* meaning to feast together, and *smilet,* a little smile.

Less overtly troublesome than the technical words but more treacherous are the words that seem readily intelligible to us but whose Elizabethan meanings differ from their modern ones. When Horatio describes the Ghost as an "erring spirit," he is saying not that the ghost has sinned or made an error but that it is wandering. Here is a short list of some of the most common words in Shakespeare's plays that often (but not always) have a meaning other than their most usual modern meaning:

'a	he
abuse	deceive
accident	occurrence
advertise	inform
an, and	if
annoy	harm
appeal	accuse
artificial	skillful
brave	fine, splendid
censure	opinion
cheer	(1) face (2) frame of mind
chorus	a single person who comments on the events
closet	small private room
competitor	partner
conceit	idea, imagination
cousin	kinsman
cunning	skillful
disaster	evil astrological influence
doom	judgment
entertain	receive into service

envy	malice
event	outcome
excrement	outgrowth (of hair)
fact	evil deed
fancy	(1) love (2) imagination
fell	cruel
fellow	(1) companion (2) low person (often an insulting term if addressed to someone of approximately equal rank)
fond	foolish
free	(1) innocent (2) generous
glass	mirror
hap, haply	chance, by chance
head	army
humor	(1) mood (2) bodily fluid thought to control one's psychology
imp	child
intelligence	news
kind	natural, acting according to nature
let	hinder
lewd	base
mere(ly)	utter(ly)
modern	commonplace
natural	a fool, an idiot
naughty	(1) wicked (2) worthless
next	nearest
nice	(1) trivial (2) fussy
noise	music
policy	(1) prudence (2) stratagem
presently	immediately
prevent	anticipate
proper	handsome
prove	test
quick	alive
sad	serious
saw	proverb
secure	without care, incautious
silly	innocent

sensible	capable of being perceived by the senses
shrewd	sharp
so	provided that
starve	die
still	always
success	that which follows
tall	brave
tell	count
tonight	last night
wanton	playful, careless
watch	keep awake
will	lust
wink	close both eyes
wit	mind, intelligence

All glosses, of course, are mere approximations; sometimes one of Shakespeare's words may hover between an older meaning and a modern one, and as we have seen, his words often have multiple meanings.

3. Grammar. A few matters of grammar may be surveyed, though it should be noted at the outset that Shakespeare sometimes made up his own grammar. As E.A. Abbott says in *A Shakespearian Grammar,* "Almost any part of speech can be used as any other part of speech": a noun as a verb ("he childed as I fathered"); a verb as a noun ("She hath made compare"); or an adverb as an adjective ("a seldom pleasure"). There are hundreds, perhaps thousands, of such instances in the plays, many of which at first glance would not seem at all irregular and would trouble only a pedant. Here are a few broad matters.

Nouns: The Elizabethans thought the *-s* genitive ending for nouns (as in *man's*) derived from *his*; thus the line " 'gainst the count his galleys I did some service," for "the count's galleys."

Adjectives: By Shakespeare's time adjectives had lost the endings that once indicated gender, number, and case. About the only difference between Shakespeare's adjectives and ours is the use of the now redundant *more* or *most* with the comparative ("some more fitter place") or superlative

("This was the most unkindest cut of all"). Like double comparatives and double superlatives, double negatives were acceptable; Mercutio "will not budge for no man's pleasure."

Pronouns: The greatest change was in pronouns. In Middle English *thou, thy,* and *thee* were used among familiars and in speaking to children and inferiors; *ye, your,* and *you* were used in speaking to superiors (servants to masters, nobles to the king) or to equals with whom the speaker was not familiar. Increasingly the "polite" forms were used in all direct address, regardless of rank, and the accusative *you* displaced the nominative *ye.* Shakespeare sometimes uses *ye* instead of *you,* but even in Shakespeare's day *ye* was archaic, and it occurs mostly in rhetorical appeals.

Thou, thy, and *thee* were not completely displaced, however, and Shakespeare occasionally makes significant use of them, sometimes to connote familiarity or intimacy and sometimes to connote contempt. In *Twelfth Night* Sir Toby advises Sir Andrew to insult Cesario by addressing him as *thou:* "If thou thou'st him some thrice, it shall not be amiss" (3.2.46–47). In *Othello* when Brabantio is addressing an unidentified voice in the dark he says, "What are you?" (1.1.91), but when the voice identifies itself as the foolish suitor Roderigo, Brabantio uses the contemptuous form, saying, "I have charged thee not to haunt about my doors" (93). He uses this form for a while, but later in the scene, when he comes to regard Roderigo as an ally, he shifts back to the polite *you,* beginning in line 163, "What said she to you?" and on to the end of the scene. For reasons not yet satisfactorily explained, Elizabethans used *thou* in addresses to God—"O God, thy arm was here," the king says in *Henry V* (4.8.108)—and to supernatural characters such as ghosts and witches. A subtle variation occurs in *Hamlet.* When Hamlet first talks with the Ghost in 1.5, he uses *thou,* but when he sees the Ghost in his mother's room, in 3.4, he uses *you,* presumably because he is now convinced that the Ghost is not a counterfeit but is his father.

Perhaps the most unusual use of pronouns, from our point of view, is the neuter singular. In place of our *its, his* was often used, as in "How far that little candle throws *his* beams." But the use of a masculine pronoun for a neuter noun came to seem unnatural, and so *it* was used for the possessive as well as the nominative: "The hedge-sparrow fed the cuckoo so long / That it had it head bit off by it young." In the late sixteenth century the possessive form *its* developed, apparently by analogy with the *-s* ending used to indicate a genitive noun, as in *book*'s, but *its* was not yet common usage in Shakespeare's day. He seems to have used *its* only ten times, mostly in his later plays. Other usages, such as "you have seen Cassio and she together" or the substitution of *who* for *whom,* cause little problem even when noticed.

Verbs, Adverbs, and Prepositions: Verbs cause almost no difficulty: The third person singular present form commonly ends in *-s,* as in modern English (e.g., "He blesses"), but sometimes in *-eth* (Portia explains to Shylock that mercy "blesseth him that gives and him that takes"). Broadly speaking, the *-eth* ending was old-fashioned or dignified or "literary" rather than colloquial, except for the words *doth, hath,* and *saith.* The *-eth* ending (regularly used in the King James Bible, 1611) is very rare in Shakespeare's dramatic prose, though not surprisingly it occurs twice in the rather formal prose summary of the narrative poem *Lucrece.* Sometimes a plural subject, especially if it has collective force, takes a verb ending in *-s,* as in "My old bones aches." Some of our strong or irregular preterites (such as *broke*) have a different form in Shakespeare (*brake*); some verbs that now have a weak or regular preterite (such as *helped*) in Shakespeare have a strong or irregular preterite (*holp*). Some adverbs that today end in *-ly* were not inflected: "grievous sick," "wondrous strange." Finally, prepositions often are not the ones we expect: "We are such stuff as dreams are made on," "I have a king here to my flatterer."

Again, none of the differences (except meanings that have substantially changed or been lost) will cause much difficulty. But it must be confessed that for some elliptical passages there is no widespread agreement on meaning. Wise editors resist saying more than they know, and when they are uncertain they add a question mark to their gloss.

Shakespeare's Theater

In Shakespeare's infancy, Elizabethan actors performed wherever they could—in great halls, at court, in the courtyards of inns. These venues implied not only different audiences but also different playing conditions. The innyards must have made rather unsatisfactory theaters: on some days they were unavailable because carters bringing goods to London used them as depots; when available, they had to be rented from the innkeeper. In 1567, presumably to avoid such difficulties, and also to avoid regulation by the Common Council of London, which was not well disposed toward theatricals, one John Brayne, brother-in-law of the carpenter turned actor James Burbage, built the Red Lion in an eastern suburb of London. We know nothing about its shape or its capacity; we can say only that it may have been the first building in Europe constructed for the purpose of giving plays since the end of antiquity, a thousand years earlier. Even after the building of the Red Lion theatrical activity continued in London in makeshift circumstances, in marketplaces and inns, and always uneasily. In 1574 the Common Council required that plays and playing places in London be licensed because

> sundry great disorders and inconveniences have been found to ensue to this city by the inordinate haunting of great multitudes of people, specially youth, to plays, interludes, and shows, namely occasion of frays and quarrels, evil practices of incontinency in great inns having chambers and secret places adjoining to their open stages and galleries.

The Common Council ordered that innkeepers who wished licenses to hold performance put up a bond and make contributions to the poor.

The requirement that plays and innyard theaters be licensed, along with the other drawbacks of playing at inns and presumably along with the success of the Red Lion, led James Burbage to rent a plot of land northeast of the city walls, on property outside the jurisdiction of the city. Here he built England's second playhouse, called simply the Theatre. About all that is known of its construction is that it was wood. It soon had imitators, the most famous being the Globe (1599), essentially an amphitheater built across the Thames (again outside the city's jurisdiction), constructed with timbers of the Theatre, which had been dismantled when Burbage's lease ran out.

Admission to the theater was one penny, which allowed spectators to stand at the sides and front of the stage that jutted into the yard. An additional penny bought a seat in a covered part of the theater, and a third penny bought a more comfortable seat and a better location. It is notoriously difficult to translate prices into today's money, since some things that are inexpensive today would have been expensive in the past and vice versa—a pipeful of tobacco (imported, of course) cost a lot of money, about three pennies, and an orange (also imported) cost two or three times what a chicken cost—but perhaps we can get some idea of the low cost of the penny admission when we realize that a penny could also buy a pot of ale. An unskilled laborer made about five or sixpence a day, an artisan about twelve pence a day, and the hired actors (as opposed to the sharers in the company, such as Shakespeare) made about ten pence a performance. A printed play cost five or sixpence. Of course a visit to the theater (like a visit to a baseball game today) usually cost more than the admission since the spectator probably would also buy food and drink. Still, the low entrance fee meant that the theater was available to all except the very poorest people, rather as movies and most athletic events are today. Evidence indicates that the audience ranged from apprentices who somehow managed to scrape together the minimum entrance fee and to escape from their masters for a few hours, to prosperous members of the middle class and aristocrats who paid the additional fee for admission to the galleries. The exact proportion of men to women cannot be determined, but women of all classes certainly were present. Theaters were open every afternoon but Sundays for much of the year, except in times of plague, when they were closed because of fear of infection. By the way, no evidence suggests the presence of toilet facilities. Presumably the patrons relieved themselves by making a quick trip to the fields surrounding the playhouses.

There are four important sources of information about the

structure of Elizabethan public playhouses—drawings, a contract, recent excavations, and stage directions in the plays. Of drawings, only the so-called de Witt drawing (c. 1596) of the Swan—really his friend Aernout van Buchell's copy of Johannes de Witt's drawing—is of much significance. The drawing, the only extant representation of the interior of an Elizabethan theater, shows an amphitheater of three tiers, with a stage jutting from a wall into the yard or

Johannes de Witt, a Continental visitor to London, made a drawing of the Swan theater in about the year 1596. The original drawing is lost; this is Aernout van Buchell's copy of it.

center of the building. The tiers are roofed, and part of the stage is covered by a roof that projects from the rear and is supported at its front on two posts, but the groundlings, who paid a penny to stand in front of the stage or at its sides, were exposed to the sky. (Performances in such a playhouse were held only in the daytime; artificial illumination was not used.) At the rear of the stage are two massive doors; above the stage is a gallery.

The second major source of information, the contract for the Fortune (built in 1600), specifies that although the Globe (built in 1599) is to be the model, the Fortune is to be square, eighty feet outside and fifty-five inside. The stage is to be forty-three feet broad, and is to extend into the middle of the yard, i.e., it is twenty-seven and a half feet deep.

The third source of information, the 1989 excavations of the Rose (built in 1587), indicate that the Rose was fourteen-sided, about seventy-two feet in diameter with an inner yard almost fifty feet in diameter. The stage at the Rose was about sixteen feet deep, thirty-seven feet wide at the rear, and twenty-seven feet wide downstage. The relatively small dimensions and the tapering stage, in contrast to the rectangular stage in the Swan drawing, surprised theater historians and have made them more cautious in generalizing about the Elizabethan theater. Excavations at the Globe have not yielded much information, though some historians believe that the fragmentary evidence suggests a larger theater, perhaps one hundred feet in diameter.

From the fourth chief source, stage directions in the plays, one learns that entrance to the stage was by the doors at the rear (*"Enter one citizen at one door, and another at the other"*). A curtain hanging across the doorway—or a curtain hanging between the two doorways—could provide a place where a character could conceal himself, as Polonius does, when he wishes to overhear the conversation between Hamlet and Gertrude. Similarly, withdrawing a curtain from the doorway could "discover" (reveal) a character or two. Such discovery scenes are very rare in Elizabethan drama, but a good example occurs in *The Tempest* (5.1.171), where a stage direction tells us, *"Here Prospero discovers Ferdinand and Miranda playing at chess."* There was also some sort of playing space "aloft" or "above" to represent, for instance, the top of a city's walls or a room above the street. Doubtless each theater had its own peculiarities, but perhaps we can talk about a "typical" Elizabethan theater if we realize that no theater need exactly fit the description, just as no mother is the average mother with 2.7 children.

This hypothetical theater is wooden, round, or polygonal (in *Henry V* Shakespeare calls it a "wooden *O*") capable of holding some eight hundred spectators who stood in the yard around the projecting elevated stage—these spectators were the "groundlings"—and some fifteen hundred additional spectators who sat in the three roofed galleries. The stage, protected by a "shadow" or "heavens" or roof, is entered from two doors; behind the doors is the "tiring house" (attiring house, i.e., dressing room), and above the stage is some sort of gallery that may sometimes hold spectators but can be used (for example) as the bedroom from which Romeo—according to a stage direction in one text—"goeth down." Some evidence suggests that a throne can be lowered onto the platform stage, perhaps from the "shadow"; certainly characters can descend from the stage through a trap or traps into the cellar or "hell." Sometimes this space beneath the stage accommodates a sound-effects man or musician (in *Antony and Cleopatra* "*music of the hautboys* [oboes] *is under the stage*") or an actor (in *Hamlet* the "*Ghost cries under the stage*"). Most characters simply walk on and off through the doors, but because there is no curtain in front of the platform, corpses will have to be carried off (Hamlet obligingly clears the stage of Polonius's corpse, when he says, "I'll lug the guts into the neighbor room"). Other characters may have fallen at the rear, where a curtain on a doorway could be drawn to conceal them.

Such may have been the "public theater," so called because its inexpensive admission made it available to a wide range of the populace. Another kind of theater has been called the "private theater" because its much greater admission charge (sixpence versus the penny for general admission at the public theater) limited its audience to the wealthy or the prodigal. The private theater was basically a large room, entirely roofed and therefore artificially illuminated, with a stage at one end. The theaters thus were distinct in two ways: One was essentially an amphitheater that catered to the general public; the other was a hall that catered to the wealthy. In 1576 a hall theater was established in Blackfriars, a Dominican priory in London that had been suppressed in 1538 and confiscated by the Crown and thus was not under the city's jurisdiction. All the actors in this Blackfriars theater were boys about eight to thirteen years old (in the public theaters similar boys played female parts; a boy Lady Macbeth played to a man Macbeth). Near the end of this section on Shakespeare's theater we will talk at some length about possible implications in this convention of using boys to play female roles, but for the moment we should say that it doubtless accounts for the relative lack of female roles in Elizabethan drama. Thus, in *A Midsummer Night's Dream*, out of twenty-one named roles, only four are female; in *Hamlet*, out of twenty-four, only two (Gertrude and Ophelia) are female. Many of Shakespeare's characters have fathers but no mothers—for instance, King Lear's daughters. We need not bring in Freud to explain the disparity; a dramatic company had only a few boys in it.

To return to the private theaters, in some of which all of the performers were children—the "eyrie of . . . little eyases" (nest of unfledged hawks—2.2.347–48) which Rosencrantz mentions when he and Guildenstern talk with Hamlet. The theater in Blackfriars had a precarious existence, and ceased operations in 1584. In 1596 James Burbage, who had already made theatrical history by building the Theatre, began to construct a second Blackfriars theater. He died in 1597, and for several years this second Blackfriars theater was used by a troupe of boys, but in 1608 two of Burbage's sons and five other actors (including Shakespeare) became joint operators of the theater, using it in the winter when the open-air Globe was unsuitable. Perhaps such a smaller theater, roofed, artificially illuminated, and with a tradition of a wealthy audience, exerted an influence in Shakespeare's late plays.

Performances in the private theaters may well have had intermissions during which music was played, but in the public theaters the action was probably uninterrupted, flowing from scene to scene almost without a break. Actors would enter, speak, exit, and others would immediately enter and establish (if necessary) the new locale by a few properties and by words and gestures. To indicate that the scene took place at night, a player or two would carry a torch. Here are some samples of Shakespeare establishing the scene:

This is Illyria, lady.   (*Twelfth Night,* 1.2.2)

Well, this is the Forest of Arden.   (*As You Like It,* 2.4.14)

This castle has a pleasant seat; the air
Nimbly and sweetly recommends itself
Unto our gentle senses.   (*Macbeth,* 1.6.1–3)

The west yet glimmers with some streaks of day.
                                                            (*Macbeth,* 3.3.5)

Sometimes a speech will go far beyond evoking the minimal setting of place and time, and will, so to speak, evoke the social world in which the characters move. For instance, early in the first scene of *The Merchant of Venice* Salerio suggests an explanation for Antonio's melancholy. (In the following passage, *pageants* are decorated wagons, floats, and *cursy* is the verb "to curtsy," or "to bow.")

Your mind is tossing on the ocean,
There where your argosies with portly sail—
Like signiors and rich burghers on the flood,
Or as it were the pageants of the sea—
Do overpeer the petty traffickers
That cursy to them, do them reverence,
As they fly by them with their woven wings.   (1.1.8–14)

Late in the nineteenth century, when Henry Irving produced the play with elaborate illusionistic sets, the first scene showed a ship moored in the harbor, with fruit vendors and dock laborers, in an effort to evoke the bustling and exotic life of Venice. But Shakespeare's words give us this exotic, rich world of commerce in his highly descriptive language when Salerio speaks of "argosies with portly sail" that fly with "woven wings"; equally important, through Salerio Shakespeare conveys a sense of the orderly, hierarchical society in which the lesser ships, "the petty traffickers," curtsy and thereby "do . . . reverence" to their superiors, the merchant prince's ships, which are "Like signiors and rich burghers."

On the other hand, it is a mistake to think that except for verbal pictures the Elizabethan stage was bare. Although Shakespeare's Chorus in *Henry V* calls the stage an "unworthy scaffold" (Prologue 1.10) and urges the spectators to "eke out our performance with your mind" (Prologue 3.35), there was considerable spectacle. The last act of *Macbeth,* for instance, has five stage directions calling for *"drum and colors,"* and another sort of appeal to the eye is indicated by the stage direction *"Enter Macduff, with Macbeth's head."* Some scenery and properties may have been substantial; doubtless a throne was used, but the pillars supporting the roof would have served for the trees on which Orlando pins his poems in *As You Like It*.

Having talked about the public theater—"this wooden *O*"—at some length, we should mention again that Shakespeare's plays were performed also in other locales. Alvin Kernan, in *Shakespeare, the King's Playwright: Theater in the Stuart Court 1603–1613* (1995) points out that "several of [Shakespeare's] plays contain brief theatrical performances, set always in a court or some noble house. When Shakespeare portrayed a theater, he did not, except for the choruses in *Henry V*, imagine a public theater" (p. 195). (Examples include episodes in *The Taming of the Shrew*, *A Midsummer Night's Dream*, *Hamlet*, and *The Tempest*.)

A Note on the Use of Boy Actors in Female Roles

Until fairly recently, scholars were content to mention that the convention existed; they sometimes also mentioned that it continued the medieval practice of using males in female roles, and that other theaters, notably in ancient Greece and in China and Japan, also used males in female roles. (In classical Noh drama in Japan, males still play the female roles.) Prudery may have been at the root of the academic failure to talk much about the use of boy actors, or maybe there really is not much more to say than that it was a convention of a male-centered culture (Stephen Greenblatt's view, in *Shakespearean Negotiations* [1988]). Further, the very nature of a convention is that it is not thought about: Hamlet is a Dane and Julius Caesar is a Roman, but in Shakespeare's plays they speak English, and we in the audience never give this odd fact a thought. Similarly, a character may speak in the presence of others and we understand, again without thinking about it, that he or she is not heard by the figures on the stage (the aside); a character alone on the stage may speak (the soliloquy), and we do not take the character to be unhinged; in a realistic (box) set, the fourth wall, which allows us to see what is going on, is miraculously missing. The no-nonsense view, then, is that the boy actor was an accepted convention, accepted unthinkingly—just as today we know that Kenneth Branagh is not Hamlet, Al Pacino is not Richard III, and Denzel Washington is not the Prince of Aragon. In this view, the audience takes the performer for the role, and that is that; such is the argument we now make for race-free casting, in which African-Americans and Asians can play roles of persons who lived in medieval Denmark and ancient Rome. But gender perhaps is different, at least today. It is a matter of abundant academic study: The Elizabethan theater is now sometimes called a transvestite theater, and we hear much about cross-dressing.

Shakespeare himself in a very few passages calls attention to the use of boys in female roles. At the end of *As You Like It* the boy who played Rosalind addresses the audience, and says, "O men, . . . if I were a woman, I would kiss as many of you as had beards that pleased me." But this is in the Epilogue; the plot is over, and the actor is stepping out of the play and into the audience's everyday world. A second reference to the practice of boys playing female roles occurs in *Antony and Cleopatra*, when Cleopatra imagines that she and Antony will be the subject of crude plays, her role being performed by a boy:

> The quick comedians
> Extemporally will stage us, and present
> Our Alexandrian revels: Antony
> Shall be brought drunken forth, and I shall see
> Some squeaking Cleopatra boy my greatness.   (5.2.216–20)

In a few other passages, Shakespeare is more indirect. For instance, in *Twelfth Night* Viola, played of course by a boy, disguises herself as a young man and seeks service in the house of a lord. She enlists the help of a Captain, and (by way of explaining away her voice and her beardlessness) says,

> I'll serve this duke
> Thou shalt present me as an eunuch to him.   (1.2.55–56)

In *Hamlet*, when the players arrive in 2.2, Hamlet jokes with the boy who plays a female role. The boy has grown since Hamlet last saw him: "By'r Lady, your ladyship is nearer to heaven than when I saw you last by the altitude of a chopine" (a lady's thick-soled shoe). He goes on: "Pray God your voice . . . be not cracked" (434–38).

Exactly how sexual, how erotic, this material was and is, is now much disputed. Again, the use of boys may have been unnoticed, or rather not thought about—an unexamined convention—by most or all spectators most of the time, perhaps *all* of the time, except when Shakespeare calls the convention to the attention of the audience, as in the passages just quoted. Still, an occasional bit seems to invite erotic thoughts. The clearest example is the name that Rosalind takes in *As You Like It*, Ganymede—the beautiful youth whom Zeus abducted. Did boys dressed to play female roles carry homoerotic appeal for straight men (Lisa Jardine's view, in *Still Harping on Daughters* [1983]), or for gay men, or for some or all women in the audience? Further, when the boy actor played a woman who (for the purposes of the plot) disguised herself as a male, as Rosalind, Viola, and Portia do—so we get a boy playing a woman playing a man—what sort of appeal was generated, and for what sort of spectator?

Some scholars have argued that the convention empowered women by letting female characters display a freedom unavailable in Renaissance patriarchal society; the convention, it is said, undermined rigid gender distinctions. In this view, the convention (along with plots in which female characters for a while disguised themselves as young men) allowed Shakespeare to say what some modern gender

critics say: Gender is a constructed role rather than a bio-
logical given, something we make, rather than a fixed binary
opposition of male and female (see Juliet Dusinberre, in
Shakespeare and the Nature of Women [1975]). On the other
hand, some scholars have maintained that the male disguise
assumed by some female characters serves only to reaffirm
traditional social distinctions since female characters who
don male garb (notably Portia in *The Merchant of Venice*
and Rosalind in *As You Like It*) return to their female garb
and at least implicitly (these critics say) reaffirm the status
quo. (For this last view, see Clara Claiborne Park, in an
essay in *The Woman's Part*, ed. Carolyn Ruth Swift Lenz et
al. [1980].) Perhaps no one answer is right for all plays; in
As You Like It cross-dressing empowers Rosalind, but in
Twelfth Night cross-dressing comically traps Viola.

Shakespeare's Dramatic Language: Costumes, Gestures and Silences; Prose and Poetry

Because Shakespeare was a dramatist, not merely a poet,
he worked not only with language but also with costume,
sound effects, gestures, and even silences. We have already
discussed some kinds of spectacle in the preceding section,
and now we will begin with other aspects of visual language;
a theater, after all, is literally a "place for seeing." Consider
the opening stage direction in *The Tempest*, the first play in
the first published collection of Shakespeare's plays: *"A
tempestuous noise of thunder and Lightning heard: Enter a
Ship-master, and a Boteswain."*

Costumes: What did that shipmaster and that boatswain
wear? Doubtless they wore something that identified them
as men of the sea. Not much is known about the costumes
that Elizabethan actors wore, but at least three points are
clear: (1) many of the costumes were splendid versions of
contemporary Elizabethan dress; (2) some attempts were
made to approximate the dress of certain occupations and of
antique or exotic characters such as Romans, Turks, and
Jews; (3) some costumes indicated that the wearer was

supernatural. Evidence for elaborate Elizabethan clothing can be found in the plays themselves and in contemporary comments about the "sumptuous" players who wore the discarded clothing of noblemen, as well as in account books that itemize such things as "a scarlet cloak with two broad gold laces, with gold buttons down the sides."

The attempts at approximation of the dress of certain occupations and nationalities also can be documented from the plays themselves, and it derives additional confirmation from a drawing of the first scene of Shakespeare's *Titus Andronicus*—the only extant Elizabethan picture of an identifiable episode in a play. (See pp. xxxviii–xxxix.) The drawing, probably done in 1594 or 1595, shows Queen Tamora pleading for mercy. She wears a somewhat medieval-looking robe and a crown; Titus wears a toga and a wreath, but two soldiers behind him wear costumes fairly close to Elizabethan dress. We do not know, however, if the drawing represents an actual stage production in the public theater, or perhaps a private production, or maybe only a reader's visualization of an episode. Further, there is some conflicting evidence: In *Julius Caesar* a reference is made to Caesar's doublet (a close-fitting jacket), which, if taken literally, suggests that even the protagonist did not wear Roman clothing; and certainly the lesser characters, who are said to wear hats, did not wear Roman garb.

It should be mentioned, too, that even ordinary clothing can be symbolic: Hamlet's "inky cloak," for example, sets him apart from the brightly dressed members of Claudius's court and symbolizes his mourning; the fresh clothes that are put on King Lear partly symbolize his return to sanity. Consider, too, the removal of disguises near the end of some plays. For instance, Rosalind in *As You Like It* and Portia and Nerissa in *The Merchant of Venice* remove their male attire, thus again becoming fully themselves.

Gestures and Silences: Gestures are an important part of a dramatist's language. King Lear kneels before his daughter Cordelia for a benediction (4.7.57–59), an act of humility that contrasts with his earlier speeches banishing her and that contrasts also with a comparable gesture, his ironic

kneeling before Regan (2.4.153–55). Northumberland's
failure to kneel before King Richard II (3.3.71–72) speaks
volumes. As for silences, consider a moment in *Coriolanus*:
Before the protagonist yields to his mother's entreaties
(5.3.182), there is this stage direction: *"Holds her by the
hand, silent."* Another example of "speech in dumbness"
occurs in *Macbeth*, when Macduff learns that his wife and
children have been murdered. He is silent at first, as Malcolm's speech indicates: "What, man! Ne'er pull your hat
upon your brows. Give sorrow words" (4.3.208–09). (For
a discussion of such moments, see Philip C. McGuire's
Speechless Dialect: Shakespeare's Open Silences [1985].)

Of course when we think of Shakespeare's work, we think
primarily of his language, both the poetry and the prose.

Prose: Although two of his plays (*Richard II* and *King John*)
have no prose at all, about half the others have at least one
quarter of the dialogue in prose, and some have notably
more: *1 Henry IV* and *2 Henry IV*, about half; *As You Like It*

and *Twelfth Night*, a little more than half; *Much Ado About
Nothing*, more than three quarters; and *The Merry Wives of
Windsor*, a little more than five sixths. We should remember
that despite Molière's joke about M. Jourdain, who was
amazed to learn that he spoke prose, most of us do not
speak prose. Rather, we normally utter repetitive, shapeless,
and often ungrammatical torrents; prose is something very
different—a sort of literary imitation of speech at its most
coherent.

Today we may think of prose as "natural" for drama; or
even if we think that poetry is appropriate for high tragedy
we may still think that prose is the right medium for comedy.
Greek, Roman, and early English comedies, however, were
written in verse. In fact, prose was not generally considered
a literary medium in England until the late fifteenth century;
Chaucer tells even his bawdy stories in verse. By the end of
the 1580s, however, prose had established itself on the
English comic stage. In tragedy, Marlowe made some use of
prose, not simply in the speeches of clownish servants but

even in the speech of a tragic hero, Doctor Faustus. Still, before Shakespeare, prose normally was used in the theater only for special circumstances: (1) letters and proclamations, to set them off from the poetic dialogue; (2) mad characters, to indicate that normal thinking has become disordered; and (3) low comedy, or speeches uttered by clowns even when they are not being comic. Shakespeare made use of these conventions, but he also went far beyond them. Sometimes he begins a scene in prose and then shifts into verse as the emotion is heightened; or conversely, he may shift from verse to prose when a speaker is lowering the emotional level, as when Brutus speaks in the Forum.

Shakespeare's prose usually is not prosaic. Hamlet's prose includes not only small talk with Rosencrantz and Guildenstern but also princely reflections on "What a piece of work is a man" (2.2.312). In conversation with Ophelia, he shifts from light talk in verse to a passionate prose denunciation of women (3.1.103), though the shift to prose here is perhaps also intended to suggest the possibility of madness. (Consult Brian Vickers, *The Artistry of Shakespeare's Prose* [1968].)

Poetry: Drama in rhyme in England goes back to the Middle Ages, but by Shakespeare's day rhyme no longer dominated poetic drama; a finer medium, blank verse (strictly speaking, unrhymed lines of ten syllables, with the stress on every second syllable) had been adopted. But before looking at unrhymed poetry, a few things should be said about the chief uses of rhyme in Shakespeare's plays. (1) A couplet (a pair of rhyming lines) is sometimes used to convey emotional heightening at the end of a blank verse speech; (2) characters sometimes speak a couplet as they leave the stage, suggesting closure; (3) except in the latest plays, scenes fairly often conclude with a couplet, and sometimes, as in *Richard II*, 2.1.145–46, the entrance of a new character within a scene is preceded by a couplet, which wraps up the earlier portion of that scene; (4) speeches of two characters occasionally are linked by rhyme, most notably in *Romeo and Juliet*, 1.5.95–108, where the lovers speak a sonnet between them; elsewhere a taunting reply occasionally rhymes with the previous speaker's last line; (5) speeches with sententious or gnomic remarks are sometimes in rhyme, as in the duke's speech in *Othello* (1.3.199–206); (6) speeches of sardonic mockery are sometimes in rhyme—for example, Iago's speech on women in *Othello* (2.1.146–58)—and they sometimes conclude with an emphatic couplet, as in Bolingbroke's speech on comforting words in *Richard II* (1.3.301–2); (7) some characters are associated with rhyme, such as the fairies in *A Midsummer Night's Dream*; (8) in the early plays, especially *The Comedy of Errors* and *The Taming of the Shrew*, comic scenes that in later plays would be in prose are in jingling rhymes; (9) prologues, choruses, plays-within-the-play, inscriptions, vows, epilogues, and so on are often in rhyme, and the songs in the plays are rhymed.

Neither prose nor rhyme immediately comes to mind when we first think of Shakespeare's medium: It is blank verse, unrhymed iambic pentameter. (In a mechanically exact line there are five iambic feet. An iambic foot consists of two syllables, the second accented, as in *away*; five feet make a pentameter line. Thus, a strict line of iambic pentameter contains ten syllables, the even syllables being stressed more heavily than the odd syllables. Fortunately, Shakespeare usually varies the line somewhat.) The first speech in *A Midsummer Night's Dream*, spoken by Duke Theseus to his betrothed, is an example of blank verse:

> Now, fair Hippolyta, our nuptial hour
> Draws on apace. Four happy days bring in
> Another moon; but, O, methinks, how slow
> This old moon wanes! She lingers my desires,
> Like to a stepdame, or a dowager,
> Long withering out a young man's revenue.   (1.1.1–6)

As this passage shows, Shakespeare's blank verse is not mechanically unvarying. Though the predominant foot is the iamb (as in *apace* or *desires*), there are numerous variations. In the first line the stress can be placed on "fair," as the regular metrical pattern suggests, but it is likely that "Now" gets almost as much emphasis; probably in the second line "Draws" is more heavily emphasized than "on," giving us a trochee (a stressed syllable followed by an unstressed one); and in the fourth line each word in the phrase "This old moon wanes" is probably stressed fairly heavily, conveying by two spondees (two feet, each of two stresses) the oppressive tedium that Theseus feels.

In Shakespeare's early plays much of the blank verse is end-stopped (that is, it has a heavy pause at the end of each line), but he later developed the ability to write iambic pentameter verse paragraphs (rather than lines) that give the illusion of speech. His chief techniques are (1) enjambing, i.e., running the thought beyond the single line, as in the first three lines of the speech just quoted; (2) occasionally replacing an iamb with another foot; (3) varying the position of the chief pause (the caesura) within a line; (4) adding an occasional unstressed syllable at the end of a line, traditionally called a feminine ending; (5) and beginning or ending a speech with a half line.

Shakespeare's mature blank verse has much of the rhythmic flexibility of his prose; both the language, though richly figurative and sometimes dense, and the syntax seem natural. It is also often highly appropriate to a particular character. Consider, for instance, this speech from *Hamlet*, in which Claudius, King of Denmark ("the Dane"), speaks to Laertes:

> And now, Laertes, what's the news with you?
> You told us of some suit. What is't, Laertes?
> You cannot speak of reason to the Dane
> And lose your voice. What wouldst thou beg, Laertes,
> That shall not be my offer, not thy asking?   (1.2.42–46)

Notice the short sentences and the repetition of the name "Laertes," to whom the speech is addressed. Notice, too, the shift from the royal "us" in the second line to the more intimate "my" in the last line, and from "you" in the first three lines to the more intimate "thou" and "thy" in the last two lines. Claudius knows how to ingratiate himself with Laertes.

For a second example of the flexibility of Shakespeare's blank verse, consider a passage from *Macbeth*. Distressed by the doctor's inability to cure Lady Macbeth and by the imminent battle, Macbeth addresses some of his remarks to the doctor and others to the servant who is arming him. The entire speech, with its pauses, interruptions, and irresolution (in "Pull't off, I say," Macbeth orders the servant to remove the armor that the servant has been putting on him), catches Macbeth's disintegration. (In the first line, *physic* means "medicine," and in the fourth and fifth lines, *cast the water* means "analyze the urine.")

> Throw physic to the dogs, I'll none of it.
> Come, put mine armor on. Give me my staff.
> Seyton, send out.—Doctor, the thanes fly from me.—
> Come, sir, dispatch. If thou couldst, doctor, cast
> The water of my land, find her disease
> And purge it to a sound and pristine health,
> I would applaud thee to the very echo,
> That should applaud again.—Pull't off, I say.—
> What rhubarb, senna, or what purgative drug,
> Would scour these English hence? Hear'st thou of them?
>
> (5.3.47–56)

Blank verse, then, can be much more than unrhymed iambic pentameter, and even within a single play Shakespeare's blank verse often consists of several styles, depending on the speaker and on the speaker's emotion at the moment.

The Play Text as a Collaboration

Shakespeare's fellow dramatist Ben Jonson reported that the actors said of Shakespeare, "In his writing, whatsoever he penned, he never blotted out line," i.e., never crossed out material and revised his work while composing. None of Shakespeare's plays survives in manuscript (with the possible exception of a scene in *Sir Thomas More*), so we cannot fully evaluate the comment, but in a few instances the published work clearly shows that he revised his manuscript. Consider the following passage (shown here in facsimile) from the best early text of *Romeo and Juliet*, the Second Quarto (1599):

Ro. Would I were sleepe and peace so sweet to rest
The grey eyde morne smiles on the frowning night,
Checkring the Easterne Clouds with streaks of light,
And darknesse fleckted like a drunkard reeles,
From forth daies pathway, made by *Tytans* wheeles.
Hence will I to my ghostly Friers close cell,
His helpe to craue, and my deare hap to tell.

                                               Exit.

Enter Frier alone with a basket.   (night,
Fri. The grey-eyed morne smiles on the frowning
Checking the Easterne clowdes with streaks of light:
And fleckeld darknesse like a drunkard reeles,
From forth daies path, and *Titans* burning wheeles:
Now ere the sun aduance his burning eie,

Romeo rather elaborately tells us that the sun at dawn is
dispelling the night (morning is smiling, the eastern clouds
are checked with light, and the sun's chariot—Titan's
wheels—advances), and he will seek out his spiritual father,
the Friar. He exits and, oddly, the Friar enters and says pretty
much the same thing about the sun. Both speakers say that
"the gray-eyed morn smiles on the frowning night," but there
are small differences, perhaps having more to do with the
business of printing the book than with the author's
composition: For Romeo's "checkring," "fleckted," and
"pathway," we get the Friar's "checking," "fleckeld," and
"path." (Notice, by the way, the inconsistency in Elizabethan
spelling: Romeo's "clouds" become the Friar's "clowdes.")
  Both versions must have been in the printer's copy, and it
seems safe to assume that both were in Shakespeare's manuscript. He must have written one version—let's say he first
wrote Romeo's closing lines for this scene—and then he
decided, no, it's better to give this lyrical passage to the
Friar, as the opening of a new scene, but he neglected to
delete the first version. Editors must make a choice, and they
may feel that the reasonable thing to do is to print the text as
Shakespeare intended it. But how can we know what he
intended? Almost all modern editors delete the lines from

Romeo's speech, and retain the Friar's lines. They don't do this because they know Shakespeare's intention, however. They give the lines to the Friar because the first published version (1597) of *Romeo and Juliet* gives only the Friar's version, and this text (though in many ways inferior to the 1599 text) is thought to derive from the memory of some actors, that is, it is thought to represent a performance, not just a script. Maybe during the course of rehearsals Shakespeare—an actor as well as an author—unilaterally decided that the Friar should speak the lines; if so (remember that we don't know this to be a fact) his final intention was to give the speech to the Friar. Maybe, however, the actors talked it over and settled on the Friar, with or without Shakespeare's approval. On the other hand, despite the 1597 version, one might argue (if only weakly) on behalf of giving the lines to Romeo rather than to the Friar, thus: (1) Romeo's comment on the coming of the daylight emphasizes his separation from Juliet, and (2) the figurative language seems more appropriate to Romeo than to the Friar. Having said this, in the Signet edition we have decided in this instance to draw on the evidence provided by earlier text and to give the lines to the Friar, on the grounds that since Q1 reflects a production, in the theater (at least on one occasion) the lines were spoken by the Friar.

A playwright sold a script to a theatrical company. The script thus belonged to the company, not the author, and author and company alike must have regarded this script not as a literary work but as the basis for a play that the actors would create on the stage. We speak of Shakespeare as the author of the plays, but readers should bear in mind that the texts they read, even when derived from a single text, such as the First Folio (1623), are inevitably the collaborative work not simply of Shakespeare with his company—doubtless during rehearsals the actors would suggest alterations—but also with other forces of the age. One force was governmental censorship. In 1606 parliament passed "an Act to restrain abuses of players," prohibiting the utterance of oaths and the name of God. So where the earliest text of *Othello* gives us "By heaven" (3.3.106), the first Folio gives "Alas," presumably reflecting the compliance of stage practice with the law. Similarly, the 1623 version of *King Lear* omits the oath "Fut" (probably from "By God's foot") at 1.2.142, again presumably reflecting the line as it was spoken on the stage. Editors who seek to give the reader the play that Shakespeare initially conceived—the "authentic" play conceived by the solitary Shakespeare—probably will restore the missing oaths and references to God. Other editors, who see the play as a collaborative work, a construction made not only by Shakespeare but also by actors and compositors and even government censors, may claim that what counts is the play as it was actually performed. Such editors regard the censored text as legitimate, since it is the play that was (presumably) finally put on. A performed text, they argue, has more historical reality than a text produced by an editor who has sought to get at what Shakespeare initially wrote. In this view, the text of a play is rather like the script of a film; the script is not the film, and the play text is not the performed play. Even if we want to talk about the play that Shakespeare "intended," we will find ourselves talking about a script that he handed over to a company with the intention that it be implemented by actors. The "intended" play is the one that the actors—we might almost say "society"—would help to construct.

Further, it is now widely held that a play is also the work of readers and spectators, who do not simply receive meaning, but who create it when they respond to the play. This idea is fully in accord with contemporary post-structuralist critical thinking, notably Roland Barthes's "The Death of the Author," in *Image-Music-Text* (1977) and Michel Foucault's "What Is an Author?," in *The Foucault Reader* (1984). The gist of the idea is that an author is not an isolated genius; rather, authors are subject to the politics and other social structures of their age. A dramatist especially is a worker in a collaborative project, working most obviously with actors—parts may be written for particular actors—but working also with the audience. Consider the words of Samuel Johnson, written to be spoken by the actor David Garrick at the opening of a theater in 1747:

> The stage but echoes back the public voice;
> The drama's laws, the drama's patrons give,
> For we that live to please, must please to live.

The audience—the public taste as understood by the play-wright—helps to determine what the play is. Moreover, even members of the public who are not part of the playwright's immediate audience may exert an influence through censorship. We have already glanced at governmental censorship, but there are also other kinds. Take one of Shakespeare's most beloved characters, Falstaff, who appears in three of Shakespeare's plays, the two parts of *Henry IV* and *The Merry Wives of Windsor*. He appears with this name in the earliest printed version of the first of these plays, *1 Henry IV*, but we know that Shakespeare originally called him (after an historical figure) Sir John Oldcastle. Oldcastle appears in Shakespeare's source (partly reprinted in the Signet edition of *1 Henry IV*), and a trace of the name survives in Shakespeare's play, 1.2.43–44, where Prince Hal punningly addresses Falstaff as "my old lad of the castle." But for some reason—perhaps because the family of the historical Oldcastle complained—Shakespeare had to change the name. In short, the play as we have it was (at least in this detail) subject to some sort of censorship. If we think that a text should present what we take to be the author's intention, we probably will want to replace *Falstaff* with *Oldcastle*. But if we recognize that a play is a collaboration, we may welcome the change, even if it was forced on Shakespeare. Somehow *Falstaff*, with its hint of *false-staff*, i.e., inadequate prop, seems just right for this fat knight who, to our delight, entertains the young prince with untruths. We can go as far as saying that, at least so far as a play is concerned, an insistence on the author's original intention (even if we could know it) can sometimes impoverish the text.

The tiny example of Falstaff's name illustrates the point that the text we read is inevitably only a version—something in effect produced by the collaboration of the playwright with his actors, audiences, compositors, and editors—of a fluid text that Shakespeare once wrote, just as the *Hamlet* that we see on the screen starring Kenneth Branagh is not the *Hamlet* that Shakespeare saw in an open-air playhouse starring Richard Burbage. *Hamlet* itself, as we shall note in a moment, also exists in several versions. It is not surprising that there is now much talk about the *instability* of Shakespeare's texts.

Because he was not only a playwright but was also an actor and a shareholder in a theatrical company, Shakespeare probably was much involved with the translation of the play from a manuscript to a stage production. He may or may not have done some rewriting during rehearsals, and he may or may not have been happy with cuts that were made. Some plays, notably *Hamlet* and *King Lear*, are so long that it is most unlikely that the texts we read were acted in their entirety. Further, for both of these plays we have more than one early text that demands consideration. In *Hamlet*, the Second Quarto (1604) includes some two hundred lines not found in the Folio (1623). Among the passages missing from the Folio are two of Hamlet's reflective speeches, the "dram of evil" speech (1.4.13–38) and "How all occasions do inform against me" (4.4.32–66). Since the Folio has more numerous and often fuller stage directions, it certainly looks as though in the Folio we get a theatrical version of the play, a text whose cuts were probably made—this is only a hunch, of course—not because Shakespeare was changing his conception of Hamlet but because the playhouse demanded a modified play. (The problem is complicated, since the Folio not only cuts some of the Quarto but adds some material. Various explanations have been offered.)

Or take an example from *King Lear*. In the First and Second Quarto (1608, 1619), the final speech of the play is given to Albany, Lear's surviving son-in-law, but in the First Folio version (1623), the speech is given to Edgar. The Quarto version is in accord with tradition—usually the highest-ranking character in a tragedy speaks the final words. Why does the Folio give the speech to Edgar? One possible answer is this: The Folio version omits some of Albany's speeches in earlier scenes, so perhaps it was decided (by Shakespeare? by the players?) not to give the final lines to so pale a character. In fact, the discrepancies are so many between the two texts, that some scholars argue we do not simply have texts showing different theatrical productions. Rather, these scholars say, Shakespeare substantially revised the play, and we really have two versions of *King Lear* (and of *Othello* also, say some)—two different plays—not simply two texts, each of which is in some ways imperfect.

In this view, the 1608 version of *Lear* may derive from Shakespeare's manuscript, and the 1623 version may derive from his later revision. The Quartos have almost three hundred lines not in the Folio, and the Folio has about a hundred lines not in the Quartos. It used to be held that all the texts were imperfect in various ways and from various causes—some passages in the Quartos were thought to have been set from a manuscript that was not entirely legible, other passages were thought to have been set by a compositor who was new to setting plays, and still other passages were thought to have been provided by an actor who misremembered some of the lines. This traditional view held that an editor must draw on the Quartos and the Folio in order to get Shakespeare's "real" play. The new argument holds (although not without considerable strain) that we have two authentic plays, Shakespeare's early version (in the Quarto) and Shakespeare's—or his theatrical company's—revised version (in the Folio). Not only theatrical demands but also Shakespeare's own artistic sense, it is argued, called for extensive revisions. Even the titles vary: Q1 is called *True Chronicle Historie of the life and death of King Lear and his three Daughters*, whereas the Folio text is called *The Tragedie of King Lear*. To combine the two texts in order to produce what the editor thinks is the play that Shakespeare intended to write is, according to this view, to produce a text that is false to the history of the play. If the new view is correct, and we do have texts of two distinct versions of *Lear* rather than two imperfect versions of one play, it supports in a textual way the poststructuralist view that we cannot possibly have an unmediated vision of (in this case) a play by Shakespeare; we can only recognize a plurality of visions.

Editing Texts

Though eighteen of his plays were published during his lifetime, Shakespeare seems never to have supervised their publication. There is nothing unusual here; when a playwright sold a play to a theatrical company he surrendered his ownership to it. Normally a company would not publish the play, because to publish it meant to allow competitors to acquire the piece. Some plays did get published: Apparently hard-up actors sometimes pieced together a play for a publisher; sometimes a company in need of money sold a play; and sometimes a company allowed publication of a play that no longer drew audiences. That Shakespeare did not concern himself with publication is not remarkable; of his contemporaries, only Ben Jonson carefully supervised the publication of his own plays.

In 1623, seven years after Shakespeare's death, John Heminges and Henry Condell (two senior members of Shakespeare's company, who had worked with him for about twenty years) collected his plays—published and unpublished—into a large volume, of a kind called a folio. (A folio is a volume consisting of large sheets that have been folded once, each sheet thus making two leaves, or four pages. The size of the page of course depends on the size of the sheet—a folio can range in height from twelve to sixteen inches, and in width from eight to eleven; the pages in the 1623 edition of Shakespeare, commonly called the First Folio, are approximately thirteen inches tall and eight inches wide.) The eighteen plays published during Shakespeare's lifetime had been issued one play per volume in small formats called quartos. (Each sheet in a quarto has been folded twice, making four leaves, or eight pages, each page being about nine inches tall and seven inches wide, roughly the size of a large paperback.)

Heminges and Condell suggest in an address "To the great variety of readers" that the republished plays are presented in better form than in the quartos:

> Before you were abused with diverse stolen and surreptitious copies, maimed and deformed by the frauds and stealths of injurious impostors that exposed them; even those, are now offered to your view cured and perfect of their limbs, and all the rest absolute in their numbers, as he [i.e., Shakespeare] conceived them.

There is a good deal of truth to this statement, but some of the quarto versions are better than others; some are in fact preferable to the Folio text.

Whoever was assigned to prepare the texts for publication

in the first Folio seems to have taken the job seriously and yet not to have performed it with uniform care. The sources of the texts seem to have been, in general, good unpublished copies or the best published copies. The first play in the collection, *The Tempest*, is divided into acts and scenes, has unusually full stage directions and descriptions of spectacle, and concludes with a list of the characters, but the editor was not able (or willing) to present all of the succeeding texts so fully dressed. Later texts occasionally show signs of carelessness: in one scene of *Much Ado About Nothing* the names of actors, instead of characters, appear as speech prefixes, as they had in the Quarto, which the Folio reprints; proofreading throughout the Folio is spotty and apparently was done without reference to the printer's copy; the pagination of *Hamlet* jumps from 156 to 257. Further, the proofreading was done while the presses continued to print, so that each play in each volume contains a mix of corrected and uncorrected pages.

Modern editors of Shakespeare must first select their copy; no problem if the play exists only in the Folio, but a considerable problem if the relationship between a Quarto and the Folio—or an early Quarto and a later one—is unclear. In the case of *Romeo and Juliet*, the First Quarto (Q1), published in 1597, is vastly inferior to the Second (Q2), published in 1599. The basis of Q1 apparently is a version put together from memory by some actors. Not surprisingly, it garbles many passages and is much shorter than Q2. On the other hand, occasionally Q1 makes better sense than Q2. For instance, near the end of the play, when the parents have assembled and learned of the deaths of Romeo and Juliet, in Q2 the Prince says (5.3.208–9),

Come, *Montague;* for thou art early vp
To see thy sonne and heire, now earling downe.

The last three words of this speech surely do not make sense, and many editors turn to Q1, which instead of "now earling downe" has "more early downe." Some modern editors take only "early" from Q1, and print "now early down"; others take "more early," and print "more early down." Further, Q1 (though, again, quite clearly a garbled and abbreviated text) includes some stage directions that are not found in Q2, and today many editors who base their text on Q2 are glad to add these stage directions, because the directions help to give us a sense of what the play looked like on Shakespeare's stage. Thus, in 4.3.58, after Juliet drinks the potion, Q1 gives us this stage direction, not in Q2: *"She falls upon her bed within the curtains."*

In short, an editor's decisions do not end with the choice of a single copy text. First of all, editors must reckon with Elizabethan spelling. If they are not producing a facsimile, they probably modernize the spelling, but ought they to preserve the old forms of words that apparently were pronounced quite unlike their modern forms—*lanthorn, alablaster*? If they preserve these forms are they really preserving Shakespeare's forms or perhaps those of a compositor in the printing house? What is one to do when one finds *lanthorn* and *lantern* in adjacent lines? (The editors of this series in general, but not invariably, assume that words should be spelled in their modern form, unless, for instance, a rhyme is involved.) Elizabethan punctuation, too, presents problems. For example, in the First Folio, the only text for the play, Macbeth rejects his wife's idea that he can wash the blood from his hand (2.2.60–62):

> No: this my Hand will rather
> The multitudinous Seas incarnardine,
> Making the Greene one, Red.

Obviously an editor will remove the superfluous capitals, and will probably alter the spelling to "incarnadine," but what about the comma before "Red"? If we retain the comma, Macbeth is calling the sea "the green one." If we drop the comma, Macbeth is saying that his bloody hand will make the sea ("the Green") *uniformly* red.

An editor will sometimes have to change more than spelling and punctuation. Macbeth says to his wife (1.7.46–47):

> I dare do all that may become a man,
> Who dares no more, is none.

For two centuries editors have agreed that the second line is unsatisfactory, and have emended "no" to "do": "Who dares do more is none." But when in the same play (4.2.21–22) Ross says that fearful persons

> Floate vpon a wilde and violent Sea
> Each way, and moue,

need we emend the passage? On the assumption that the compositor misread the manuscript, some editors emend "each way, and move" to "and move each way"; others emend "move" to "none" (i.e., "Each way and none"). Other editors, however, let the passage stand as in the original. The editors of the Signet Classic Shakespeare have restrained themselves from making abundant emendations. In their minds they hear Samuel Johnson on the dangers of emendation: "I have adopted the Roman sentiment, that it is more honorable to save a citizen than to kill an enemy." Some departures (in addition to spelling, punctuation, and lineation) from the copy text have of course been made, but the original readings are listed in a note following the play, so that readers can evaluate the changes for themselves.

Following tradition, the editors of the Signet Classic Shakespeare have prefaced each play with a list of characters, and throughout the play have regularized the names of the speakers. Thus, in our text of *Romeo and Juliet*, all speeches by Juliet's mother are prefixed "Lady Capulet," although the 1599 Quarto of the play, which provides our copy text, uses at various points seven speech tags for this one character: *Capu. Wi.* (i.e., Capulet's wife), *Ca. Wi., Wi., Wife, Old La.* (i.e., Old Lady), *La.,* and *Mo.* (i.e., Mother). Similarly, in *All's Well That Ends Well*, the character whom we regularly call "Countess" is in the Folio (the copy text) variously identified as *Mother, Countess, Old Countess, Lady,* and *Old Lady.* Admittedly there is some loss in regularizing, since the various prefixes may give us a hint of the way Shakespeare (or a scribe who copied Shakespeare's manuscript) was thinking of the character in a particular scene—for instance, as a mother, or as an old lady. But too much can be made of these differing prefixes, since the social relationships implied are *not* always relevant to the given scene.

We have also added line numbers and in many cases act and scene divisions as well as indications of locale at the beginning of scenes. The Folio divided most of the plays into acts and some into scenes. Early eighteenth-century editors increased the divisions. These divisions, which provide a convenient way of referring to passages in the plays, have been retained, but when not in the text chosen as the basis for the Signet Classic text they are enclosed within square brackets, [ ], to indicate that they are editorial additions. Similarly, though no play of Shakespeare's was equipped with indications of the locale at the heads of scene divisions, locales have here been added in square brackets for the convenience of readers, who lack the information that costumes, properties, gestures, and scenery afford to spectators. Spectators can tell at a glance they are in the throne room, but without an editorial indication the reader may be puzzled for a while. It should be mentioned, incidentally, that there are a few authentic stage directions—perhaps Shakespeare's, perhaps a prompter's—that suggest locales, such as *"Enter Brutus in his orchard,"* and *"They go up into the Senate house."* It is hoped that the bracketed additions in the Signet text will provide readers with the sort of help provided by these two authentic directions, but it is equally hoped that the reader will remember that the stage was not loaded with scenery.

Shakespeare on the Stage

Each volume in the Signet Classic Shakespeare includes a brief stage (and sometimes film) history of the play. When we read about earlier productions, we are likely to find them eccentric, obviously wrongheaded—for instance, Nahum Tate's version of *King Lear*, with a happy ending, which held the stage for about a century and a half, from the late seventeenth century until the end of the first quarter of the nineteenth. We see engravings of David Garrick, the greatest actor of the eighteenth century, in eighteenth-century garb as King Lear, and we smile, thinking how absurd the production must have been. If we are more thoughtful, we say, with the English novelist L. P. Hartley, "The past is a foreign country: they do things differently there." But if the eighteenth-century staging is a foreign country, what of the plays of the late sixteenth and seventeenth centuries? A foreign language, a foreign theater, a foreign audience.

Probably all viewers of Shakespeare's plays, beginning with Shakespeare himself, at times have been unhappy with the plays on the stage. Consider three comments about production that we find in the plays themselves, which suggest Shakespeare's concerns. The Chorus in *Henry V* complains that the heroic story cannot possibly be adequately staged:

> But pardon, gentles all,
> The flat unraisèd spirits that hath dared
> On this unworthy scaffold to bring forth
> So great an object. Can this cockpit hold
> The vasty fields of France? Or may we cram
> Within this wooden *O* the very casques
> That did affright the air at Agincourt?
>
> . . . .
>
> Piece out our imperfections with your thoughts.
>
> (Prologue 1.8–14,23)

Second, here are a few sentences (which may or may not represent Shakespeare's own views) from Hamlet's longish lecture to the players:

Speak the speech, I pray you, as I pronounced it to you, trippingly on the tongue. But if you mouth it, as many of our players do, I had as lief the town crier spoke my lines. . . . O, it offends me to the soul to hear a robustious periwig-pated fellow tear a passion to tatters, to very rags, to split the ears of the groundlings. . . . And let those that play your clowns speak no more than is set down for them, for there be of them that will themselves laugh, to set on some quantity of barren spectators to laugh too, though in the meantime some necessary question of the play be then to be considered. That's villainous and shows a most pitiful ambition in the fool that uses it. (3.2.1–47)

Finally, we can quote again from the passage cited earlier in this introduction, concerning the boy actors who played the female roles. Cleopatra imagines with horror a theatrical version of her activities with Antony:

> The quick comedians
> Extemporally will stage us, and present
> Our Alexandrian revels: Antony
> Shall be brought drunken forth, and I shall see
> Some squeaking Cleopatra boy my greatness
> I' th' posture of a whore.   (5.2.216–21)

It is impossible to know how much weight to put on such passages—perhaps Shakespeare was just being modest about his theater's abilities—but it is easy enough to think that he was unhappy with some aspects of Elizabethan production. Probably no production can fully satisfy a playwright, and for that matter, few productions can fully satisfy *us;* we regret this or that cut, this or that way of costuming the play, this or that bit of business.

One's first thought may be this: Why don't they just do "authentic" Shakespeare, "straight" Shakespeare, the play as Shakespeare wrote it? But as we read the plays—words written to be performed—it sometimes becomes clear that we do not know *how* to perform them. For instance, in *Antony and Cleopatra* Antony, the Roman general who has succumbed to Cleopatra and to Egyptian ways, says, "The nobleness of life / Is to do thus" (1.1.36–37). But what is "thus"? Does Antony at this point embrace Cleopatra? Does he embrace and kiss her? (There are, by the way, very few scenes of kissing on Shakespeare's stage, possibly because boys played the female roles.) Or does he make a sweeping gesture, indicating the Egyptian way of life?

This is not an isolated example; the plays are filled with lines that call for gestures, but we are not sure what the gestures should be. *Interpretation* is inevitable. Consider a passage in *Hamlet*. In 3.1, Polonius persuades his daughter, Ophelia, to talk to Hamlet while Polonius and Claudius eavesdrop. The two men conceal themselves, and Hamlet encounters Ophelia. At 3.1.131 Hamlet suddenly says to her, "Where's your father?" Why does Hamlet, apparently out of nowhere—they have not been talking about Polonius—ask this question? Is this an example of the "antic disposition" (fantastic behavior) that Hamlet earlier (1.5.172) had told Horatio and others—including us—he would display? That is, is the question about the whereabouts of her father a seemingly irrational one, like his earlier question (3.1.103) to Ophelia, "Ha, ha! Are you honest?" Or, on the other hand, has Hamlet (as in many productions) suddenly glimpsed Polonius's foot protruding from beneath a drapery at the rear? That is, does Hamlet ask the question because he has suddenly seen something suspicious and now is testing Ophelia? (By the way, in productions that do give Hamlet a physical cue, it is almost always Polonius rather than Claudius who provides the clue. This itself is an act of interpretation on the part of the director.) Or (a third possibility) does Hamlet get a clue from Ophelia, who inadvertently betrays the spies by nervously glancing at their place of hiding? This is the interpretation used in the BBC television version, where Ophelia glances in fear toward the hiding place just after Hamlet says "Why wouldst thou be a breeder of sinners?" (121–22). Hamlet, realizing that he is being observed, glances here and there *before* he asks "Where's your father?" The question thus is a climax to what he has been doing while speaking the preceding lines. Or (a fourth interpretation) does Hamlet suddenly, without the aid of any clue whatsoever, intuitively (insightfully, mysteriously, wonderfully) sense that someone is spying? Directors must decide, of course—and so must readers.

Recall, too, the preceding discussion of the texts of the plays, which argued that the texts—though they seem to be before us in permanent black on white—are unstable. The Signet text of *Hamlet*, which draws on the Second Quarto (1604) and the First Folio (1623) is considerably longer than any version staged in Shakespeare's time. Our version, even if spoken very briskly and played without any intermission, would take close to four hours, far beyond "the two hours' traffic of our stage" mentioned in the Prologue to *Romeo and Juliet*. (There are a few contemporary references to the duration of a play, but none mentions more than three hours.) Of Shakespeare's plays, only *The Comedy of Errors*, *Macbeth*, and *The Tempest* can be done in less than three hours without cutting. And even if we take a play that exists only in a short text, *Macbeth*, we cannot claim that we are experiencing the very play that Shakespeare conceived, partly because some of the Witches' songs almost surely are non-Shakespearean additions, and partly because we are not willing to watch the play performed without an intermission and with boys in the female roles.

Further, as the earlier discussion of costumes mentioned, the plays apparently were given chiefly in contemporary, that is, in Elizabethan dress. If today we give them in the costumes that Shakespeare probably saw, the plays seem not contemporary but curiously dated. Yet if we use our own dress, we find lines of dialogue that are at odds with what we see; we may feel that the language, so clearly not our own, is inappropriate coming out of people in today's dress. A common solution, incidentally, has been to set the plays in the nineteenth century, on the grounds that this attractively distances the plays (gives them a degree of foreignness, allowing for interesting costumes) and yet doesn't put them into a museum world of Elizabethan England.

Inevitably our productions are adaptations, *our* adaptations, and inevitably they will look dated, not in a century but in twenty years, or perhaps even in a decade. Still, we cannot escape from our own conceptions. As the director Peter Brook has said, in *The Empty Space* (1968):

> It is not only the hair-styles, costumes and make-ups that look dated. All the different elements of staging—the shorthands of behavior that stand for emotions; gestures, gesticulations and tones of voice—are all fluctuating on an invisible stock exchange all the time. . . . A living theatre that thinks it can stand aloof from anything as trivial as fashion will wilt. (p. 16)

As Brook indicates, it is through today's hairstyles, costumes, makeup, gestures, gesticulations, tones of voice—this includes our *conception* of earlier hairstyles, costumes, and so forth if we stage the play in a period other than our own—that we inevitably stage the plays.

It is a truism that every age invents its own Shakespeare, just as, for instance, every age has invented its own classical world. Our view of ancient Greece, a slave-holding society in which even free Athenian women were severely circumscribed, does not much resemble the Victorians' view of ancient Greece as a glorious democracy, just as, perhaps, our view of Victorianism itself does not much resemble theirs. We cannot claim that the Shakespeare on our stage is the true Shakespeare, but in our stage productions we find a Shakespeare that speaks to us, a Shakespeare that our ancestors doubtless did not know but one that seems to us to be the true Shakespeare—at least for a while.

Our age is remarkable for the wide variety of kinds of staging that it uses for Shakespeare, but one development deserves special mention. This is the now common practice of race-blind or color-blind or nontraditional casting, which allows persons who are not white to play in Shakespeare. Previously blacks performing in Shakespeare were limited to a mere three roles, Othello, Aaron (in *Titus Andronicus*), and the Prince of Morocco (in *The Merchant of Venice*), and there were no roles at all for Asians. Indeed, African-Americans rarely could play even one of these three roles, since they were not welcome in white companies. Ira Aldridge (c.1806–1867), a black actor of undoubted talent, was forced to make his living by performing Shakespeare in England and in Europe, where he could play not only Othello but also—in whiteface—other tragic roles such as King Lear. Paul Robeson (1898–1976) made theatrical history when he played Othello in London in 1930, and there was some talk about bringing the production to the United States, but there was more talk about whether American audiences would tolerate the sight of a black man—a real black man, not a white man in blackface—kissing and then killing a white woman. The idea was tried out in summer stock in 1942, the reviews were enthusiastic, and in the following year Robeson opened on Broadway in a production that ran an astounding 296 performances. An occasional all-black company sometimes performed Shakespeare's plays, but otherwise blacks (and other minority members) were in effect shut out from performing Shakespeare. Only since about 1970 has it been common for nonwhites to play major roles along with whites. Thus, in a 1996–97 production of *Antony and Cleopatra*, a white Cleopatra, Vanessa Redgrave, played opposite a black Antony, David Harewood.

Multiracial casting is now especially common at the New York Shakespeare Festival, founded in 1954 by Joseph Papp, and in England, where even siblings such as Claudio and Isabella in *Measure for Measure* or Lear's three daughters may be of different races. Probably most viewers today soon stop worrying about the lack of realism, and move beyond the color of the performers' skin to the quality of the performance.

Nontraditional casting is not only a matter of color or race; it includes sex. In the past, occasionally a distinguished woman of the theater has taken on a male role—Sarah Bernhardt (1844–1923) as Hamlet is perhaps the most famous example—but such performances were widely regarded as eccentric. Although today there have been some performances involving cross-dressing (a drag *As You Like It* staged by the National Theatre in England in 1966 and in the United States in 1974 has achieved considerable fame in the annals of stage history), what is more interesting is the casting of women in roles that traditionally are male but that need not be. Thus, a 1993–94 English production of *Henry V* used a woman—*not* cross-dressed—in the role of the governor of Harfleur. According to Peter Holland, who reviewed the production in *Shakespeare Survey* 48 (1995), "having a female Governor of Harfleur feminized the city and provided a direct response to the horrendous threat of rape and murder that Henry had offered, his language and her body in direct connection and opposition" (p. 210). Ten years from now the device may not play so effectively, but today it speaks to us. Shakespeare, born in the Elizabethan Age, has been dead nearly four hundred years, yet he is, as Ben Jonson said, "not of an age but for all time." We must understand, however, that he is "for all time" precisely because each age finds in his abundance something for itself and something of itself.

And here we come back to two issues discussed earlier in this introduction—the instability of the text and, curiously, the Bacon/Oxford heresy concerning the authorship of the plays. *Of course* Shakespeare wrote the plays, and we should daily fall on our knees to thank him for them—and yet there is something to the idea that he is not their only author. Every editor, every director and actor, and every reader to some degree shapes them, too, for when we edit, direct, act, or read, we inevitably become Shakespeare's collaborator and re-create the plays. The plays, one might say, are so cunningly contrived that they guide our responses, tell us how we ought to feel, and make a mark on us, but (for better or for worse) we also make a mark on them.

—SYLVAN BARNET
Tufts University

Introduction

The date of *Macbeth*, like that of many of Shakespeare's plays, is not beyond all dispute, but there are good reasons for believing it was written in 1605–1606 and was performed at Hampton Court on 7 August 1606 before King James I of England and his brother-in-law, King Christian of Denmark. (James, the son of Mary Stuart, Mary Queen of Scots, had succeeded to the English throne at the death of Elizabeth I in 1603.) The play seems to have been written to please James (and perhaps thus to further the fortunes of Shakespeare's theatrical company, which in 1603 had become "His Majesty's Servants," more familiarly called the King's Men. The evidence that Shakespeare sought to please James ranges from the highly favorable portrait of Banquo, from whom the Stuarts claimed descent (the pageant in 4.1. of Banquo and the eight kings seems to be a polite tribute to James, who was the ninth Stuart monarch), to such a small detail as the omission of a defeat of the Danes—this to avoid embarrassing the visiting Danish king. Among the conspicuous contemporary allusions we can comment on three, the witches, the drunken Porter's allusion to equivocation in 2.3.8–9, and the passage about the king's healing touch in 4.3.146–59. James was deeply interested in witchcraft, and had written a book that dealt with the topic, *Daemonologie* (published in Scotland in 1597, and in England in 1603). The Porter's reference to equivocators was probably stimulated by the testimony of Father Henry Garnet, a Jesuit priest involved in the Gunpowder Plot, an unsuccessful scheme in November 1605 to blow up the Houses of Parliament and thereby kill the king and his ministers. Garnet testified that equivocation—the giving of a misleading answer under oath—was morally permissible in certain circumstances. Touching for "the King's Evil" (scrofula, or tuberculosis of the skin) was a practice that James disliked but was persuaded to adopt in order to show his concern for his subjects and also in order to enhance the mystique that a king rules by divine authority. In fact, he refused to actually touch, but he did engage in the practice of hanging a token around the neck of afflicted persons.

For a discussion of much additional evidence, a reader should consult Henry N. Paul's *The Royal Play of Macbeth* (1950), or for a highly readable brief discussion, Alvin Kernan, *Shakespeare, the King's Playwright: Theater in the Stuart Court 1603–1613* (1995). Our concern here will not be with the play Shakespeare wrote for the two kings, but with the play he wrote for us.

Although *Macbeth* draws its material from Holinshed's *Chronicles,* a historical compilation that provided Shakespeare with much of the material for the ten plays that in the Folio of 1623 comprise the section labeled "Histories," *Macbeth* was entitled a tragedy and was printed among the tragedies in the Folio. James may have looked on the play as history, but it is not history. (Banquo, for example, was a convenient invention of a Scottish historian who in the early sixteenth century needed to give the Stuart line a proper beginning.) It is something that poets and literary critics customarily consider superior to history: a vision of life that has the concreteness of history and yet the wisdom of philosophy. Of course none of Shakespeare's history plays is satisfactory history; the exclusion of *Macbeth* from the "Histories" does not mean that the editors of the Folio recognized in it any unusual departure from fact. Perhaps *Macbeth* was excluded simply because its dramatis personae are Scottish, not English. But its presence among the "Tragedies" may mean that the editors saw a fundamental difference between *Macbeth* and, say, *Richard III,* which had earlier been published as a tragedy and which is called a tragedy even while it is placed among the "Histories." When one reads or sees *Richard III,* one cannot help feeling—even despite some familiarity with modern historical accounts that have demonstrated Shakespeare's distortions of fact—that one is experiencing a re-creation or re-presentation of what men did to other men during a segment of English history. When one reads or sees *Macbeth,* one cannot help feeling that one is experiencing a re-creation or re-presentation of what a man is, in the present, even in the timeless.

Suppose we take a definition of tragedy and apply it to *Macbeth.* We may find that the play helps to support the definition, and that when we apply this touchstone we see things in the play that we might otherwise have missed. (But we will also see that the definition shrinks the play, and that after it has served its purpose it must be discarded for another that may further illuminate the play.) Let us take as our first touchstone a line uttered in Cyril Tourneur's *The Revenger's Tragedy,* a play apparently written about the same time as *Macbeth*:

> When the bad bleed, then is the tragedy good.

In this view, tragedy shows the punishment of evildoers; at its conclusion (to quote the Duke of Albany, in *King Lear*)

> All friends shall taste
> The wages of their virtue, and all foes
> The cup of their deservings.   (5.3.304–6)

What is there of this in *Macbeth?* If Tourneur's "bad" includes, as it must, a man who knowingly kills his benefactor, and who follows this murder with tyrannical assaults upon the lives of his countrymen (including women and children), then the formula has some relevance to *Macbeth.* For although most discussions of tragedy start from Aristotle's assumption that the best tragedy concerns a man who does a deed of horror in ignorance (Oedipus kills an old man who unknown to him is his father, Othello kills Desdemona in the mistaken belief that she is unchaste, Brutus makes errors of judgment that undercut his high-minded aspirations), Macbeth is not confused about the criminal nature of his deed. When he kills the king who is his guest and generous lord, he knows, as Oedipus, Othello, and Brutus do not, that he does a "horrid deed." Even before he does the deed he foresees the outcome, apparently sensing that in the nature of things something rather like Albany's view will come about through the workings of even-handed justice. In his first soliloquy he says:

> we but teach
> Bloody instructions, which, being taught, return
> To plague th' inventor: this even-handed justice
> Commends th' ingredients of our poisoned chalice
> To our own lips.[1]
>
> (1.7.8–12)

Nor does Macbeth lose his moral sense after his first crime. Midway in the play, when he has already suffered violent feelings of guilt, he determines to toughen himself in villainous practice; he has seen the ghost of one of his victims because (he thinks) he is still a fearful novice in crime and he has not yet inured himself by "hard use." A little later, when he fears he is losing his control, he determines that his course must be bloodier:

> From this moment
> The very firstlings of my heart shall be
> The firstlings of my hand. And even now,
> To crown my thoughts with acts, be it thought and
>   done:
> The castle of Macduff I will surprise;
> Seize upon Fife; give to th' edge o' th' sword
> His wife, his babes, and all unfortunate souls
> That trace him in his line. No boasting like a fool;
> This deed I'll do before this purpose cool.
>
> (4.1.146–54)

Another way of seeing something of Macbeth's calculated villainy—something of the quality that puts him in Tourneur's classification of "the bad"—is to see what his

---

[1]By the way, although the idea that an evil act engenders its own punishment is scarcely novel, Shakespeare's use of it here is probably indebted to a passage in Holinshed's *Chronicles*: "For the prick of conscience, as it chanceth ever in tyrants and such as attain to any estate by unrighteous means, caused him ever to fear, lest he should be served of the same cup as he had ministered to his predecessors."

opponents are like. Who are they? Chief of them is Malcolm, the heir to the throne—a man chaste, trustworthy, and patriotic—and they include men who are distressed to hear that Macbeth has made "each new morn / New widows howl, new orphans cry" (4.3.4–5). To these enemies of Macbeth, he is a butcher, a tyrant, a hell-kite, a hell-hound. Malcolm and his allies, on the other hand, are the instruments of the powers above, and are God's soldiers. The concluding speech sharply contrasts the defeated tyrant (at whose fall, Dr. Johnson says, "every reader rejoices") and the rightful king:

> What's more to do,
> Which would be planted newly with the time—
> As calling home our exiled friends abroad
> That fled the snares of watchful tyranny,
> Producing forth the cruel ministers
> Of this dead butcher and his fiendlike queen,
> Who, as 'tis thought, by self and violent hands
> Took off her life—this, and what needful else
> That calls upon us, by the grace of Grace
> We will perform in measure, time, and place:
> So thanks to all at once and to each one,
> Whom we invite to see us crowned at Scone.
>
>   (5.8.64–75)

Macbeth has been allied with witches or fiends, but the rightful ruler will work "by the grace of Grace." Macbeth has been unable to "buckle his distempered cause / Within the belt of rule" (5.2.15–16), but the rightful ruler will perform his actions "in measure, time, and place." Macbeth had heard Duncan say to him "I have begun to plant thee, and will labor / To make thee full of growing" (1.4.28–29), yet he had turned against the source of his growth, killed Duncan (and so made of himself a rootless branch that must become desiccated); the rightful ruler's mind turns to planting newly with the time.

It can be put this way: Macbeth's action is contrary to nature, and he knows it. The mere thought of his deed makes his body function unnaturally. The witches' solicitation, he says,

> doth unfix my hair
> And make my seated heart knock at my ribs,
> Against the use of nature.   (1.3.135–37)

The wounds inflicted on Duncan look like "a breach in nature" (2.3.115), and the sun feels the effect of the murder:

> By th' clock 'tis day,
> And yet dark night strangles the traveling lamp:
> Is't night's predominance, or the day's shame,
> That darkness does the face of earth entomb,
> When living light should kiss it?   (2.4.6–10)

To which the Old Man replies: " 'Tis unnatural, / Even like the deed that's done."

By turning against the source of his growth, then, Macbeth becomes infected:

> Who then shall blame
> His pestered senses to recoil and start,
> When all that is within him does condemn
> Itself for being there?   (5.2.22–25)

But of course this is not the whole story, and the Macbeth that has been thus far discussed is only a part of Shakespeare's Macbeth. At the outset of the play we meet not Macbeth but the Weird Sisters. The next time they assemble, the third one says, it will be to meet with Macbeth. The incantatory quality of their verse—the power of the rhyme, the alliteration, and the mysterious paradoxes—can be felt even in a single couplet:

> Fair is foul, and foul is fair.
> Hover through the fog and filthy air.
>   (1.1.10–11)

We may insist, on reflection, that Macbeth is a free agent who need not have yielded to the witches' hints; certainly he harbors within him what they present to our eye. Yet can we feel sure that he has not been ensnared: the charm has been wound up, and if he is the tyrant, viewed another way he is the victim of infernal tyranny. "The instruments of darkness tell us truths, / Win us with honest trifles, to betray 's / In deepest consequence" (1.3.124–26). The witches can control the winds, and we first see Macbeth on a "blasted heath" (77). The very air he breathes, as it is in part made up of the witches who "melted as breath into the wind" (81–82), is infected. This second view, of Macbeth as victim, though it must not be pressed (the noble Duncan finds the air sweet— but, in another way, he too is a victim), finds support in Shakespeare's other tragedies and even in his use of the word "tragedy" and its derivatives. He seems never to use it in a context that bears much resemblance to Tourneur's line, "When the bad bleed, then is the tragedy good." Always, or almost always, the word is linked with a violent death that evokes woe or is said to be woeful. Because he does not mention "tragedy" in *Macbeth*, an example must be drawn from another play. One of his earliest uses of the word will suffice. In *1 Henry VI*, Salisbury, an English commander, has been killed by a hidden French gunner. Talbot, Salisbury's cohort, laments the sudden fall:

> Accursèd tower! Accursèd fatal hand
> That hath contrived this woeful tragedy.
>
> (1.4.76–77)

The reference to the tower and the word "fatal" ("destined," "fated") are important, for they suggest that tragedy sets its woeful happenings against a mysterious backdrop of inhuman and inscrutable forces.

The Weird Sisters in *Macbeth* are of course part of this inscrutable surrounding. In the Folio their name is spelled "weyard" or "weyward" (perhaps with a glance at "wayward"?) but the stage directions and speech prefixes call them witches. They have the traditional petty malice (and beards) of witches, and they acknowledge "masters," but they also have properties not associated with witches: they vanish like bubbles, and they speak authoritatively. In the fourth act they are closer to the Furies than to mischievous hags. No English play before *Macbeth* has such imposing witches, and if the Weird Sisters resemble witches in their ability to sail in a sieve and in their animal-killing and in their cookery and in their revenge on the sailor's wife, they nevertheless seem also to merit the title Macbeth gives them—"juggling fiends" (5.18.19). Their name suggests the Fates (Old English *wyrd,* fate), and Holinshed conjectures that they may be "The goddesses of destiny," though of course Holinshed's view need not be Shakespeare's.

Is it, then, Macbeth's bad luck that the witches wait for him? Or is there something within himself that has attracted them, and that makes him recognize his kinship with them? Are they the dramatist's concrete embodiments of a part of Macbeth? As soon as we ask these questions we realize that debate is futile; we cannot reply by pointing to Elizabethan treatises on demonology; we can only repeat portions of the play; and the play does not provide unequivocal answers.

Equivocation, in fact, is in part what the play is about. The Porter soliloquizes about an equivocator (2.3.8–12), but we do not have to wait for him to introduce the theme of doubleness or ambiguity. The Weird Sisters, in the first scene, will meet "when the battle's lost and won," and for them "fair is foul, and foul is fair." A few moments later Macbeth will enter, and his first line will be

<blockquote>So foul and fair a day I have not seen.   (1.3.38)</blockquote>

One aspect of this pervasive doubleness is in the wordplay. The Porter has his quibbles, of course, but so do Macbeth and Lady Macbeth. Second meanings, however, lurk not only under words (e.g., *gild-guilt*); there are second meanings under whole speeches and actions. This is not surprising in a play in which the protagonist is advised to "look like th' innocent flower, / But be the serpent under 't" (1.5.66–67), and in which we hear "Away, and mock the time with fairest show: / False face must hide what the false heart doth know" (1.7.81–82). Still, it was not inevitable that Shakespeare should so brilliantly follow the innocent Duncan's observation that "There's no art / To find the mind's construction in the face: / He was a gentleman on whom I built / An absolute trust" (1.4.11–14) with a stage direction, *"Enter Macbeth,"* i.e., enter another whose appearance will deceive Duncan.

It is time that we look more closely at Macbeth's double nature, for if he is the "devilish Macbeth" that Malcolm says he is, he is also something else.

Very early in the play—immediately after the odd ritual of a dozen lines in which the Weird Sisters inform us that they will meet with Macbeth, we get a report of Macbeth's loyalty and courage. He is "brave Macbeth," "valiant cousin! Worthy gentleman," and "noble Macbeth" (1.2.16, 24, 67), and by his deeds against rebels and foreign invaders he has earned these words. His first appearance on the stage does not quite confirm this report, but if anything it even more potently engages our sympathetic interest; he starts and seems "to fear / Things that do sound so fair" (1.3.51–52). With hindsight we can say that he starts because he has already harbored criminal impulses that respond to the witches' words, but what is more important is that his apprehensiveness suggests both an apartness from others and a self-division that will make us see in him a good deal more than the blackguard. Twice in this first view of Macbeth we hear him described as "rapt," and his asides— confessing his uncertainties—complicate him and make him more than the hero described in the previous scene. There he had unseamed a rebel from the nave to the chops, had been an eagle, a cannon, and valor's minion. That is, when we first hear of Macbeth we hear of a man of noble and unambiguous action; when we first see Macbeth, we see a man of uncertainty. His first appearance puts him in the company of sympathetic tragic heroes such as Hamlet and Romeo. (Hamlet's first remark is an aside, and his next few speeches reveal he is not at one with his surroundings or himself. When we first see Romeo he is so abstracted that he is unaware of the time of day, and he endures "sad hours.") Conversely, Macbeth is far from the evil Richard III, whose history Shakespeare presented in the tragic shape of a rise and fall. Richard is unambiguously a villain. As early as the thirtieth line of the play he begins

> I am determined to prove a villain,
> And hate the idle pleasures of these days.
> Plots have I laid, inductions dangerous,
> By drunken prophecies, libels, and dreams,

> To set my brother Clarence and the King
> In deadly hate, the one against the other.
> And if King Edward be as true and just
> As I am subtle, false, and treacherous . . .

This unmitigated villainy is not without its attractions, but contrast it with Macbeth's recoil at his own murderous thoughts:

> My thought, whose murder yet is but fantastical,
> Shakes so my single state of man that function
> Is smothered in surmise, and nothing is
> But what is not.   (1.3.139–42)

It is not, then, that he commits crimes and at the end suffers; he suffers even before he commits his first criminal action, and because he is his own tormentor he scarcely needs the spectator's punishing eyes. Immediately after killing Duncan he is afflicted with doubts and has a premonition of the sleeplessness that will ensue. Lady Macbeth takes a simpler view: "Consider it not so deeply," "These deeds must not be thought / After these ways; so, it will make us mad," "A little water clears us of this deed: / How easy is it then!" (2.2.29,32–33,66. But if she here seems as black as the evil angel that prompts Mankind to illicit deeds in the old morality plays, she too reveals inner depths in the sleepwalking scene, when we see that like her husband she is troubled with thick-coming fancies that keep her from her rest.)

Macbeth early recognizes the unnaturalness of his thoughts, and, as the asides in the first act make clear, they estrange him from his fellows and even almost from himself. They

> make my seated heart knock at my ribs,
> Against the use of nature.   (1.3.136–37)

The soldier who fought along with his countrymen—who is described as a savior—becomes, by the last act, a man who knows that he has no friends (enemy troops, rather than troops of friends, surround him); his soldiers at the end—those who do not desert him—are mere "constrainèd things / Whose hearts are absent too" (5.4.13–14). His course in blood has separated him not only from God ("wherefore could I not pronounce 'Amen'?"—2.2.30), and from his subjects (he cannot banquet at ease with them), but even from his wife. At the start of the play she is his "dearest partner of greatness," and his "dearest love" (1.5.12,59). But midway in the play (though she is "dearest chuck"—3.2.45) he keeps from her the plot against Banquo, and at the end he seems almost insensible to her death: "She should have died hereafter" (5.5.17). There are many ways of responding to the news of the death of a beloved one, and in this play Shakespeare gives us three. It is instructive to compare Macduff's response (4.3) and Old Siward's (5.8), very different yet not totally so, and to contrast them to Macbeth's utterly dissimilar response.

What of Macbeth's own death? Its effect on us is complex. When his severed head is brought in, perhaps we sense a parallel between Macbeth's career and that of the treacherous Macdonwald, whose head Macbeth had justly fixed upon the battlements, and a contrast between, first, Macbeth and the Thane of Cawdor, who confessed his treasons and yielded up his life "as 'twere a . . . trifle" (1.4.11), and, second, between Macbeth and Young Siward, who died as "God's soldier" (5.8.47); but perhaps too we feel that there is something of the soldierly Macbeth in his final contest, and, equally important, that his death is the release (hence it is not wholly painful to him) of one who knows he harvested what he sowed, and who is aweary of the sun.

The speech Macbeth makes before he dies can here be used to remind us that he holds our interest partly by his language. It is not a matter of confusing the character with the author, but simply a matter of recognizing that one of the things that makes us interested in Macbeth (and in all of the people embodied in the play, or rather, the people who embody the play) is memorable speech. The point might be made by printing the lines he utters on the nothingness of life just after he learns of Lady Macbeth's death—lines so potent that although they fit exactly into their place in the drama they have often been taken out and held to represent Shakespeare's own view—yet the role that Macbeth's language plays can be still better seen by quoting a dying speech that

David Garrick composed for Macbeth in the eighteenth century. Even the reader who has read only as much of the play as has been quoted in this introduction must recognize that every word of Shakespeare's Macbeth will engage him as Garrick's does not. Garrick's Macbeth says:

> Hell drags me down. I sink,
> I sink. Oh! my soul is lost forever.
> Oh!   *Dies.*

The final speech of Shakespeare's Macbeth is an almost indescribable blend of corrupted pride, desperation, animal fury, and courage; it is not one of the meditative or descriptive passages that even out of context has a life of its own, but like all the other lines in the play it holds us rapt.

—SYLVAN BARNET
Tufts University

The Tragedy of
MACBETH

Duncan, King of Scotland
Malcolm ⎱
Donalbain ⎰ his sons
Macbeth ⎫
Banquo ⎪
Macduff ⎪
Lennox ⎪
Ross ⎬ noblemen of Scotland
Menteith ⎪
Angus ⎪
Caithness ⎭
Fleance, son to Banquo
Siward, Earl of Northumberland, general of the
    English forces
Young Siward, his son
Seyton, an officer attending on Macbeth
Son to Macduff
An English Doctor
A Scottish Doctor
A Porter
An Old Man
Three Murderers
Lady Macbeth
Lady Macduff
A Gentlewoman attending on Lady Macbeth
Hecate
Witches
Apparitions
Lords, Officers, Soldiers, Attendants, and Mes-
    sengers

Scene: Scotland; England]

The Tragedy of Macbeth

ACT 1

Scene 1.   [*An open place.*]

Thunder and lightning. Enter Three Witches.

First Witch. When shall we three meet again?
  In thunder, lightning, or in rain?

Second Witch. When the hurlyburly's done,
  When the battle's lost and won.

Third Witch. That will be ere the set of sun.   5

First Witch. Where the place?

Second Witch.   Upon the heath.

Third Witch. There to meet with Macbeth.

First Witch. I come, Graymalkin.° ¹

Second Witch. Paddock° calls.

Third Witch.   Anon!°

All. Fair is foul, and foul is fair.   10
  Hover through the fog and filthy air.

                                        Exeunt.

---

¹ The degree sign (°) indicates a footnote, which is keyed to the text by
line number. Text references are printed in **boldface** type; the annotation
follows in roman type.
1.1. 8 **Graymalkin** (the witch's attendant spirit, a gray cat)   9 **Paddock**
toad   9 **Anon** at once

Scene 2.   [*A camp.*]

Alarum within.° *Enter King* [*Duncan*], *Malcolm, Donalbain, Lennox, with Attendants, meeting a bleeding Captain.*

King. What bloody man is that? He can report,
　　As seemeth by his plight, of the revolt
　　The newest state.

Malcolm.　　　　　　This is the sergeant°
　　Who like a good and hardy soldier fought
5　　'Gainst my captivity. Hail, brave friend!
　　Say to the king the knowledge of the broil°
　　As thou didst leave it.

Captain.　　　　　　　Doubtful it stood,
　　As two spent swimmers, that do cling together
　　And choke their art.° The merciless Macdonwald—
10　　Worthy to be a rebel for to that
　　The multiplying villainies of nature
　　Do swarm upon him—from the Western Isles°
　　Of kerns and gallowglasses° is supplied;
　　And Fortune, on his damnèd quarrel° smiling,
15　　Showed like a rebel's whore:° but all's too weak:
　　For brave Macbeth—well he deserves that name—
　　Disdaining Fortune, with his brandished steel,
　　Which smoked with bloody execution,
　　Like valor's minion° carved out his passage

1.2.s.d. **Alarum within** trumpet call offstage 3 **sergeant** i.e., officer
(he is called, perhaps with no inconsistency in Shakespeare's day,
a captain in the s.d. and speech prefixes. *Sergeant* is trisyllabic)
6 **broil** quarrel 9 **choke their art** hamper each other's doings 12 **Western Isles** Hebrides 13 **Of kerns and gallowglasses** with lightly armed
Irish foot soldiers and heavily armed ones 14 **damnèd quarrel** accursed
cause 15 **Showed like a rebel's whore** i.e., falsely appeared to favor
Macdonwald 19 **minion** (trisyllabic) favorite

Till he faced the slave;   20
Which nev'r shook hands, nor bade farewell to him,
Till he unseamed him from the nave to th' chops,°
And fixed his head upon our battlements.

King. O valiant cousin! Worthy gentleman!

Captain. As whence the sun 'gins his reflection°   25
Shipwracking storms and direful thunders break,
So from that spring whence comfort seemed to come
Discomfort swells. Mark, King of Scotland, mark:
No sooner justice had, with valor armed,
Compelled these skipping kerns to trust their heels   30
But the Norweyan lord, surveying vantage,°
With furbished arms and new supplies of men,
Began a fresh assault.

King.   Dismayed not this
Our captains, Macbeth and Banquo?

Captain.   Yes;
As sparrows eagles, or the hare the lion.   35
If I say sooth,° I must report they were
As cannons overcharged with double cracks;°
So they doubly redoubled strokes upon the foe.
Except° they meant to bathe in reeking wounds,
Or memorize another Golgotha,°   40
I cannot tell—
But I am faint; my gashes cry for help.

King. So well thy words become thee as thy wounds;
They smack of honor both. Go get him surgeons.

                              [*Exit Captain, attended.*]

                    Enter Ross and Angus.

Who comes here?

---

22 **nave to th' chops** navel to the jaws   25 **reflection** (four syllables;
the ending *ion*—here and often elsewhere in the play—is disyllabic)
31 **surveying vantage** seeing an opportunity   36 **sooth** truth   37 **cracks**
explosives   39 **Except** unless   40 **memorize another Golgotha** make
the place as memorable as Golgotha, "the place of the skull"

45 *Malcolm.*   The worthy Thane° of Ross.

Lennox. What a haste looks through his eyes! So
    should he look
  That seems to° speak things strange.

Ross.   God save the king!

King. Whence cam'st thou, worthy Thane?

Ross.   From Fife, great King;
  Where the Norweyan banners flout the sky
50 And fan our people cold.
  Norway° himself, with terrible numbers,
  Assisted by that most disloyal traitor
  The Thane of Cawdor, began a dismal° conflict;
  Till that Bellona's bridegroom, lapped in proof,°
55 Confronted him with self-comparisons,°
  Point against point, rebellious arm 'gainst arm,
  Curbing his lavish° spirit: and, to conclude,
  The victory fell on us.

King.   Great happiness!

Ross.   That now
  Sweno, the Norways' king, craves composition;°
60 Nor would we deign him burial of his men
  Till he disbursèd, at Saint Colme's Inch,°
  Ten thousand dollars° to our general use.

King. No more that Thane of Cawdor shall deceive
  Our bosom interest:° go pronounce his present°
    death,
65 And with his former title greet Macbeth.

Ross. I'll see it done.

King. What he hath lost, noble Macbeth hath won.
                        Exeunt.

---

45 **Thane** (a Scottish title of nobility) 47 **seems to** seems about to
51 **Norway** the King of Norway 53 **dismal** threatening 54 **Bellona's
... proof** the mate of the goddess of war, clad in tested (proved)
armor 55 **self-comparisons** counter-movements 57 **lavish** insolent
59 **composition** terms of peace 61 **Inch** island 62 **dollars** (Spanish and
Dutch currency) 64 **Our bosom interest** my (plural of royalty)
heart's trust 64 **present** immediate

Scene 3.   [*A heath.*]

Thunder. Enter the Three Witches.

First Witch. Where hast thou been, sister?

Second Witch. Killing swine.

Third Witch. Sister, where thou?

First Witch. A sailor's wife had chestnuts in her lap,
    And mounched, and mounched, and mounched.
      "Give me," quoth I.   5
    "Aroint thee,° witch!" the rump-fed ronyon° cries.
    Her husband's to Aleppo gone, master o' th' Tiger:
    But in a sieve I'll thither sail,
    And, like a rat without a tail,
    I'll do, I'll do, and I'll do.   10

Second Witch. I'll give thee a wind.

First Witch. Th' art kind.

Third Witch. And I another.

First Witch. I myself have all the other;
    And the very ports they blow,°   15
    All the quarters that they know
    I' th' shipman's card.°
    I'll drain him dry as hay:
    Sleep shall neither night nor day
    Hang upon his penthouse lid;°   20
    He shall live a man forbid:°
    Weary sev'nights nine times nine
    Shall he dwindle, peak,° and pine:

1.3. 6 **Aroint thee** begone 6 **rump-fed ronyon** fat-rumped scabby creature 15 **ports they blow** harbors to which the winds blow (?)
17 **card** compass card 20 **penthouse lid** eyelid (the figure is of a lean-to)
21 **forbid** cursed 23 **peak** waste away

Though his bark cannot be lost,
25 Yet it shall be tempest-tossed.
Look what I have.

Second Witch. Show me, show me.

First Witch. Here I have a pilot's thumb,
Wracked as homeward he did come.

                        Drum within.

30 *Third Witch.* A drum, a drum!
Macbeth doth come.

All. The weïrd° sisters, hand in hand,
Posters° of the sea and land,
Thus do go about, about:
35 Thrice to thine, and thrice to mine,
And thrice again, to make up nine.
Peace! The charm's wound up.

                Enter Macbeth and Banquo.

Macbeth. So foul and fair a day I have not seen.

Banquo. How far is 't called to Forres? What are these
40 So withered, and so wild in their attire,
That look not like th' inhabitants o' th' earth,
And yet are on 't? Live you, or are you aught
That man may question?° You seem to understand me,
By each at once her choppy° finger laying
45 Upon her skinny lips. You should be women,
And yet your beards forbid me to interpret
That you are so.

Macbeth.   Speak, if you can: what are you?

First Witch. All hail, Macbeth! Hail to thee, Thane of Glamis!

Second Witch. All hail, Macbeth! Hail to thee, Thane of
Cawdor!

---

32 **weïrd** destiny-serving (? Shakespeare's chief source, Holinshed's *Chronicles*, reports that one common opinion held that the women were "the weird sisters . . . the goddesses of destiny." The spelling in the First Folio (1623) text of *Macbeth*, however, is *weyward* here and at 2.1.20; at 3.1.2, 3.4.134, and 4.1.136 it is *weyard*. The word may glance at *wayward*, and probably is dissyllabic. We use *weïrd* consistently)   33 **Posters** swift travelers   43 **question** talk to   44 **choppy** chapped

Third Witch. All hail, Macbeth, that shalt be King
    hereafter!   50

Banquo. Good sir, why do you start, and seem to fear
    Things that do sound so fair? I' th' name of truth,
    Are ye fantastical,° or that indeed
    Which outwardly ye show? My noble partner
    You greet with present grace° and great prediction   55
    Of noble having° and of royal hope,
    That he seems rapt withal:° to me you speak not.
    If you can look into the seeds of time,
    And say which grain will grow and which will not,
    Speak then to me, who neither beg nor fear   60
    Your favors nor your hate.

First Witch. Hail!

Second Witch. Hail!

Third Witch. Hail!

First Witch. Lesser than Macbeth, and greater.   65

Second Witch. Not so happy,° yet much happier.

Third Witch. Thou shalt get° kings, though thou be
    none.
    So all hail, Macbeth and Banquo!

First Witch. Banquo and Macbeth, all hail!

Macbeth. Stay, you imperfect° speakers, tell me more: 70
    By Sinel's° death I know I am Thane of Glamis;
    But how of Cawdor? The Thane of Cawdor lives,
    A prosperous gentleman; and to be King
    Stands not within the prospect of belief,
    No more than to be Cawdor. Say from whence   75
    You owe° this strange intelligence?° Or why
    Upon this blasted heath you stop our way

---

53 **fantastical** imaginary   55 **grace** honor   56 **having** possession   57 **rapt withal** entranced by it   66 **happy** fortunate   67 **get** beget   70 **imperfect** incomplete   71 **Sinel** (Macbeth's father)   76 **owe** own, have   76 **intelligence** information

With such prophetic greeting? Speak, I charge
   you.

                                  Witches vanish.

Banquo. The earth hath bubbles as the water has,
80   And these are of them. Whither are they vanished?

Macbeth. Into the air, and what seemed corporal°
   melted
   As breath into the wind. Would they had stayed!

Banquo. Were such things here as we do speak about?
   Or have we eaten on the insane° root
85   That takes the reason prisoner?

Macbeth. Your children shall be kings.

Banquo.   You shall be King.

Macbeth. And Thane of Cawdor too. Went it not so?

Banquo. To th' selfsame tune and words. Who's here?

           Enter Ross and Angus.

Ross. The King hath happily received, Macbeth,
90   The news of thy success; and when he reads°
   Thy personal venture in the rebels' fight,
   His wonders and his praises do contend
   Which should be thine or his.° Silenced with that,
   In viewing o'er the rest o' th' selfsame day,
95   He finds thee in the stout Norweyan ranks,
   Nothing afeard of what thyself didst make,
   Strange images of death. As thick as tale
   Came post with post,° and every one did bear
   Thy praises in his kingdom's great defense,
   And poured them down before him.

100 *Angus.*   We are sent
   To give thee, from our royal master, thanks;

---

81 **corporal** corporeal 84 **insane** insanity-producing 90 **reads** considers
92–93 **His wonders ... his** i.e., Duncan's speechless admiration, appropriate to him, contends with his desire to praise you (?) 97–98 **As
thick ... post** as fast as could be counted came messenger after messenger

Only to herald thee into his sight,
Not pay thee.

Ross. And for an earnest° of a greater honor,
He bade me, from him, call thee Thane of Cawdor;　105
In which addition,° hail, most worthy Thane!
For it is thine.

Banquo.　　　　What, can the devil speak true?

Macbeth. The Thane of Cawdor lives: why do you dress
　me
In borrowed robes?

Angus.　　　　　Who was the thane lives yet,
But under heavy judgment bears that life　　　　110
Which he deserves to lose. Whether he was com-
　bined°
With those of Norway, or did line° the rebel
With hidden help and vantage,° or that with both
He labored in his country's wrack,° I know not;
But treasons capital, confessed and proved,　　115
Have overthrown him.

Macbeth.　　　[*Aside*] Glamis, and Thane of Cawdor:
The greatest is behind.° [*To Ross and Angus*] Thanks
　for your pains.
[*Aside to Banquo*] Do you not hope your children
　shall be kings,
When those that gave the Thane of Cawdor to me
Promised no less to them?

Banquo.　　　[*Aside to Macbeth*] That, trusted home,°　120
Might yet enkindle you unto the crown,
Besides the Thane of Cawdor. But 'tis strange:
And oftentimes, to win us to our harm,
The instruments of darkness tell us truths,
Win us with honest trifles, to betray 's　　　　125

---

104 **earnest** pledge　106 **addition** title　111 **combined** allied　112 **line** support　113 **vantage** opportunity　114 **wrack** ruin　117 **behind** i.e., to follow　120 **home** all the way

In deepest consequence.°
Cousins,° a word, I pray you.

Macbeth.   [*Aside*] Two truths are told,
    As happy prologues to the swelling° act
    Of the imperial theme.—I thank you, gentlemen.—
130 [*Aside*] This supernatural soliciting°
    Cannot be ill, cannot be good. If ill,
    Why hath it given me earnest of success,
    Commencing in a truth? I am Thane of Cawdor:
    If good, why do I yield to that suggestion
135 Whose horrid image doth unfix my hair
    And make my seated° heart knock at my ribs,
    Against the use of nature?° Present fears
    Are less than horrible imaginings.
    My thought, whose murder yet is but fantastical,°
140 Shakes so my single° state of man that function
    Is smothered in surmise, and nothing is
    But what is not.

Banquo.   Look, how our partner's rapt.

Macbeth. [*Aside*] If chance will have me King, why,
        chance may crown me,
    Without my stir.

Banquo.   New honors come upon him,
    Like our strange° garments, cleave not to their
145   mold
    But with the aid of use.

Macbeth.   [*Aside*] Come what come may,
    Time and the hour runs through the roughest day.

Banquo. Worthy Macbeth, we stay upon your leisure.°

Macbeth. Give me your favor.° My dull brain was
        wrought

126 **In deepest consequence** in the most significant sequel 127 **Cousins**
i.e., fellow noblemen 128 **swelling** stately 130 **soliciting** inviting
136 **seated** fixed 137 **Against the use of nature** contrary to my natural
way 139 **fantastical** imaginary 140 **single** unaided, weak (or "entire"?)
145 **strange** new 148 **stay upon your leisure** await your convenience
149 **favor** pardon

With things forgotten. Kind gentlemen, your pains   *150*
Are registered where every day I turn
The leaf to read them. Let us toward the King.
[*Aside to Banquo*] Think upon what hath
    chanced, and at more time,
The interim having weighed it,° let us speak
Our free hearts° each to other.

Banquo.   Very gladly.   *155*

Macbeth. Till then, enough. Come, friends.

                                        Exeunt.

Scene 4.   [*Forres. The palace.*]

*Flourish.° Enter King [Duncan], Lennox,
Malcolm, Donalbain, and Attendants.*

King. Is execution done on Cawdor? Are not
    Those in commission° yet returned?

Malcolm.   My liege,
    They are not yet come back. But I have spoke
    With one that saw him die, who did report
    That very frankly he confessed his treasons,   *5*
    Implored your Highness' pardon and set forth
    A deep repentance: nothing in his life
    Became him like the leaving it. He died
    As one that had been studied° in his death,
    To throw away the dearest thing he owed°   *10*
    As 'twere a careless° trifle.

154 **The interim having weighed it** i.e., when we have had time to
think   155 **Our free hearts** our minds freely   1.4.s.d. **Flourish** fanfare
2 **in commission** i.e., commissioned to oversee the execution   9 **studied**
rehearsed   10 **owed** owned   11 **careless** uncared-for

King.   There's no art
To find the mind's construction in the face:
He was a gentleman on whom I built
An absolute trust.

    Enter Macbeth, Banquo, Ross, and Angus.

                      O worthiest cousin!
15   The sin of my ingratitude even now
Was heavy on me: thou art so far before,
That swiftest wing of recompense is slow
To overtake thee. Would thou hadst less deserved,
That the proportion° both of thanks and payment
20   Might have been mine! Only I have left to say,
More is thy due than more than all can pay.

Macbeth. The service and the loyalty I owe,
In doing it, pays itself.° Your Highness' part
Is to receive our duties: and our duties
25   Are to your throne and state children and servants;
Which do but what they should, by doing every
      thing
Safe toward° your love and honor.

King.   Welcome hither.
I have begun to plant thee, and will labor
To make thee full of growing. Noble Banquo,
30   That hast no less deserved, nor must be known
No less to have done so, let me enfold thee
And hold thee to my heart.

Banquo.   There if I grow,
The harvest is your own.

King.   My plenteous joys,
Wanton° in fullness, seek to hide themselves
35   In drops of sorrow. Sons, kinsmen, thanes,
And you whose places are the nearest, know,
We will establish our estate° upon
Our eldest, Malcolm, whom we name hereafter

19 **proportion** preponderance   23 **pays itself** is its own reward   27 **Safe toward** safeguarding (?)   34 **Wanton** unrestrained   37 **establish our estate** settle the succession

The Prince of Cumberland: which honor must
Not unaccompanied invest him only,   *40*
But signs of nobleness, like stars, shall shine
On all deservers. From hence to Inverness,
And bind us further to you.

Macbeth. The rest is labor, which is not used for you.°
    I'll be myself the harbinger, and make joyful   *45*
The hearing of my wife with your approach;
So, humbly take my leave.

King.   My worthy Cawdor!

Macbeth. [*Aside*] The Prince of Cumberland! That
    is a step
On which I must fall down, or else o'erleap,
For in my way it lies. Stars, hide your fires;   *50*
Let not light see my black and deep desires:
The eye wink at the hand;° yet let that be
Which the eye fears, when it is done, to see.

                                   Exit.

King. True, worthy Banquo; he is full so valiant,
    And in his commendations° I am fed;   *55*
It is a banquet to me. Let's after him,
Whose care is gone before to bid us welcome.
It is a peerless kinsman.   *Flourish. Exeunt.*

Scene 5. [*Inverness. Macbeth's castle.*]

Enter Macbeth's wife, alone, with a letter.

Lady Macbeth. [*Reads*] "They met me in the day
    of success; and I have learned by the perfect'st

---

44 **The rest ... you** i.e., repose is laborious when not employed for
you   52 **wink at the hand** i.e., be blind to the hand's deed   55 **his commendations** commendations of him

report they have more in them than mortal knowledge. When I burned in desire to question them
further, they made themselves air, into which they
vanished. Whiles I stood rapt in the wonder of it,
came missives° from the King, who all-hailed me
'Thane of Cawdor'; by which title, before, these
weïrd sisters saluted me, and referred me to the
coming on of time, with 'Hail, King that shalt
be!' This have I thought good to deliver thee,° my
dearest partner of greatness, that thou mightst not
lose the dues of rejoicing, by being ignorant of
what greatness is promised thee. Lay it to thy heart,
and farewell."

Glamis thou art, and Cawdor, and shalt be
What thou art promised. Yet do I fear thy nature;
It is too full o' th' milk of human kindness°
To catch the nearest way. Thou wouldst be great,
Art not without ambition, but without
The illness° should attend it. What thou wouldst
    highly,
That wouldst thou holily; wouldst not play false,
And yet wouldst wrongly win. Thou'dst have,
    great Glamis,
That which cries "Thus thou must do" if thou have
    it;
And that which rather thou dost fear to do
Than wishest should be undone. Hie thee hither,
That I may pour my spirits in thine ear,
And chastise with the valor of my tongue
All that impedes thee from the golden round°
Which fate and metaphysical° aid doth seem
To have thee crowned withal.°

Enter Messenger.

1.5.   7 **missives** messengers   11 **deliver thee** report to you   18 **milk of
human kindness** i.e., gentle quality of human nature   21 **illness** wickedness   29 **round** crown   30 **metaphysical** supernatural   31 **withal** with

　　　　　　　　　　　　What is your tidings?

Messenger. The King comes here tonight.

Lady Macbeth.　　　　　　　　Thou 'rt mad to say it!
　Is not thy master with him, who, were 't so,
　Would have informed for preparation?

Messenger. So please you, it is true. Our thane is
　　coming.　　　　　　　　　　　　　　　　　　*35*
　One of my fellows had the speed of him,°
　Who, almost dead for breath, had scarcely more
　Than would make up his message.

Lady Macbeth.　　　　　　　Give him tending;
　He brings great news.　　　　*Exit Messenger.*
　　　　　　　　　The raven himself is hoarse
　That croaks the fatal entrance of Duncan　　　*40*
　Under my battlements. Come, you spirits
　That tend on mortal° thoughts, unsex me here,
　And fill me, from the crown to the toe, top-full
　Of direst cruelty! Make thick my blood,
　Stop up th' access and passage to remorse,°　　*45*
　That no compunctious visitings of nature°
　Shake my fell° purpose, nor keep peace between
　Th' effect° and it! Come to my woman's breasts,
　And take my milk for° gall, you murd'ring ministers,°
　Wherever in your sightless° substances　　　*50*
　You wait on° nature's mischief! Come, thick night,
　And pall° thee in the dunnest° smoke of hell,
　That my keen knife see not the wound it makes,
　Nor heaven peep through the blanket of the dark,
　To cry "Hold, hold!"

　　　　　　　　　Enter Macbeth.

　　　　　　　Great Glamis! Worthy Cawdor!　*55*
　Greater than both, by the all-hail hereafter!°

36 **had the speed of him** outdistanced him　42 **mortal** deadly　45 **re-morse** compassion　46 **compunctious visitings of nature** natural feel-ings of compassion　47 **fell** savage　48 **effect** fulfillment　49 **for** in ex-change for　49 **ministers** agents　50 **sightless** invisible　51 **wait on** assist　52 **pall** enshroud　52 **dunnest** darkest　56 **all-hail hereafter** the third all-hail (?) the all-hail of the future (?)

Thy letters have transported me beyond
This ignorant° present, and I feel now
The future in the instant.°

Macbeth.   My dearest love,
Duncan comes here tonight.

60 *Lady Macbeth.*   And when goes hence?

Macbeth. Tomorrow, as he purposes.

Lady Macbeth.   O, never
Shall sun that morrow see!
Your face, my Thane, is as a book where men
May read strange matters. To beguile the time,°
65 Look like the time; bear welcome in your eye,
Your hand, your tongue: look like th' innocent
          flower,
But be the serpent under 't. He that's coming
Must be provided for: and you shall put
This night's great business into my dispatch;°
70 Which shall to all our nights and days to come
Give solely sovereign sway and masterdom.

Macbeth. We will speak further.

Lady Macbeth.   Only look up clear.°
To alter favor ever is to fear.°
Leave all the rest to me.   *Exeunt.*

---

58 **ignorant** unknowing   59 **instant** present   64 **To beguile the time** i.e.,
to deceive people of the day   69 **dispatch** management   72 **look up clear**
appear undisturbed   73 **To alter ... fear** to show a disturbed face is
dangerous

Scene 6.   [*Before Macbeth's castle.*]

*Hautboys° and torches. Enter King [Duncan],
Malcolm, Donalbain, Banquo, Lennox, Macduff,
Ross, Angus, and Attendants.*

King. This castle hath a pleasant seat;° the air
  Nimbly and sweetly recommends itself
  Unto our gentle° senses.

Banquo.   This guest of summer,
  The temple-haunting martlet,° does approve°
  By his loved mansionry° that the heaven's breath   5
  Smells wooingly here. No jutty,° frieze,
  Buttress, nor coign of vantage,° but this bird
  Hath made his pendent bed and procreant° cradle.
  Where they most breed and haunt,° I have observed
  The air is delicate.

Enter Lady [Macbeth].

King.   See, see, our honored hostess!   10
  The love that follows us sometime is our trouble,
  Which still we thank as love.° Herein I teach you
  How you shall bid God 'ield° us for your pains
  And thank us for your trouble.

Lady Macbeth.   All our service
  In every point twice done, and then done double,   15
  Were poor and single business° to contend
  Against those honors deep and broad wherewith

1.6.s.d. **Hautboys** oboes   1 **seat** site   3 **gentle** soothed   4 **temple-haunting martlet** martin (swift) nesting in churches   4 **approve** prove   5 **mansionry** nests   6 **jutty** projection   7 **coign of vantage** advantageous corner   8 **procreant** breeding   9 **haunt** visit   11–12 **The love . . . love** the love offered me sometimes inconveniences me, but still I value it as love   13 **'ield** reward   16 **single business** feeble service

Your Majesty loads our house: for those of old,
And the late dignities heaped up to them,
We rest your hermits.°

20 *King.*   Where's the Thane of Cawdor?
We coursed° him at the heels, and had a purpose
To be his purveyor:° but he rides well,
And his great love, sharp as his spur, hath holp°
    him
To his home before us. Fair and noble hostess,
We are your guest tonight.

25 *Lady Macbeth.*   Your servants ever
Have theirs, themselves, and what is theirs, in
    compt,°
To make their audit at your Highness' pleasure,
Still° to return your own.

King.   Give me your hand.
Conduct me to mine host: we love him highly,
30 And shall continue our graces towards him.
By your leave, hostess.   *Exeunt.*

Scene 7.   [*Macbeth's castle.*]

Hautboys. Torches. Enter a Sewer,° and diverse Ser-
vants with dishes and service over the stage. Then
enter Macbeth.

Macbeth. If it were done° when 'tis done, then 'twere
    well
It were done quickly. If th' assassination

20 **your hermits** dependents bound to pray for you   21 **coursed** pursued
22 **purveyor** advance-supply officer   23 **holp** helped   26 **Have theirs . . .**
compt have their dependents, themselves, and their possessions in trust
28 **Still** always   1.7.s.d. **Sewer** chief butler   1 **done** over and done
with

Could trammel up° the consequence, and catch,
With his surcease,° success;° that but this blow
Might be the be-all and the end-all—here,   5
But here, upon this bank and shoal of time,
We'd jump° the life to come. But in these cases
We still° have judgment here; that we but teach
Bloody instructions, which, being taught, return
To plague th' inventor: this even-handed° justice   10
Commends° th' ingredients of our poisoned
    chalice
To our own lips. He's here in double trust:
First, as I am his kinsman and his subject,
Strong both against the deed; then, as his host,
Who should against his murderer shut the door,   15
Not bear the knife myself. Besides, this Duncan
Hath borne his faculties° so meek, hath been
So clear° in his great office, that his virtues
Will plead like angels trumpet-tongued against
The deep damnation of his taking-off;   20
And pity, like a naked newborn babe,
Striding° the blast, or heaven's cherubin horsed
Upon the sightless couriers° of the air,
Shall blow the horrid deed in every eye,
That° tears shall drown the wind. I have no spur   25
To prick the sides of my intent, but only
Vaulting ambition, which o'erleaps itself
And falls on th' other———

                    Enter Lady [Macbeth].

                              How now! What news?

Lady Macbeth. He has almost supped. Why have you
    left the chamber?

---

3 **trammel up** catch in a net   4 **his surcease** Duncan's death(?) the
consequence's cessation(?)   4 **success** what follows   7 **jump** risk   8 **still**
always   10 **even-handed** impartial   11 **Commends** offers   17 **faculties**
powers   18 **clear** spotless   22 **Striding** bestriding   23 **sightless couriers**
invisible coursers (i.e., the winds)   25 **That** so that

Macbeth. Hath he asked for me?

30   *Lady Macbeth.*   Know you not he has?

Macbeth. We will proceed no further in this business:
He hath honored me of late, and I have bought°
Golden opinions from all sorts of people,
Which would be worn now in their newest gloss,
Not cast aside so soon.

35   *Lady Macbeth.*   Was the hope drunk
Wherein you dressed yourself? Hath it slept since?
And wakes it now, to look so green° and pale
At what it did so freely? From this time
Such I account thy love. Art thou afeard
40   To be the same in thine own act and valor
As thou art in desire? Wouldst thou have that
Which thou esteem'st the ornament of life,
And live a coward in thine own esteem,
Letting "I dare not" wait upon° "I would,"
Like the poor cat° i' th' adage?

45   *Macbeth.*   Prithee, peace!
I dare do all that may become a man;
Who dares do more is none.

Lady Macbeth.   What beast was 't then
That made you break° this enterprise to me?
When you durst do it, then you were a man;
50   And to be more than what you were, you would
Be so much more the man. Nor time nor place
Did then adhere,° and yet you would make both.
They have made themselves, and that their° fitness
          now
Does unmake you. I have given suck, and know
55   How tender 'tis to love the babe that milks me:
I would, while it was smiling in my face,
Have plucked my nipple from his boneless gums,

---

32 **bought** acquired   37 **green** sickly   44 **wait upon** follow   45 **cat** (who
wants fish but fears to wet its paws)   48 **break** broach   52 **adhere** suit
53 **that their** their very

And dashed the brains out, had I so sworn as you
Have done to this.

Macbeth.   If we should fail?

Lady Macbeth.   We fail?
But° screw your courage to the sticking-place,°   60
And we'll not fail. When Duncan is asleep—
Whereto the rather shall his day's hard journey
Soundly invite him—his two chamberlains
Will I with wine and wassail° so convince,°
That memory, the warder° of the brain,   65
Shall be a fume, and the receipt of reason
A limbeck only:° when in swinish sleep
Their drenchèd natures lies° as in a death,
What cannot you and I perform upon
Th' unguarded Duncan, what not put upon   70
His spongy° officers, who shall bear the guilt
Of our great quell?°

Macbeth.   Bring forth men-children only;
For thy undaunted mettle° should compose
Nothing but males. Will it not be received,
When we have marked with blood those sleepy two   75
Of his own chamber, and used their very daggers,
That they have done 't?

Lady Macbeth.   Who dares receive it other,°
As we shall make our griefs and clamor roar
Upon his death?

Macbeth.   I am settled, and bend up
Each corporal agent to this terrible feat.   80
Away, and mock the time° with fairest show:
False face must hide what the false heart doth know.

                                        Exeunt.

---

60 **But** only   60 **sticking-place** notch (holding the bowstring of a taut
crossbow)   64 **wassail** carousing   64 **convince** overpower   65 **warder**
guard   66–67 **receipt ... only** i.e., the receptacle (*receipt*), which
should collect the distillate of thought—reason—will be a mere vessel
(*limbeck*) of undistilled liquids   68 **lies** lie   71 **spongy** sodden   72 **quell**
killing   73 **mettle** substance   77 **other** otherwise   81 **mock the time** beguile the world

ACT 2

Scene 1.   [*Inverness. Court of Macbeth's castle.*]

Enter Banquo, and Fleance, with a torch before him.

Banquo. How goes the night, boy?

Fleance. The moon is down; I have not heard the
     clock.

Banquo. And she goes down at twelve.

Fleance.   I take't, 'tis later, sir.

Banquo. Hold, take my sword. There's husbandry° in
     heaven.
5   Their candles are all out. Take thee that too.
     A heavy summons° lies like lead upon me,
     And yet I would not sleep. Merciful powers,
     Restrain in me the cursèd thoughts that nature
     Gives way to in repose!

     Enter Macbeth, and a Servant with a torch.

                                Give me my sword!
10   Who's there?

Macbeth. A friend.

Banquo. What, sir, not yet at rest? The King's a-bed:
     He hath been in unusual pleasure, and
     Sent forth great largess to your offices:°
15   This diamond he greets your wife withal,
     By the name of most kind hostess; and shut up°
     In measureless content.

2.1. 4 **husbandry** frugality   6 **summons** call (to sleep)   14 **largess to
your offices** gifts to your servants' quarters   16 **shut up** concluded

24

Macbeth.   Being unprepared,
Our will became the servant to defect,°
Which else should free have wrought.

Banquo.   All's well.
I dreamt last night of the three weïrd sisters: 20
To you they have showed some truth.

Macbeth.   I think not of them.
Yet, when we can entreat an hour to serve,
We would spend it in some words upon that
    business,
If you would grant the time.

Banquo.   At your kind'st leisure.

Macbeth. If you shall cleave to my consent, when
    'tis,°   25
It shall make honor for you.

Banquo.   So° I lose none
In seeking to augment it, but still keep
My bosom franchised° and allegiance clear,°
I shall be counseled.

Macbeth.   Good repose the while!

Banquo. Thanks, sir. The like to you!   30

                    Exit Banquo [with Fleance].

Macbeth. Go bid thy mistress, when my drink is ready,
She strike upon the bell. Get thee to bed.

                    Exit [Servant].

Is this a dagger which I see before me,
The handle toward my hand? Come, let me clutch
    thee.
I have thee not, and yet I see thee still.   35
Art thou not, fatal vision, sensible°
To feeling as to sight, or art thou but
A dagger of the mind, a false creation,

---

18 **Our ... defect** our good will was hampered by our deficient preparations   25 **cleave ... 'tis** join my cause, when the time comes
26 **So** provided that   28 **franchised** free (from guilt)   28 **clear** spotless
36 **sensible** perceptible

Proceeding from the heat-oppressèd brain?
40   I see thee yet, in form as palpable
As this which now I draw.
Thou marshal'st me the way that I was going;
And such an instrument I was to use.
Mine eyes are made the fools o' th' other senses,
45   Or else worth all the rest. I see thee still;
And on thy blade and dudgeon° gouts° of blood,
Which was not so before. There's no such thing.
It is the bloody business which informs°
Thus to mine eyes. Now o'er the one half-world
50   Nature seems dead, and wicked dreams abuse°
The curtained sleep; witchcraft celebrates
Pale Hecate's offerings;° and withered murder,
Alarumed° by his sentinel, the wolf,
Whose howl's his watch, thus with his stealthy pace,
55   With Tarquin's° ravishing strides, towards his design
Moves like a ghost. Thou sure and firm-set earth,
Hear not my steps, which way they walk, for fear
Thy very stones prate of my whereabout,
And take the present horror from the time,
Which now suits with it.° Whiles I threat, he
60   lives:
Words to the heat of deeds too cold breath gives.

A bell rings.

I go, and it is done: the bell invites me.
Hear it not, Duncan, for it is a knell
That summons thee to heaven, or to hell.

Exit.

---

46 **dudgeon** wooden hilt   46 **gouts** large drops   48 **informs** gives shape
(?)   50 **abuse** deceive   52 **Hecate's offerings** offerings to Hecate (goddess of sorcery)   53 **Alarumed** called to action   55 **Tarquin** (Roman
tyrant who ravished Lucrece)   59–60 **take ... it** remove (by noise) the
horrible silence attendant on this moment and suitable to it (?)

Scene 2.   [*Macbeth's Castle.*]

Enter Lady [Macbeth].

Lady Macbeth. That which hath made them drunk hath
    made me bold;
  What hath quenched them hath given me fire. Hark!
    Peace!
  It was the owl that shrieked, the fatal bellman,
  Which gives the stern'st good-night.° He is about it.
  The doors are open, and the surfeited grooms   5
  Do mock their charge with snores. I have drugged
    their possets,°
  That death and nature° do contend about them,
  Whether they live or die.

Macbeth.   [*Within*] Who's there? What, ho?

Lady Macbeth. Alack, I am afraid they have awaked
  And 'tis not done! Th' attempt and not the deed   10
  Confounds° us. Hark! I laid their daggers ready;
  He could not miss 'em. Had he not resembled
  My father as he slept, I had done 't.

Enter Macbeth.

                         My husband!

Macbeth. I have done the deed. Didst thou not hear a
  noise?

Lady Macbeth. I heard the owl scream and the crickets
  cry.   15
  Did not you speak?

Macbeth.   When?

2.2.3–4 **bellman ... good-night** i.e., the owl's call, portending death,
is like the town crier's call to a condemned man   6 **possets** (bedtime
drinks)   7 **nature** natural vitality   11 **Confounds** ruins

Lady Macbeth.   Now.

Macbeth.   As I descended?

Lady Macbeth. Ay.

Macbeth. Hark!
   Who lies i' th' second chamber?

Lady Macbeth.   Donalbain.

20 *Macbeth.* This is a sorry° sight.

Lady Macbeth. A foolish thought, to say a sorry sight.

Macbeth. There's one did laugh in 's sleep, and one
      cried "Murder!"
   That they did wake each other. I stood and heard
      them.
   But they did say their prayers, and addressed them
   Again to sleep.

25 *Lady Macbeth.*   There are two lodged together.

Macbeth. One cried "God bless us!" and "Amen" the
      other,
   As they had seen me with these hangman's° hands:
   List'ning their fear, I could not say "Amen,"
   When they did say "God bless us!"

Lady Macbeth.   Consider it not so deeply.

Macbeth. But wherefore could not I pronounce
30   "Amen"?
   I had most need of blessing, and "Amen"
   Stuck in my throat.

Lady Macbeth.   These deeds must not be thought
   After these ways; so, it will make us mad.

Macbeth. Methought I heard a voice cry "Sleep no
      more!
35   Macbeth does murder sleep"—the innocent sleep,
   Sleep that knits up the raveled sleave° of care,

20 **sorry** miserable   27 **hangman's** executioner's (i.e., bloody)   36 **knits
up the raveled sleave** straightens out the tangled skein

The death of each day's life, sore labor's bath,
Balm of hurt minds, great nature's second course,°
Chief nourisher in life's feast——

Lady Macbeth.   What do you mean?

Macbeth. Still it cried "Sleep no more!" to all the
    house: 40
"Glamis hath murdered sleep, and therefore
    Cawdor
Shall sleep no more: Macbeth shall sleep no more."

Lady Macbeth. Who was it that thus cried? Why,
    worthy Thane,
You do unbend° your noble strength, to think
So brainsickly of things. Go get some water,   45
And wash this filthy witness° from your hand.
Why did you bring these daggers from the place?
They must lie there: go carry them, and smear
The sleepy grooms with blood.

Macbeth.   I'll go no more.
I am afraid to think what I have done;   50
Look on 't again I dare not.

Lady Macbeth.   Infirm of purpose!
Give me the daggers. The sleeping and the dead
Are but as pictures. 'Tis the eye of childhood
That fears a painted° devil. If he do bleed,
I'll gild° the faces of the grooms withal,   55
For it must seem their guilt.

                        Exit. Knock within.

Macbeth.   Whence is that knocking?
How is 't with me, when every noise appalls me?
What hands are here? Ha! They pluck out mine
    eyes!
Will all great Neptune's ocean wash this blood
Clean from my hand? No; this my hand will rather   60

---

38 **second course** i.e., sleep (the less substantial first course is food)
44 **unbend** relax   46 **witness** evidence   54 **painted** depicted   55 **gild** paint

The multitudinous seas incarnadine,°
Making the green one red.°

Enter Lady [Macbeth].

Lady Macbeth. My hands are of your color, but I
    shame
To wear a heart so white. (*Knock.*) I hear a
    knocking
65 At the south entry. Retire we to our chamber.
A little water clears us of this deed:
How easy is it then! Your constancy
Hath left you unattended.° (*Knock.*) Hark! more
    knocking.
Get on your nightgown,° lest occasion call us
70 And show us to be watchers.° Be not lost
So poorly° in your thoughts.

Macbeth. To know my deed, 'twere best not know
    myself. (*Knock.*)
Wake Duncan with thy knocking! I would thou
    couldst!
                                            Exeunt.

Scene 3.   [*Macbeth's castle.*]

Enter a Porter. Knocking within.

Porter. Here's a knocking indeed! If a man were
    porter of hell gate, he should have old° turning the
    key. (*Knock.*) Knock, knock, knock! Who's there,

61 **incarnadine** redden   62 **the green one red** (perhaps "the green one"
means "the ocean," but perhaps "one" here means "totally," "uniformly")
67–68 **Your . . . unattended** your firmness has deserted you   69 **nightgown**
dressing-gown   70 **watchers** i.e., up late   71 **poorly** weakly   2.3. 2 **should
have old** would certainly have plenty of

i' th' name of Beelzebub? Here's a farmer, that
hanged himself on th' expectation of plenty.° Come   5
in time! Have napkins enow° about you; here you'll
sweat for 't. (*Knock.*) Knock, knock! Who's there,
in th' other devil's name? Faith, here's an equivocator,° that could swear in both the scales against
either scale; who committed treason enough for   10
God's sake, yet could not equivocate to heaven. O,
come in, equivocator. (*Knock.*) Knock, knock,
knock! Who's there? Faith, here's an English tailor
come hither for stealing out of a French hose:°
come in, tailor. Here you may roast your goose.°   15
(*Knock.*) Knock, knock; never at quiet! What are
you? But this place is too cold for hell. I'll devil-
porter it no further. I had thought to have let in
some of all professions that go the primrose way
to th' everlasting bonfire. (*Knock.*) Anon, anon!   20
[*Opens an entrance.*] I pray you, remember the
porter.

Enter Macduff and Lennox.

Macduff. Was it so late, friend, ere you went to bed,
    That you do lie so late?

Porter. Faith, sir, we were carousing till the second   25
    cock:° and drink, sir, is a great provoker of three
    things.

Macduff. What three things does drink especially pro-
    voke?

Porter. Marry, sir, nose-painting, sleep, and urine.   30
    Lechery, sir, it provokes and unprovokes; it pro-
    vokes the desire, but it takes away the perfor-
    mance: therefore much drink may be said to be an
    equivocator with lechery: it makes him and it mars

4–5 **farmer ... plenty** (the farmer hoarded so he could later sell high,
but when it looked as though there would be a crop surplus he hanged
himself)   6 **enow** enough   8–9 **equivocator** i.e., Jesuit (who allegedly
employed deceptive speech to further God's ends)   14 **French hose** tight-
fitting hose   15 **goose** pressing iron   25–26 **second cock** (about 3 a.m.)

35   him; it sets him on and it takes him off; it per-
     suades him and disheartens him; makes him stand
     to and not stand to; in conclusion, equivocates
     him in a sleep, and giving him the lie, leaves him.

Macduff. I believe drink gave thee the lie° last night.

40   *Porter.* That it did, sir, i' the very throat on me: but
     I requited him for his lie, and, I think, being too
     strong for him, though he took up my legs some-
     time, yet I make a shift to cast° him.

Macduff. Is thy master stirring?

                    Enter Macbeth.

45   Our knocking has awaked him; here he comes.

Lennox. Good morrow, noble sir.

Macbeth.   Good morrow, both.

Macduff. Is the king stirring, worthy Thane?

Macbeth.   Not yet.

Macduff. He did command me to call timely° on him:
     I have almost slipped° the hour.

Macbeth.   I'll bring you to him.

50   *Macduff.* I know this is a joyful trouble to you;
     But yet 'tis one.

Macbeth. The labor we delight in physics pain.°
     This is the door.

Macduff.   I'll make so bold to call,
     For 'tis my limited service.°

                         Exit Macduff.

Lennox. Goes the king hence today?

55   *Macbeth.*   He does: he did appoint so.

---

39 **gave thee the lie** called you a liar (with a pun on "stretched you
out") 43 **cast** (with a pun on "cast," meaning "vomit") 48 **timely**
early 49 **slipped** let slip 52 **The labor ... pain** labor that gives us
pleasure cures discomfort 54 **limited service** appointed duty

Lennox. The night has been unruly. Where we lay,
  Our chimneys were blown down, and, as they say,
  Lamentings heard i' th' air, strange screams of
      death,
  And prophesying with accents terrible
  Of dire combustion° and confused events   60
  New hatched to th' woeful time: the obscure bird°
  Clamored the livelong night. Some say, the earth
  Was feverous and did shake.

Macbeth.   'Twas a rough night.

Lennox. My young remembrance cannot parallel
  A fellow to it.   65

Enter Macduff.

Macduff. O horror, horror, horror! Tongue nor heart
  Cannot conceive nor name thee.

Macbeth and Lennox.   What's the matter?

Macduff. Confusion° now hath made his masterpiece.
  Most sacrilegious murder hath broke ope
  The Lord's anointed temple, and stole thence   70
  The life o' th' building.

Macbeth.   What is 't you say? The life?

Lennox. Mean you his Majesty?

Macduff. Approach the chamber, and destroy your
      sight
  With a new Gorgon:° do not bid me speak;
  See, and then speak yourselves. Awake, awake!   75

Exeunt Macbeth and Lennox.

  Ring the alarum bell. Murder and Treason!
  Banquo and Donalbain! Malcolm! Awake!
  Shake off this downy sleep, death's counterfeit,°
  And look on death itself! Up, up, and see
  The great doom's image!° Malcolm! Banquo!   80

---

60 **combustion** tumult 61 **obscure bird** bird of darkness, i.e., the owl
68 **Confusion** destruction 74 **Gorgon** (creature capable of turning be-
holders to stone) 78 **counterfeit** imitation 80 **great doom's image** likeness of Judgment Day

As from your graves rise up, and walk like sprites,°
To countenance° this horror. Ring the bell.

Bell rings. Enter Lady [Macbeth].

Lady Macbeth. What's the business,
    That such a hideous trumpet calls to parley
    The sleepers of the house? Speak, speak!

85 *Macduff.*   O gentle lady,
    'Tis not for you to hear what I can speak:
    The repetition,° in a woman's ear,
    Would murder as it fell.

Enter Banquo.

                    O Banquo, Banquo!
    Our royal master's murdered.

Lady Macbeth.   Woe, alas!
    What, in our house?

90 *Banquo.*   Too cruel anywhere.
    Dear Duff, I prithee, contradict thyself,
    And say it is not so.

Enter Macbeth, Lennox, and Ross.

Macbeth. Had I but died an hour before this chance,
    I had lived a blessèd time; for from this instant
95 There's nothing serious in mortality:°
    All is but toys.° Renown and grace is dead,
    The wine of life is drawn, and the mere lees°
    Is left this vault° to brag of.

Enter Malcolm and Donalbain.

Donalbain. What is amiss?

Macbeth.   You are, and do not know 't.
100 The spring, the head, the fountain of your blood
    Is stopped; the very source of it is stopped.

Macduff. Your royal father's murdered.

---

81 **sprites** spirits   82 **countenance** be in keeping with   87 **repetition** report   95 **serious in mortality** worthwhile in mortal life   96 **toys** trifles   97 **lees** dregs   98 **vault** (1) wine vault (2) earth, with the sky as roof (?)

Malcolm. 　　　　　　　　　　　O, by whom?

Lennox. Those of his chamber, as it seemed, had
　　done 't:
　　Their hands and faces were all badged° with blood;
　　So were their daggers, which unwiped we found　　　*105*
　　Upon their pillows. They stared, and were
　　　distracted.
　　No man's life was to be trusted with them.

Macbeth. O, yet I do repent me of my fury,
　　That I did kill them.

Macduff. 　　　　　　　Wherefore did you so?

Macbeth. Who can be wise, amazed,° temp'rate and
　　furious,　　　　　　　　　　　　　　　　　　　*110*
　　Loyal and neutral, in a moment? No man.
　　The expedition° of my violent love
　　Outrun the pauser, reason. Here lay Duncan,
　　His silver skin laced with his golden blood,
　　And his gashed stabs looked like a breach in nature　*115*
　　For ruin's wasteful entrance: there, the murderers,
　　Steeped in the colors of their trade, their daggers
　　Unmannerly breeched with gore.° Who could
　　　refrain,°
　　That had a heart to love, and in that heart
　　Courage to make 's love known?

Lady Macbeth. 　　　　　　　Help me hence, ho!　*120*

Macduff. Look to° the lady.

Malcolm. [*Aside to Donalbain*] Why do we hold
　　our tongues,
　　That most may claim this argument for ours?°

Donalbain. [*Aside to Malcolm*] What should be
　　spoken here,
　　Where our fate, hid in an auger-hole,°

---

104 **badged** marked　110 **amazed** bewildered　112 **expedition** haste
118 **Unmannerly breeched with gore** covered with unseemly breeches of
blood　118 **refrain** check oneself　121 **Look to** look after　123 **That
most ... ours?** who are the most concerned with this topic　124 **auger-
hole** i.e., unsuspected place

125   May rush, and seize us? Let's away:
        Our tears are not yet brewed.

Malcolm. [*Aside to Donalbain*] Nor our strong
        sorrow
        Upon the foot of motion.°

Banquo.   Look to the lady.

                    [*Lady Macbeth is carried out.*]

        And when we have our naked frailties hid,°
        That suffer in exposure, let us meet
130   And question° this most bloody piece of work,
        To know it further. Fears and scruples° shake us.
        In the great hand of God I stand, and thence
        Against the undivulged pretense° I fight
        Of treasonous malice.

Macduff.   And so do I.

All.   So all.

135   *Macbeth.* Let's briefly° put on manly readiness,
        And meet i' th' hall together.

All.   Well contented.

                    Exeunt [*all but Malcolm and Donalbain*].

Malcolm. What will you do? Let's not consort with
        them.
        To show an unfelt sorrow is an office°
        Which the false man does easy. I'll to England.

140   *Donalbain.* To Ireland, I; our separated fortune
        Shall keep us both the safer. Where we are
        There's daggers in men's smiles; the near in blood,
        The nearer bloody.

Malcolm.   This murderous shaft that's shot
        Hath not yet lighted, and our safest way

126–27 **Our tears ... motion** i.e., we have not yet had time for tears
nor to express our sorrows in action (?)   128 **naked frailties hid** poor
bodies clothed   130 **question** discuss   131 **scruples** suspicions   133 **un-
divulged pretense** hidden purpose   135 **briefly** quickly   138 **office** function

Is to avoid the aim. Therefore to horse;　　　　　　*145*
And let us not be dainty of° leave-taking,
But shift away. There's warrant° in that theft
Which steals itself° when there's no mercy left.

　　　　　　　　　　　　　　　　　　Exeunt.

Scene 4.　　[*Outside Macbeth's castle.*]

Enter Ross with an Old Man.

Old Man. Threescore and ten I can remember well:
　Within the volume of which time I have seen
　Hours dreadful and things strange, but this sore°
　　night
　Hath trifled former knowings.°

Ross.　　　　　　　　　　　Ha, good father,
　Thou seest the heavens, as troubled with man's act,　　*5*
　Threatens his bloody stage. By th' clock 'tis day,
　And yet dark night strangles the traveling lamp:°
　Is 't night's predominance,° or the day's shame,
　That darkness does the face of earth entomb,
　When living light should kiss it?

Old Man.　　　　　　　　　'Tis unnatural,　　*10*
　Even like the deed that's done. On Tuesday last
　A falcon, tow'ring in her pride of place,°
　Was by a mousing° owl hawked at and killed.

Ross. And Duncan's horses—a thing most strange
　　and certain—
　Beauteous and swift, the minions° of their race,　　*15*

146 **dainty of** fussy about　147 **warrant** justification　148 **steals itself**
steals oneself away　2.4.　3 **sore** grievous　4 **trifled former knowings**
made trifles of former experiences　7 **traveling lamp** i.e., the sun　8 **predominance** astrological supremacy　12 **tow'ring ... place** soaring at
her summit　13 **mousing** i.e., normally mouse-eating　15 **minions** darlings

Turned wild in nature, broke their stalls, flung out,°
Contending 'gainst obedience, as they would make
War with mankind.

Old Man.   'Tis said they eat° each other.

Ross. They did so, to th' amazement of mine eyes,
That looked upon 't.

Enter Macduff.

20   Here comes the good Macduff
How goes the world, sir, now?

Macduff.   Why, see you not?

Ross. Is 't known who did this more than bloody deed?

Macduff. Those that Macbeth hath slain.

Ross.   Alas, the day!
What good could they pretend?°

Macduff.   They were suborned:°
25   Malcolm and Donalbain, the king's two sons,
Are stol'n away and fled, which puts upon them
Suspicion of the deed.

Ross.   'Gainst nature still.
Thriftless° ambition, that will ravin up°
Thine own life's means! Then 'tis most like
30   The sovereignty will fall upon Macbeth.

Macduff. He is already named,° and gone to Scone
To be invested.°

Ross.   Where is Duncan's body?

Macduff. Carried to Colmekill,
The sacred storehouse of his predecessors
And guardian of their bones.

35 *Ross.*   Will you to Scone?

Macduff. No, cousin, I'll to Fife.

---

16 **flung out** lunged wildly 18 **eat** ate 24 **pretend** hope for 24 **sub-**
orned bribed 28 **Thriftless** wasteful 28 **ravin up** greedily devour
31 **named** elected 32 **invested** installed as king

Ross. Well, I will thither.

Macduff. Well, may you see things well done there.
    Adieu,
  Lest our old robes sit easier than our new!

Ross. Farewell, father.

Old Man. God's benison° go with you, and with those   40
  That would make good of bad, and friends of foes!

                                    Exeunt omnes.

40 **benison** blessing

ACT 3

Scene 1.   [*Forres. The palace.*]

Enter Banquo.

Banquo. Thou hast it now: King, Cawdor, Glamis, all,
    As the weïrd women promised, and I fear
    Thou play'dst most foully for 't. Yet it was said
    It should not stand° in thy posterity,
5   But that myself should be the root and father
    Of many kings. If there come truth from them—
    As upon thee, Macbeth, their speeches shine—
    Why, by the verities on thee made good,
    May they not be my oracles as well
10   And set me up in hope? But hush, no more!

*Sennet° sounded. Enter Macbeth as King, Lady
[Macbeth], Lennox, Ross, Lords, and Attendants*

Macbeth. Here's our chief guest.

Lady Macbeth.   If he had been forgotten,
    It had been as a gap in our great feast,
    And all-thing° unbecoming.

Macbeth. Tonight we hold a solemn° supper, sir,
    And I'll request your presence.

15 *Banquo.*   Let your Highness
    Command upon me, to the which my duties

3.1. 4 **stand** continue   s.d. **Sennet** trumpet call   13 **all-thing** altogether
14 **solemn** ceremonious

    Are with a most indissoluble tie
    For ever knit.

Macbeth. Ride you this afternoon?

Banquo.   Ay, my good lord.

Macbeth. We should have else desired your good advice   20
    (Which still° hath been both grave and
      prosperous°)
    In this day's council; but we'll take tomorrow.
    Is 't far you ride?

Banquo. As far, my lord, as will fill up the time
    'Twixt this and supper. Go not my horse the
      better,°   25
    I must become a borrower of the night
    For a dark hour or twain.

Macbeth.   Fail not our feast.

Banquo. My lord, I will not.

Macbeth. We hear our bloody cousins are bestowed°
    In England and in Ireland, not confessing   30
    Their cruel parricide, filling their hearers
    With strange invention.° But of that tomorrow,
    When therewithal we shall have cause of state
    Craving us jointly.° Hie you to horse. Adieu,
    Till you return at night. Goes Fleance with you?   35

Banquo. Ay, my good lord: our time does call upon 's.

Macbeth. I wish your horses swift and sure of foot,
    And so I do commend you to their backs.
    Farewell.   *Exit Banquo.*
    Let every man be master of his time   40
    Till seven at night. To make society
    The sweeter welcome, we will keep ourself

---

21 **still** always   21 **grave and prosperous** weighty and profitable   25 **Go ... better** unless my horse goes better than I expect   29 **are bestowed** have taken refuge   32 **invention** lies   33–34 **cause ... jointly** matters of state demanding our joint attention

Till supper-time alone. While° then, God be with
  you!

Exeunt Lords [and all but Macbeth and a Servant].

Sirrah,° a word with you: attend° those men
45 Our pleasure?

Attendant. They are, my lord, without° the palace
  gate.

Macbeth. Bring them before us.   *Exit Servant.*
  To be thus is nothing, but° to be safely thus—
  Our fears in° Banquo stick deep,
50 And in his royalty of nature reigns that
  Which would° be feared. 'Tis much he dares;
  And, to° that dauntless temper° of his mind,
  He hath a wisdom that doth guide his valor
  To act in safety. There is none but he
55 Whose being I do fear: and under him
  My genius is rebuked,° as it is said
  Mark Antony's was by Cæsar. He chid the sisters,
  When first they put the name of King upon me,
  And bade them speak to him; then prophetlike
60 They hailed him father to a line of kings.
  Upon my head they placed a fruitless crown
  And put a barren scepter in my gripe,°
  Thence to be wrenched with an unlineal hand,
  No son of mine succeeding. If 't be so,
65 For Banquo's issue have I filed° my mind;
  For them the gracious Duncan have I murdered;
  Put rancors° in the vessel of my peace
  Only for them, and mine eternal jewel°
  Given to the common enemy of man,°
70 To make them kings, the seeds of Banquo kings!

43 **While** until   44 **Sirrah** (common address to an inferior)   44 **attend**
await   46 **without** outside   48 **but** unless   49 **in** about   51 **would** must
52 **to** added to   52 **temper** quality   56 **genius is rebuked** guardian spirit
is cowed   62 **gripe** grasp   65 **filed** defiled   67 **rancors** bitter enmities
68 **eternal jewel** i.e., soul   69 **common enemy of man** i.e., the Devil

Rather than so, come, fate, into the list,°
And champion me to th' utterance!° Who's there?

Enter Servant and Two Murderers.

Now go to the door, and stay there till we call.

Exit Servant.

Was it not yesterday we spoke together?

Murderers. It was, so please your Highness.

Macbeth.   Well then, now   75
Have you considered of my speeches? Know
That it was he in the times past, which held you
So under fortune,° which you thought had been
Our innocent self: this I made good to you
In our last conference; passed in probation° with
  you,   80
How you were borne in hand,° how crossed;° the
  instruments,°
Who wrought with them, and all things else that
  might
To half a soul° and to a notion° crazed
Say "Thus did Banquo."

First Murderer.   You made it known to us.

Macbeth. I did so; and went further, which is now   85
Our point of second meeting. Do you find
Your patience so predominant in your nature,
That you can let this go? Are you so gospeled,°
To pray for this good man and for his issue,
Whose heavy hand hath bowed you to the grave   90
And beggared yours for ever?

First Murderer.   We are men, my liege.

Macbeth. Ay, in the catalogue ye go for° men;

---

71 **list** lists   72 **champion me to th' utterance** fight against me to the
death   77–78 **held . . . fortune** kept you from good fortune (?)   80 **passed
in probation** reviewed the proofs   81 **borne in hand** deceived   81 **crossed**
thwarted   81 **instruments** tools   83 **half a soul** a halfwit   83 **notion** mind
88 **gospeled** i.e., made meek by the gospel   92 **go for** pass as

As hounds and greyhounds, mongrels, spaniels,
    curs,
    Shoughs, water-rugs° and demi-wolves, are clept°
95 All by the name of dogs: the valued file°
    Distinguishes the swift, the slow, the subtle,
    The housekeeper,° the hunter, every one
    According to the gift which bounteous nature
    Hath in him closed,° whereby he does receive
100 Particular addition, from the bill°
    That writes them all alike: and so of men.
    Now if you have a station in the file,
    Not i' th' worst rank of manhood, say 't,
    And I will put that business in your bosoms
105 Whose execution takes your enemy off,
    Grapples you to the heart and love of us,
    Who wear our health but sickly in his life,°
    Which in his death were perfect.

Second Murderer.   I am one, my liege,
    Whom the vile blows and buffets of the world
110 Hath so incensed that I am reckless what
    I do to spite the world.

First Murderer.   And I another
    So weary with disasters, tugged with fortune,
    That I would set° my life on any chance,
    To mend it or be rid on 't.

Macbeth.   Both of you
    Know Banquo was your enemy.

115 *Both Murderers.*   True, my lord.

Macbeth. So is he mine, and in such bloody distance°
    That every minute of his being thrusts
    Against my near'st of life:° and though I could

---

94 **Shoughs, water-rugs** shaggy dogs, long-haired water dogs   94 **clept**
called   95 **valued file** classification by valuable traits   97 **housekeeper**
watchdog   99 **closed** enclosed   100 **Particular addition, from the bill**
special distinction in opposition to the list   107 **wear ... life** have
only imperfect health while he lives   113 **set** risk   116 **distance** quarrel
118 **near'st of life** most vital spot

With barefaced power sweep him from my sight
And bid my will avouch° it, yet I must not,   120
For° certain friends that are both his and mine,
Whose loves I may not drop, but wail his fall°
Who I myself struck down: and thence it is
That I to your assistance do make love,
Masking the business from the common eye   125
For sundry weighty reasons.

Second Murderer.   We shall, my lord,
Perform what you command us.

First Murderer.   Though our lives——

Macbeth. Your spirits shine through you. Within this
    hour at most
I will advise you where to plant yourselves,
Acquaint you with the perfect spy° o' th' time,   130
The moment on 't;° for 't must be done tonight,
And something° from the palace; always thought°
That I require a clearness:° and with him—
To leave no rubs° nor botches in the work—
Fleance his son, that keeps him company,   135
Whose absence is no less material to me
Than is his father's, must embrace the fate
Of that dark hour. Resolve yourselves apart:°
I'll come to you anon.

Murderers.   We are resolved, my lord.

Macbeth. I'll call upon you straight.° Abide within.   140
    It is concluded: Banquo, thy soul's flight,
    If it find heaven, must find it out tonight.   *Exeunt.*

---

120 **avouch** justify   121 **For** because of   122 **wail his fall** bewail his death
130 **perfect spy** exact information (?) (*spy* literally means "observation";
apparently Macbeth already has the Third Murderer in mind)   131 **on 't**
of it   132 **something** some distance   132 **thought** remembered   133 **clearness** freedom from suspicion   134 **rubs** flaws   138 **Resolve yourselves
apart** decide by yourself   140 **straight** immediately

Scene 2.   [*The palace.*]

Enter Macbeth's Lady and a Servant.

Lady Macbeth. Is Banquo gone from court?

Servant. Ay, madam, but returns again tonight.

Lady Macbeth. Say to the King, I would attend his
 leisure
 For a few words.

Servant.   Madam, I will.   *Exit.*

Lady Macbeth.   Nought's had, all's spent,
5 Where our desire is got without content:
 'Tis safer to be that which we destroy
 Than by destruction dwell in doubtful joy.

Enter Macbeth.

 How now, my lord! Why do you keep alone,
 Of sorriest° fancies your companions making,
 Using those thoughts which should indeed have
10 died
 With them they think on? Things without° all
 remedy
 Should be without regard: what's done is done.

Macbeth. We have scorched° the snake, not killed it:
 She'll close° and be herself, whilst our poor malice°
15 Remains in danger of her former tooth.
 But let the frame of things disjoint,° both the
 worlds° suffer,
 Ere we will eat our meal in fear, and sleep
 In the affliction of these terrible dreams

3.2. 9 **sorriest** most despicable 11 **without** beyond 13 **scorched**
slashed, scored 14 **close** heal 14 **poor malice** feeble enmity 16 **frame
of things disjoint** universe collapse 16 **both the worlds** heaven and
earth (?)

That shake us nightly: better be with the dead,
Whom we, to gain our peace, have sent to peace,   20
Than on the torture° of the mind to lie
In restless ecstasy.° Duncan is in his grave;
After life's fitful fever he sleeps well.
Treason has done his° worst: nor steel, nor poison,
Malice domestic,° foreign levy, nothing,   25
Can touch him further.

Lady Macbeth.   Come on.
Gentle my lord, sleek° o'er your rugged° looks;
Be bright and jovial among your guests tonight.

Macbeth. So shall I, love; and so, I pray, be you:
Let your remembrance apply to Banquo;°   30
Present him eminence,° both with eye and tongue:
Unsafe the while, that we must lave°
Our honors in these flattering streams
And make our faces vizards° to our hearts,
Disguising what they are.

Lady Macbeth.   You must leave this.   35

Macbeth. O, full of scorpions is my mind, dear wife!
Thou know'st that Banquo, and his Fleance, lives.

Lady Macbeth. But in them nature's copy's° not eterne.

Macbeth. There's comfort yet; they are assailable.
Then be thou jocund. Ere the bat hath flown   40
His cloistered flight, ere to black Hecate's summons
The shard-borne° beetle with his drowsy hums
Hath rung night's yawning peal, there shall be done
A deed of dreadful note.

Lady Macbeth.   What's to be done?

---

21 **torture** i.e., rack   22 **ecstasy** frenzy   24 **his** its   25 **Malice domestic**
civil war   27 **sleek** smooth   27 **rugged** furrowed   30 **Let ... Banquo**
focus your thoughts on Banquo   31 **Present him eminence** honor him
32 **Unsafe ... lave** i.e., you and I are unsafe because we must dip
34 **vizards** masks   38 **nature's copy** nature's lease (?) imitation (i.e., a
son) made by nature (?)   42 **shard-borne** borne on scaly wings (?)
dung-bred (?)

Macbeth. Be innocent of the knowledge, dearest
45   chuck,°
     Till thou applaud the deed. Come, seeling° night,
     Scarf up° the tender eye of pitiful day,
     And with thy bloody and invisible hand
     Cancel and tear to pieces that great bond°
50   Which keeps me pale! Light thickens, and the crow
     Makes wing to th' rooky° wood.
     Good things of day begin to droop and drowse,
     Whiles night's black agents to their preys do rouse.
     Thou marvel'st at my words: but hold thee still;
55   Things bad begun make strong themselves by ill:
     So, prithee, go with me.   *Exeunt.*

Scene 3.   [*Near the palace.*]

Enter Three Murderers.

First Murderer. But who did bid thee join with us?

Third Murderer.   Macbeth.

Second Murderer. He needs not our mistrust; since he
     delivers
     Our offices and what we have to do
     To the direction just.°

First Murderer.   Then stand with us.
5   The west yet glimmers with some streaks of day.
     Now spurs the lated° traveler apace
     To gain the timely inn, and near approaches
     The subject of our watch.

---

45 **chuck** chick (a term of endearment)   46 **seeling** eye-closing   47 **Scarf
up** blindfold   49 **bond** i.e., between Banquo and fate (?) Banquo's lease
on life (?) Macbeth's link to humanity (?)   51 **rooky** full of rooks
3.3.   2–4 **He needs ... just** we need not mistrust him (i.e., the Third
Murderer) since he describes our duties according to our exact directions   6 **lated** belated

Third Murderer.   Hark! I hear horses.

Banquo. (Within) Give us a light there, ho!

Second Murderer.   Then 'tis he. The rest
   That are within the note of expectation°   *10*
   Already are i' th' court.

First Murderer.   His horses go about.

Third Murderer. Almost a mile: but he does usually—
   So all men do—from hence to th' palace gate
   Make it their walk.

     Enter Banquo and Fleance, with a torch.

Second Murderer. A light, a light!

Third Murderer.   'Tis he.

First Murderer.   Stand to 't.   *15*

Banquo. It will be rain tonight.

First Murderer.   Let it come down.

     [They set upon Banquo.]

Banquo. O, treachery! Fly, good Fleance, fly, fly, fly!

       [Exit Fleance.]

   Thou mayst revenge. O slave! *[Dies.]*

Third Murderer. Who did strike out the light?

First Murderer.   Was 't not the way?°

Third Murderer. There's but one down; the son is fled.   *20*

Second Murderer. We have lost best half of our affair.

First Murderer. Well, let's away and say how much is
   done.   *Exeunt.*

---

10 **within the note of expectation** on the list of expected guests   19 **way**
i.e., thing to do

Scene 4.   [*The palace.*]

Banquet prepared. Enter Macbeth, Lady [Macbeth], Ross, Lennox, Lords, and Attendants.

Macbeth. You know your own degrees;° sit down:
At first and last, the hearty welcome.

Lords. Thanks to your Majesty.

Macbeth. Ourself will mingle with society°
5   And play the humble host.
Our hostess keeps her state,° but in best time
We will require° her welcome.

Lady Macbeth. Pronounce it for me, sir, to all our
      friends,
For my heart speaks they are welcome.

Enter First Murderer.

Macbeth. See, they encounter° thee with their hearts'
10   thanks.
Both sides are even: here I'll sit i' th' midst:
Be large in mirth; anon we'll drink a measure°
The table round. [*Goes to Murderer*] There's
      blood upon thy face.

Murderer. 'Tis Banquo's then.

15   *Macbeth.* 'Tis better thee without than he within.°
Is he dispatched?

Murderer. My lord, his throat is cut; that I did for
      him.

Macbeth. Thou art the best o' th' cutthroats.

3.4.   1 **degrees** ranks   4 **society** the company   6 **keeps her state** remains
seated in her chair of state   7 **require** request   10 **encounter** meet
12 **measure** goblet   15 **thee without than he within** outside you than
inside him

Yet he's good that did the like for Fleance;
If thou didst it, thou art the nonpareil.   20

Murderer. Most royal sir, Fleance is 'scaped.

Macbeth. [*Aside*] Then comes my fit again: I had
    else been perfect,
Whole as the marble, founded° as the rock,
As broad and general as the casing° air:
But now I am cabined, cribbed,° confined, bound in   25
To saucy° doubts and fears.—But Banquo's safe?

Murderer. Ay, my good lord: safe in a ditch he bides,
With twenty trenchèd° gashes on his head,
The least a death to nature.

Macbeth.   Thanks for that.
[*Aside*] There the grown serpent lies; the worm°
    that's fled   30
Hath nature that in time will venom breed,
No teeth for th' present. Get thee gone. Tomorrow
We'll hear ourselves° again.   *Exit Murderer.*

Lady Macbeth.   My royal lord,
You do not give the cheer.° The feast is sold
That is not often vouched, while 'tis a-making,   35
'Tis given with welcome. To feed were best at
    home;°
From thence, the sauce to meat° is ceremony;
Meeting were bare without it.

    Enter the Ghost of Banquo, and sits in
    Macbeth's place.

Macbeth.   Sweet remembrancer!°
Now good digestion wait on appetite,
And health on both!

---

23 **founded** firmly based   24 **broad ... casing** unconfined as the surrounding   25 **cribbed** penned up   26 **saucy** insolent   28 **trenchèd** trench-
like   30 **worm** serpent   33 **hear ourselves** talk it over   34 **the cheer** a
sense of cordiality   34–36 **The feast ... home** i.e., the feast seems sold
(not given) during which the host fails to welcome the guests. Mere eat-
ing is best done at home   37 **meat** food   38 **remembrancer** reminder

40 *Lennox.*   May 't please your Highness sit.

Macbeth. Here had we now our country's honor
    roofed,°
    Were the graced person of our Banquo present—
    Who may I rather challenge for unkindness
    Than pity for mischance!°

Ross.   His absence, sir,
    Lays blame upon his promise. Please 't your
45   Highness
    To grace us with your royal company?

Macbeth. The table's full.

Lennox.   Here is a place reserved, sir.

Macbeth. Where?

Lennox. Here, my good lord. What is 't that moves
    your Highness?

Macbeth. Which of you have done this?

50 *Lords.*   What, my good lord?

Macbeth. Thou canst not say I did it. Never shake
    Thy gory locks at me.

Ross. Gentlemen, rise, his Highness is not well.

Lady Macbeth. Sit, worthy friends. My lord is often
    thus,
55   And hath been from his youth. Pray you, keep seat.
    The fit is momentary; upon a thought°
    He will again be well. If much you note him,
    You shall offend him and extend his passion.°
    Feed, and regard him not.—Are you a man?

60 *Macbeth.* Ay, and a bold one, that dare look on that
    Which might appall the devil.

Lady Macbeth.   O proper stuff!
    This is the very painting of your fear.
    This is the air-drawn dagger which, you said,

---

41 **our country's honor roofed** our nobility under one roof   43–44 **Who
... mischance** whom I hope I may reprove because he is unkind rather
than pity because he has encountered an accident   56 **upon a thought**
as quick as thought   58 **extend his passion** lengthen his fit

Led you to Duncan. O, these flaws° and starts,
Impostors to° true fear, would well become　　　　　65
A woman's story at a winter's fire,
Authorized° by her grandam. Shame itself!
Why do you make such faces? When all's done,
You look but on a stool.

Macbeth.　　　　　　　　　Prithee, see there!
Behold! Look! Lo! How say you?　　　　　　70
Why, what care I? If thou canst nod, speak too.
If charnel houses° and our graves must send
Those that we bury back, our monuments
Shall be the maws of kites.°　　　　　[*Exit Ghost.*]

Lady Macbeth.　　　　　　What, quite unmanned in folly?

Macbeth. If I stand here, I saw him.

Lady Macbeth.　　　　　　　　Fie, for shame!　　75

Macbeth. Blood hath been shed ere now, i' th' olden
　　time,
Ere humane statute purged the gentle weal;°
Ay, and since too, murders have been performed
Too terrible for the ear. The times has been
That, when the brains were out, the man would die,　80
And there an end; but now they rise again,
With twenty mortal murders on their crowns,°
And push us from our stools. This is more strange
Than such a murder is.

Lady Macbeth.　　　　　My worthy lord,
Your noble friends do lack you.

Macbeth.　　　　　　　　I do forget.　　85
Do not muse at me, my most worthy friends;
I have a strange infirmity, which is nothing
To those that know me. Come, love and health to
　　all!

---

64 **flaws** gusts, outbursts　65 **to** compared with　67 **Authorized** vouched
for　72 **charnel houses** vaults containing bones　73–74 **our ... kites**
our tombs shall be the bellies of rapacious birds　77 **purged the gentle
weal** i.e., cleansed the state and made it gentle　82 **mortal murders on
their crowns** deadly wounds on their heads

Then I'll sit down. Give me some wine, fill full.

Enter Ghost.

90   I drink to th' general joy o' th' whole table,
And to our dear friend Banquo, whom we miss;
Would he were here! To all and him we thirst,°
And all to all.°

Lords.   Our duties, and the pledge.

Macbeth. Avaunt! and quit my sight! Let the earth hide
thee!
95   Thy bones are marrowless, thy blood is cold;
Thou hast no speculation° in those eyes
Which thou dost glare with.

Lady Macbeth.   Think of this, good peers,
But as a thing of custom; 'tis no other.
Only it spoils the pleasure of the time.

100 *Macbeth.* What man dare, I dare.
Approach thou like the rugged Russian bear,
The armed rhinoceros, or th' Hyrcan° tiger;
Take any shape but that, and my firm nerves°
Shall never tremble. Or be alive again,
105   And dare me to the desert° with thy sword.
If trembling I inhabit then, protest me
The baby of a girl.° Hence, horrible shadow!
Unreal mock'ry, hence!   [*Exit Ghost.*]
                   Why, so: being gone,
I am a man again. Pray you, sit still.

Lady Macbeth. You have displaced the mirth, broke the
110   good meeting,
With most admired° disorder.

Macbeth.   Can such things be,
And overcome us° like a summer's cloud,

---

92 **thirst** desire to drink 93 **all to all** everything to everybody (?) let
everybody drink to everybody (?) 96 **speculation** sight 102 **Hyrcan** of
Hyrcania (near the Caspian Sea) 103 **nerves** sinews 105 **the desert** a
lonely place 106–07 **If . . . girl** if then I tremble, proclaim me a baby
girl 111 **admired** amazing 112 **overcome us** come over us

Without our special wonder? You make me strange
Even to the disposition that I owe,°
When now I think you can behold such sights,   *115*
And keep the natural ruby of your cheeks,
When mine is blanched with fear.

Ross.   What sights, my lord?

Lady Macbeth. I pray you, speak not: he grows worse
and worse;
Question enrages him: at once, good night.
Stand not upon the order of your going,°   *120*
But go at once.

Lennox.   Good night; and better health
Attend his Majesty!

Lady Macbeth.   A kind good night to all!

                              Exeunt Lords.

Macbeth. It will have blood, they say: blood will have
blood.
Stones have been known to move and trees to
speak;
Augures and understood relations° have   *125*
By maggot-pies and choughs and rooks brought
forth°
The secret'st man of blood. What is the night?°

Lady Macbeth. Almost at odds° with morning, which is
which.

Macbeth. How say'st thou, that Macduff denies his
person
At our great bidding?

Lady Macbeth.   Did you send to him, sir?   *130*

Macbeth. I hear it by the way,° but I will send:

113–14 **You ... owe** i.e., you make me wonder what my nature is
120 **Stand ... going** do not insist on departing in your order of rank
125 **Augures and understood relations** auguries and comprehended reports 126 **By ... forth** by magpies, choughs, and rooks (telltale
birds) revealed 127 **What is the night** what time of night is it
128 **at odds** striving 131 **by the way** incidentally

  There's not a one of them but in his house
  I keep a servant fee'd.° I will tomorrow,
  And betimes° I will, to the weïrd sisters:
135 More shall they speak, for now I am bent° to know
  By the worst means the worst. For mine own good
  All causes° shall give way. I am in blood
  Stepped in so far that, should I wade no more,
  Returning were as tedious as go o'er.
140 Strange things I have in head that will to hand,
  Which must be acted ere they may be scanned.°

Lady Macbeth. You lack the season of all natures,°
  sleep.

Macbeth. Come, we'll to sleep. My strange and self-
  abuse°
  Is the initiate fear that wants hard use.°
145 We are yet but young in deed.   *Exeunt.*

Scene 5. [*A Witches' haunt.*]

*Thunder. Enter the Three Witches, meeting
Hecate.*

First Witch. Why, how now, Hecate! you look
  angerly.

Hecate. Have I not reason, beldams° as you are,
  Saucy and overbold? How did you dare
  To trade and traffic with Macbeth
5 In riddles and affairs of death;

133 **fee'd** i.e., paid to spy 134 **betimes** quickly 135 **bent** determined
137 **causes** considerations 141 **may be scanned** can be examined
142 **season of all natures** seasoning (preservative) of all living creatures
143 **My strange and self-abuse** my strange delusion 144 **initiate ...
use** beginner's fear that lacks hardening practice 3.5. 2 **beldams** hags

And I, the mistress of your charms,
The close contriver° of all harms,
Was never called to bear my part,
Or show the glory of our art?
And, which is worse, all you have done   10
Hath been but for a wayward son,
Spiteful and wrathful; who, as others do,
Loves for his own ends, not for you.
But make amends now: get you gone,
And at the pit of Acheron°   15
Meet me i' th' morning: thither he
Will come to know his destiny.
Your vessels and your spells provide,
Your charms and everything beside.
I am for th' air; this night I'll spend   20
Unto a dismal and a fatal end:
Great business must be wrought ere noon.
Upon the corner of the moon
There hangs a vap'rous drop profound;°
I'll catch it ere it come to ground: 25
And that distilled by magic sleights°
Shall raise such artificial sprites°
As by the strength of their illusion
Shall draw him on to his confusion.°
He shall spurn fate, scorn death, and bear   30
His hopes 'bove wisdom, grace, and fear:
And you all know security°
Is mortals' chiefest enemy.

                Music and a song.

Hark! I am called; my little spirit, see,
Sits in a foggy cloud and stays for me.   [*Exit.*]   35
    Sing within, "Come away, come away," &c.

First Witch. Come, let's make haste; she'll soon be
    back again.   *Exeunt.*

---

7 **close contriver** secret inventor   15 **Acheron** (river of Hades)   24 **profound** heavy   26 **sleights** arts   27 **artificial sprites** spirits created by magic arts (?) artful (cunning) spirits (?)   29 **confusion** ruin   32 **security** overconfidence

Scene 6.   [*The palace.*]

Enter Lennox and another Lord.

Lennox. My former speeches have but hit your
        thoughts,°
     Which can interpret farther. Only I say
     Things have been strangely borne.° The gracious
        Duncan
     Was pitied of Macbeth: marry, he was dead.
5   And the right-valiant Banquo walked too late;
     Whom, you may say, if 't please you, Fleance
        killed,
     For Fleance fled. Men must not walk too late.
     Who cannot want the thought,° how monstrous
     It was for Malcolm and for Donalbain
10   To kill their gracious father? Damnèd fact!°
     How it did grieve Macbeth! Did he not straight,
     In pious rage, the two delinquents tear,
     That were the slaves of drink and thralls° of sleep?
     Was not that nobly done? Ay, and wisely too;
15   For 'twould have angered any heart alive
     To hear the men deny 't. So that I say
     He has borne° all things well: and I do think
     That, had he Duncan's sons under his key—
     As, an 't° please heaven, he shall not—they should
        find
20   What 'twere to kill a father. So should Fleance.
     But, peace! for from broad words,° and 'cause he
        failed
     His presence at the tyrant's feast, I hear,

3.6. 1 **My ... thoughts** i.e., my recent words have only coincided
with what you have in your mind   3 **borne** managed   8 **cannot want
the thought** can fail to think   10 **fact** evil deed   13 **thralls** slaves
17 **borne** managed   19 **an 't** if it   21 **for from broad words** because of
frank talk

Macduff lives in disgrace. Sir, can you tell
Where he bestows himself?

Lord.   The son of Duncan,
From whom this tyrant holds the due of birth,°   25
Lives in the English court, and is received
Of the most pious Edward° with such grace
That the malevolence of fortune nothing
Takes from his high respect.° Thither Macduff
Is gone to pray the holy King, upon his aid°   30
To wake Northumberland° and warlike Siward;
That by the help of these, with Him above
To ratify the work, we may again
Give to our tables meat, sleep to our nights,
Free from our feasts and banquets bloody knives,   35
Do faithful homage and receive free° honors:
All which we pine for now. And this report
Hath so exasperate the King that he
Prepares for some attempt of war.

Lennox.   Sent he to Macduff?

Lord. He did: and with an absolute "Sir, not I,"   40
The cloudy° messenger turns me his back,
And hums, as who should say "You'll rue the time
That clogs° me with this answer."

Lennox.   And that well might
Advise him to a caution, t' hold what distance
His wisdom can provide. Some holy angel   45
Fly to the court of England and unfold
His message ere he come, that a swift blessing
May soon return to this our suffering country
Under a hand accursed!

Lord.   I'll send my prayers with him.

                                        Exeunt.

25 **due of birth** birthright   27 **Edward** Edward the Confessor (reigned 1042–1066)   28–29 **nothing ... respect** does not diminish the high respect in which he is held   30 **upon his aid** to aid him (Malcolm) 31 **To wake Northumberland** i.e., to arouse the people in an English county near Scotland   36 **free** freely granted   41 **cloudy** disturbed 43 **clogs** burdens

ACT 4

Scene 1. [*A Witches' haunt.*]

Thunder. Enter the Three Witches.

First Witch. Thrice the brinded° cat hath mewed.

Second Witch. Thrice and once the hedge-pig°
    whined.

Third Witch. Harpier° cries. 'Tis time, 'tis time.

First Witch. Round about the caldron go:
5   In the poisoned entrails throw.
    Toad, that under cold stone
    Days and nights has thirty-one
    Swelt'red venom sleeping got,°
    Boil thou first i' th' charmèd pot.

10 *All.* Double, double, toil and trouble;
    Fire burn and caldron bubble.

Second Witch. Fillet° of a fenny° snake,
    In the caldron boil and bake;
    Eye of newt and toe of frog,
15   Wool of bat and tongue of dog,
    Adder's fork° and blindworm's° sting,
    Lizard's leg and howlet's° wing,

4.1. 1 **brinded** brindled 2 **hedge-pig** hedgehog 3 **Harpier** (an attendant spirit, like Graymalkin and Paddock in 1.1) 8 **Swelt'red venom sleeping got** venom sweated out while sleeping 12 **Fillet** slice 12 **fenny** from a swamp 16 **fork** forked tongue 16 **blindworm** (a legless lizard) 17 **howlet** owlet

For a charm of pow'rful trouble,
Like a hell-broth boil and bubble.

All. Double, double, toil and trouble;   20
Fire burn and caldron bubble.

Third Witch. Scale of dragon, tooth of wolf,
Witch's mummy,° maw and gulf°
Of the ravined° salt-sea shark,
Root of hemlock digged i' th' dark,   25
Liver of blaspheming Jew,
Gall of goat, and slips of yew
Slivered in the moon's eclipse,
Nose of Turk and Tartar's lips,
Finger of birth-strangled babe   30
Ditch-delivered by a drab,°
Make the gruel thick and slab:°
Add thereto a tiger's chaudron,°
For th' ingredience of our caldron.

All. Double, double, toil and trouble;   35
Fire burn and caldron bubble.

Second Witch. Cool it with a baboon's blood,
Then the charm is firm and good.

    Enter Hecate and the other Three Witches.

Hecate. O, well done! I commend your pains;
And every one shall share i' th' gains: 40
And now about the caldron sing,
Like elves and fairies in a ring,
Enchanting all that you put in.

    Music and a song: "Black Spirits," &c.

    [*Exeunt Hecate and the other Three Witches.*]

Second Witch. By the pricking of my thumbs,
Something wicked this way comes: 45
    Open, locks,
    Whoever knocks!

23 **Witch's mummy** mummified flesh of a witch   23 **maw and gulf**
stomach and gullet   24 **ravined** ravenous   31 **Ditch-delivered by a drab**
born in a ditch of a harlot   32 **slab** viscous   33 **chaudron** entrails

Macbeth. How now, you secret, black, and midnight
    hags!
    What is 't you do?

All.   A deed without a name.

50 *Macbeth.* I conjure you, by that which you profess,
    Howe'er you come to know it, answer me:
    Though you untie the winds and let them fight
    Against the churches; though the yesty° waves
    Confound° and swallow navigation up;
    Though bladed corn be lodged° and trees blown
55   down;
    Though castles topple on their warders' heads;
    Though palaces and pyramids do slope°
    Their heads to their foundations; though the treas-
      ure
    Of nature's germens° tumble all together,
60   Even till destruction sicken,° answer me
    To what I ask you.

First Witch.   Speak.

Second Witch.   Demand.

Third Witch.   We'll answer.

First Witch. Say, if th' hadst rather hear it from our
    mouths,
    Or from our masters?

Macbeth.   Call 'em, let me see 'em.

First Witch. Pour in sow's blood, that hath eaten
65   Her nine farrow;° grease that's sweaten°
    From the murderer's gibbet throw
    Into the flame.

All.   Come, high or low,
    Thyself and office° deftly show!

---

53 **yesty** foamy   54 **Confound** destroy   55 **bladed corn be lodged** grain
in the ear be beaten down   57 **slope** bend   59 **nature's germens** seeds
of all life   60 **sicken** i.e., sicken at its own work   65 **farrow** young pigs
65 **sweaten** sweated   68 **office** function

Thunder. First Apparition: an Armed Head.

Macbeth. Tell me, thou unknown power———

First Witch.　　　　　　　　　He knows thy thought:
　Hear his speech, but say thou nought.　　　　　70

First Apparition. Macbeth! Macbeth! Macbeth! Beware
　Macduff!
　Beware the Thane of Fife. Dismiss me: enough.

　　　　　　　　　　　　　　　He descends.

Macbeth. Whate'er thou art, for thy good caution
　thanks:
　Thou hast harped° my fear aright. But one word
　more———

First Witch. He will not be commanded. Here's an-
　other,　　　　　　　　　　　　　　　　75
　More potent than the first.

　　　Thunder. Second Apparition: a Bloody Child.

Second Apparition. Macbeth! Macbeth! Macbeth!

Macbeth. Had I three ears, I'd hear thee.

Second Apparition. Be bloody, bold, and resolute!
　Laugh to scorn
　The pow'r of man, for none of woman born　　80
　Shall harm Macbeth.　　　　　　*Descends.*

Macbeth. Then live, Macduff: what need I fear of
　thee?
　But yet I'll make assurance double sure,
　And take a bond of fate.° Thou shalt not live;
　That I may tell pale-hearted fear it lies,　　　85
　And sleep in spite of thunder.

　　　Thunder. Third Apparition: a Child Crowned,
　　　　　　with a tree in his hand.

74 **harped** hit upon, struck the note of　84 **take a bond of fate** get a
guarantee from fate (i.e., he will kill Macduff and thus will compel
fate to keep its word)

                                        What is this,
That rises like the issue° of a king,
And wears upon his baby-brow the round
And top of sovereignty?°

All.   Listen, but speak not to 't.

Third Apparition. Be lion-mettled, proud, and take
90   no care
        Who chafes, who frets, or where conspirers are:
        Macbeth shall never vanquished be until
        Great Birnam Wood to high Dunsinane Hill
        Shall come against him.   *Descends.*

Macbeth.   That will never be.
95   Who can impress° the forest, bid the tree
        Unfix his earth-bound root? Sweet bodements,°
            good!
        Rebellious dead,° rise never, till the Wood
        Of Birnam rise, and our high-placed Macbeth
        Shall live the lease of nature,° pay his breath
100   To time and mortal custom.° Yet my heart
        Throbs to know one thing. Tell me, if your art
        Can tell so much: shall Banquo's issue ever
        Reign in this kingdom?

All.   Seek to know no more.

Macbeth. I will be satisfied.° Deny me this,
105   And an eternal curse fall on you! Let me know.
        Why sinks that caldron? And what noise° is this?

                            Hautboys.

First Witch. Show!

Second Witch. Show!

Third Witch. Show!

---

87 **issue** offspring 88–89 **round/And top of sovereignty** i.e., crown
95 **impress** conscript 96 **bodements** prophecies 97 **Rebellious dead**
(perhaps a reference to Banquo; but perhaps a misprint for "rebellion's
head") 99 **lease of nature** natural lifespan 100 **mortal custom** natural
death 104 **satisfied** i.e., fully informed 106 **noise** music

All. Show his eyes, and grieve his heart;   *110*
   Come like shadows, so depart!

> *A show of eight Kings and Banquo, last [King]*
> *with a glass° in his hand.*

Macbeth. Thou art too like the spirit of Banquo.
   Down!
   Thy crown does sear mine eyelids. And thy hair,
   Thou other gold-bound brow, is like the first.
   A third is like the former. Filthy hags!   *115*
   Why do you show me this? A fourth! Start,° eyes!
   What, will the line stretch out to th' crack of
      doom?°
   Another yet! A seventh! I'll see no more.
   And yet the eighth appears, who bears a glass
   Which shows me many more; and some I see   *120*
   That twofold balls and treble scepters° carry:
   Horrible sight! Now I see 'tis true;
   For the blood-boltered° Banquo smiles upon me,
   And points at them for his. What, is this so?

First Witch. Ay, sir, all this is so. But why   *125*
   Stands Macbeth thus amazedly?
   Come, sisters, cheer we up his sprites,°
   And show the best of our delights:
   I'll charm the air to give a sound,
   While you perform your antic round,°   *130*
   That this great king may kindly say
   Our duties did his welcome pay.

> *Music. The Witches dance, and vanish.*

Macbeth. Where are they? Gone? Let this pernicious
   hour
   Stand aye accursèd in the calendar!
   Come in, without there!

111.s.d. **glass** mirror   116 **Start** i.e., from the sockets   117 **crack of doom**
blast (of a trumpet?) at doomsday   121 **twofold balls and treble**
scepters (coronation emblems)   123 **blood-boltered** matted with blood
127 **sprites** spirits   130 **antic round** grotesque circular dance

Enter Lennox.

135 *Lennox.*   What's your Grace's will?

Macbeth. Saw you the weïrd sisters?

Lennox.   No, my lord.

Macbeth. Came they not by you?

Lennox.   No indeed, my lord.

Macbeth. Infected be the air whereon they ride,
   And damned all those that trust them! I did hear
140   The galloping of horse.° Who was 't came by?

Lennox. 'Tis two or three, my lord, that bring you
      word
   Macduff is fled to England.

Macbeth.   Fled to England?

Lennox. Ay, my good lord.

Macbeth. [*Aside*] Time, thou anticipat'st° my
      dread exploits.
145   The flighty purpose never is o'ertook
   Unless the deed go with it.° From this moment
   The very firstlings of my heart° shall be
   The firstlings of my hand. And even now,
   To crown my thoughts with acts, be it thought and
      done:
150   The castle of Macduff I will surprise;°
   Seize upon Fife; give to th' edge o' th' sword
   His wife, his babes, and all unfortunate souls
   That trace him in his line.° No boasting like a fool;
   This deed I'll do before this purpose cool:
155   But no more sights!—Where are these gentlemen?
   Come, bring me where they are.   *Exeunt.*

---

140 **horse** horses (or "horsemen")   144 **anticipat'st** foretold   145–46 **The
flighty ... it** the fleeting plan is never fulfilled unless an action ac-
companies it   147 **firstlings of my heart** i.e., first thoughts, impulses
150 **surprise** attack suddenly   153 **trace him in his line** are of his lineage

Scene 2.   [*Macduff's castle.*]

Enter Macduff's wife, her Son, and Ross.

Lady Macduff. What had he done, to make him fly the
    land?

Ross. You must have patience, madam.

Lady Macduff.   He had none:
    His flight was madness. When our actions do not,
    Our fears do make us traitors.

Ross.   You know not
    Whether it was his wisdom or his fear.   *5*

Lady Macduff. Wisdom! To leave his wife, to leave his
    babes,
    His mansion and his titles,° in a place
    From whence himself does fly? He loves us not;
    He wants the natural touch:° for the poor wren,
    The most diminutive of birds, will fight,   *10*
    Her young ones in her nest, against the owl.
    All is the fear and nothing is the love;
    As little is the wisdom, where the flight
    So runs against all reason.

Ross.   My dearest coz,°
    I pray you, school° yourself. But, for your husband,   *15*
    He is noble, wise, judicious, and best knows
    The fits o' th' season.° I dare not speak much
    further:
    But cruel are the times, when we are traitors
    And do not know ourselves; when we hold rumor
    From what we fear,° yet know not what we fear,   *20*

4.2.   **7 titles** possessions   **9 wants the natural touch** i.e., lacks natural affection for his wife and children   14 **coz** cousin   15 **school** control   17 **fits
o' th' season** disorders of the time   19–20 **hold rumor/From what we fear**
believe rumors because we fear

But float upon a wild and violent sea
Each way and move. I take my leave of you.
Shall not be long but I'll be here again.
Things at the worst will cease,° or else climb up-
        ward
25   To what they were before. My pretty cousin,
Blessing upon you!

Lady Macduff. Fathered he is, and yet he's fatherless.

Ross. I am so much a fool, should I stay longer,
It would be my disgrace° and your discomfort.
I take my leave at once.   *Exit Ross.*

30   *Lady Macduff.*   Sirrah,° your father's dead:
And what will you do now? How will you live?

Son. As birds do, mother.

Lady Macduff.   What, with worms and flies?

Son. With what I get, I mean; and so do they.

Lady Macduff. Poor bird! thou'dst never fear the net
        nor lime,°
35   The pitfall nor the gin.°

Son. Why should I, mother? Poor birds they are not
        set for.
My father is not dead, for all your saying.

Lady Macduff. Yes, he is dead: how wilt thou do for a
        father?

Son. Nay, how will you do for a husband?

Lady Macduff. Why, I can buy me twenty at any
40   market.

Son. Then you'll buy 'em to sell° again.

Lady Macduff. Thou speak'st with all thy wit, and yet,
        i' faith,
With wit enough for thee.°

---

24 **cease** i.e., cease worsening   29 **It would be my disgrace** i.e., I would
weep   30 **Sirrah** (here an affectionate address to a child)   34 **lime** bird-
lime (smeared on branches to catch birds)   35 **gin** trap   41 **sell** betray
43 **for thee** i.e., for a child

Son. Was my father a traitor, mother?

Lady Macduff. Ay, that he was.   *45*

Son. What is a traitor?

Lady Macduff. Why, one that swears and lies.°

Son. And be all traitors that do so?

Lady Macduff. Every one that does so is a traitor, and must be hanged.

Son. And must they all be hanged that swear and lie?   *50*

Lady Macduff. Every one.

Son. Who must hang them?

Lady Macduff. Why, the honest men.

Son. Then the liars and swearers are fools; for there are liars and swearers enow° to beat the honest   *55* men and hang up them.

Lady Macduff. Now, God help thee, poor monkey! But how wilt thou do for a father?

Son. If he were dead, you'd weep for him. If you would not, it were a good sign that I should quickly   *60* have a new father.

Lady Macduff. Poor prattler, how thou talk'st!

Enter a Messenger.

Messenger. Bless you, fair dame! I am not to you known,
Though in your state of honor I am perfect.°
I doubt° some danger does approach you nearly: *65*
If you will take a homely° man's advice,
Be not found here; hence, with your little ones.
To fright you thus, methinks I am too savage;
To do worse to you were fell° cruelty,
Which is too nigh your person. Heaven preserve you!   *70*

---

47 **swears and lies** i.e., takes an oath and breaks it   55 **enow** enough
64 **in ... perfect** I am fully informed of your honorable rank   65 **doubt**
fear   66 **homely** plain   69 **fell** fierce

I dare abide no longer.   *Exit Messenger.*

Lady Macduff.   Whither should I fly?
I have done no harm. But I remember now
I am in this earthly world, where to do harm
Is often laudable, to do good sometime
75   Accounted dangerous folly. Why then, alas,
Do I put up that womanly defense,
To say I have done no harm?—What are these faces?

          Enter Murderers.

Murderer. Where is your husband?

Lady Macduff. I hope, in no place so unsanctified
Where such as thou mayst find him.

80 *Murderer.*   He's a traitor.

Son. Thou li'st, thou shag-eared° villain!

Murderer.   What, you egg!

          [*Stabbing him.*]

Young fry° of treachery!

Son.   He has killed me, mother:
Run away, I pray you!

               [*Dies.*]
          Exit [*Lady Macduff*], *crying "Murder!"* [*fol-
               lowed by Murderers*].

Scene 3. [*England. Before the King's palace.*]
          Enter Malcolm and Macduff.

Malcolm. Let us seek out some desolate shade, and
     there
     Weep our sad bosoms empty.

81 **shag-eared** hairy-eared (?), with shaggy hair hanging over the ears
(?)   82 **fry** spawn

Macduff.   Let us rather
　　Hold fast the mortal° sword, and like good men
　　Bestride our down-fall'n birthdom.° Each new
　　　　morn
　　New widows howl, new orphans cry, new sorrows   5
　　Strike heaven on the face, that° it resounds
　　As if it felt with Scotland and yelled out
　　Like syllable of dolor.°

Malcolm.   What I believe, I'll wail;
　　What know, believe; and what I can redress,
　　As I shall find the time to friend,° I will.   10
　　What you have spoke, it may be so perchance.
　　This tyrant, whose sole° name blisters our tongues,
　　Was once thought honest:° you have loved him
　　　　well;
　　He hath not touched you yet. I am young; but
　　　　something
　　You may deserve of him through me;° and wisdom°   15
　　To offer up a weak, poor, innocent lamb
　　T' appease an angry god.

Macduff. I am not treacherous.

Malcolm.   But Macbeth is.
　　A good and virtuous nature may recoil
　　In° an imperial charge. But I shall crave your
　　　　pardon;   20
　　That which you are, my thoughts cannot
　　　　transpose:°
　　Angels are bright still, though the brightest° fell:
　　Though all things foul would wear° the brows of
　　　　grace,
　　Yet grace must still look so.°

4.3.　3 **mortal** deadly　4 **Bestride our down-fall'n birthdom** protectively
stand over our native land　6 **that** so that　8 **Like syllable of dolor**
similar sound of grief　10 **to friend** friendly, propitious　12 **sole** very
13 **honest** good　15 **deserve of him through me** i.e., earn by betraying
me to Macbeth　15 **wisdom** it may be wise　19–20 **recoil/In** give way
under　21 **transpose** transform　22 **the brightest** i.e., Lucifer　23 **would
wear** desire to wear　24 **so** i.e., like itself

Macduff.   I have lost my hopes.

Malcolm. Perchance even there where I did find my
25   doubts.
      Why in that rawness° left you wife and child,
      Those precious motives, those strong knots of
        love,
      Without leave-taking? I pray you,
      Let not my jealousies° be your dishonors,
30   But mine own safeties. You may be rightly just°
      Whatever I shall think.

Macduff.   Bleed, bleed, poor country:
      Great tyranny, lay thou thy basis° sure,
      For goodness dare not check° thee: wear thou thy
        wrongs;
      The title is affeered.° Fare thee well, lord:
35   I would not be the villain that thou think'st
      For the whole space that's in the tyrant's grasp
      And the rich East to boot.

Malcolm.   Be not offended:
      I speak not as in absolute fear of you.
      I think our country sinks beneath the yoke;
40   It weeps, it bleeds, and each new day a gash
      Is added to her wounds. I think withal°
      There would be hands uplifted in my right;°
      And here from gracious England° have I offer
      Of goodly thousands: but, for° all this,
45   When I shall tread upon the tyrant's head,
      Or wear it on my sword, yet my poor country
      Shall have more vices than it had before,
      More suffer, and more sundry ways than ever,
      By him that shall succeed.

Macduff.   What should he be?

50 *Malcolm.* It is myself I mean, in whom I know

---

26 **rawness** unprotected condition   29 **jealousies** suspicions   30 **rightly just**
perfectly honorable   32 **basis** foundation   33 **check** restrain   34 **affeered**
legally confirmed   41 **withal** moreover   42 **in my right** on behalf of my
claim   43 **England** i.e., the King of England   44 **for** despite

All the particulars° of vice so grafted°
That, when they shall be opened,° black Macbeth
Will seem as pure as snow, and the poor state
Esteem him as a lamb, being compared
With my confineless harms.°

Macduff.   Not in the legions   55
Of horrid hell can come a devil more damned
In evils to top Macbeth.

Malcolm.   I grant him bloody,
Luxurious,° avaricious, false, deceitful,
Sudden,° malicious, smacking of every sin
That has a name: but there's no bottom, none,   60
In my voluptuousness:° your wives, your daughters,
Your matrons and your maids, could not fill up
The cistern of my lust, and my desire
All continent° impediments would o'erbear,
That did oppose my will. Better Macbeth   65
Than such an one to reign.

Macduff.   Boundless intemperance
In nature° is a tyranny; it hath been
Th' untimely emptying of the happy throne,
And fall of many kings. But fear not yet
To take upon you what is yours: you may   70
Convey° your pleasures in a spacious plenty,
And yet seem cold, the time° you may so hoodwink.
We have willing dames enough. There cannot be
That vulture in you, to devour so many
As will to greatness dedicate themselves,   75
Finding it so inclined.

Malcolm.   With this there grows
In my most ill-composed affection° such

51 **particulars** special kinds   51 **grafted** engrafted   52 **opened** in bloom,
i.e., revealed   55 **confineless harms** unbounded evils   58 **Luxurious** lech-
erous   59 **Sudden** violent   61 **voluptuousness** lust   64 **continent** restraining
67 **In nature** in man's nature   71 **Convey** secretly manage   72 **time** age,
i.e., people   77 **ill-composed affection** evilly compounded character

A stanchless° avarice that, were I King,
I should cut off the nobles for their lands,
80   Desire his jewels and this other's house:
And my more-having would be as a sauce
To make me hunger more, that I should forge
Quarrels unjust against the good and loyal,
Destroying them for wealth.

Macduff.   This avarice
85   Sticks deeper, grows with more pernicious root
Than summer-seeming° lust, and it hath been
The sword of our slain kings.° Yet do not fear.
Scotland hath foisons to fill up your will
Of your mere own.° All these are portable,°
90   With other graces weighed.

Malcolm. But I have none: the king-becoming graces,
As justice, verity, temp'rance, stableness,
Bounty, perseverance, mercy, lowliness,
Devotion, patience, courage, fortitude,
95   I have no relish of° them, but abound
In the division of each several crime,°
Acting it many ways. Nay, had I pow'r, I should
Pour the sweet milk of concord into hell,
Uproar° the universal peace, confound
All unity on earth.

100   *Macduff.*   O Scotland, Scotland!

Malcolm. If such a one be fit to govern, speak:
I am as I have spoken.

Macduff.   Fit to govern!
No, not to live. O nation miserable!
With an untitled tyrant bloody-sceptered,
105   When shalt thou see thy wholesome days again,

---

78 **stanchless** never-ending   86 **summer-seeming** befitting summer, i.e.,
youthful (?) transitory (?)   87 **sword of our slain kings** i.e., the cause
of death to our kings   88–89 **foisons . . . own** enough abundance of
your own to satisfy your covetousness   89 **portable** bearable   95 **relish
of** taste for (?) trace of (?)   96 **division of each several crime** variations of each kind of crime   99 **Uproar** put into a tumult

Since that the truest issue of thy throne
By his own interdiction° stands accursed,
And does blaspheme his breed?° Thy royal father
Was a most sainted king: the queen that bore thee,
Oft'ner upon her knees than on her feet,   *110*
Died° every day she lived. Fare thee well!
These evils thou repeat'st upon thyself
Hath banished me from Scotland. O my breast,
Thy hope ends here!

Malcolm.   Macduff, this noble passion,
Child of integrity, hath from my soul   *115*
Wiped the black scruples,° reconciled my thoughts
To thy good truth and honor. Devilish Macbeth
By many of these trains° hath sought to win me
Into his power; and modest wisdom° plucks me
From over-credulous haste: but God above   *120*
Deal between thee and me! For even now
I put myself to° thy direction, and
Unspeak mine own detraction; here abjure
The taints and blames I laid upon myself,
For° strangers to my nature. I am yet   *125*
Unknown to woman, never was forsworn,
Scarcely have coveted what was mine own,
At no time broke my faith, would not betray
The devil to his fellow, and delight
No less in truth than life. My first false speaking   *130*
Was this upon myself. What I am truly,
Is thine and my poor country's to command:
Whither indeed, before thy here-approach,
Old Siward, with ten thousand warlike men,
Already at a point,° was setting forth.   *135*
Now we'll together, and the chance of goodness
Be like our warranted quarrel!° Why are you
   silent?

---

107 **interdiction** curse, exclusion   108 **breed** ancestry   111 **Died** i.e., prepared for heaven   116 **scruples** suspicions   118 **trains** plots   119 **modest
wisdom** i.e., prudence   122 **to** under   125 **For** as   135 **at a point** prepared
136–37 **the chance ... quarrel** i.e., may our chance of success equal the
justice of our cause

Macduff. Such welcome and unwelcome things at once
    'Tis hard to reconcile.

Enter a Doctor.

Malcolm. Well, more anon. Comes the King forth, I
140   pray you?

Doctor. Ay, sir. There are a crew of wretched souls
    That stay° his cure: their malady convinces
    The great assay of art;° but at his touch,
    Such sanctity hath heaven given his hand,
    They presently amend.°

145 *Malcolm.*   I thank you, doctor.

Exit [*Doctor*].

Macduff. What's the disease he means?

Malcolm.   'Tis called the evil:°
    A most miraculous work in this good King,
    Which often since my here-remain in England
    I have seen him do. How he solicits heaven,
150   Himself best knows: but strangely-visited° people,
    All swoll'n and ulcerous, pitiful to the eye,
    The mere° despair of surgery, he cures,
    Hanging a golden stamp° about their necks,
    Put on with holy prayers: and 'tis spoken,
155   To the succeeding royalty he leaves
    The healing benediction. With this strange virtue°
    He hath a heavenly gift of prophecy,
    And sundry blessings hang about his throne
    That speak° him full of grace.

Enter Ross.

Macduff.   See, who comes here?

160 *Malcolm.* My countryman; but yet I know him not.

---

142 **stay** await   142–43 **convinces/The great assay of art** i.e., defies the
efforts of medical science   145 **presently amend** immediately recover
146 **evil** (scrofula, called "the king's evil" because it could allegedly be
cured by the king's touch)   150 **strangely-visited** oddly afflicted   152 **mere**
utter   153 **stamp** coin   156 **virtue** power   159 **speak** proclaim

Macduff. My ever gentle° cousin, welcome hither.

Malcolm. I know him now: good God, betimes°
   remove
The means that makes us strangers!

Ross.   Sir, amen.

Macduff. Stands Scotland where it did?

Ross.   Alas, poor country!
Almost afraid to know itself! It cannot   *165*
Be called our mother but our grave, where nothing°
But who knows nothing is once seen to smile;
Where sighs and groans, and shrieks that rent the
   air,
Are made, not marked;° where violent sorrow seems
A modern ecstasy.° The dead man's knell   *170*
Is there scarce asked for who, and good men's lives
Expire before the flowers in their caps,
Dying or ere they sicken.

Macduff.   O, relation
Too nice,° and yet too true!

Malcolm.   What's the newest grief?

Ross. That of an hour's age doth hiss the speaker;°   *175*
Each minute teems° a new one.

Macduff.   How does my wife?

Ross. Why, well.

Macduff.   And all my children?

Ross.   Well, too.

Macduff. The tyrant has not battered at their peace?

Ross. No; they were well at peace when I did leave
   'em.

---

161 **gentle** noble   162 **betimes** quickly   166 **nothing** no one   169 **marked**
noticed   170 **modern ecstasy** i.e., ordinary emotion   173–74 **relation/Too
nice** tale too accurate   175 **That . . . speaker** i.e., the report of the
grief of an hour ago is hissed as stale news   176 **teems** gives birth to

180 *Macduff.* Be not a niggard of your speech: how goes 't?

   Ross. When I came hither to transport the tidings,
     Which I have heavily° borne, there ran a rumor
     Of many worthy fellows that were out;°
     Which was to my belief witnessed° the rather,
185   For that I saw the tyrant's power° afoot.
     Now is the time of help. Your eye in Scotland
     Would create soldiers, make our women fight,
     To doff their dire distresses.

   Malcolm.   Be 't their comfort
     We are coming thither. Gracious England hath
190   Lent us good Siward and ten thousand men;
     An older and a better soldier none
     That Christendom gives out.°

   Ross.   Would I could answer
     This comfort with the like! But I have words
     That would° be howled out in the desert air,
     Where hearing should not latch° them.

195 *Macduff.*   What concern they?
     The general cause or is it a fee-grief
     Due to some single breast?°

   Ross.   No mind that's honest
     But in it shares some woe, though the main part
     Pertains to you alone.

   Macduff.   If it be mine,
200   Keep it not from me, quickly let me have it.

   Ross. Let not your ears despise my tongue for ever,
     Which shall possess them with the heaviest sound
     That ever yet they heard.

   Macduff.   Humh! I guess at it.

   Ross. Your castle is surprised;° your wife and babes

---

182 **heavily** sadly 183 **out** i.e., up in arms 184 **witnessed** attested 185 **power** army 192 **gives out** reports 194 **would** should 195 **latch** catch 196–97 **fee-grief/Due to some single breast** i.e., a personal grief belonging to an individual 204 **surprised** suddenly attacked

Savagely slaughtered. To relate the manner,   205
Were, on the quarry° of these murdered deer,
To add the death of you.

Malcolm.   Merciful heaven!
What, man! Ne'er pull your hat upon your brows;
Give sorrow words. The grief that does not speak
Whispers the o'er-fraught heart,° and bids it break.   210

Macduff. My children too?

Ross.   Wife, children, servants, all
That could be found.

Macduff.   And I must be from thence!
My wife killed too?

Ross.   I have said.

Malcolm.   Be comforted.
Let's make us med'cines of our great revenge,
To cure this deadly grief.   215

Macduff. He has no children. All my pretty ones?
Did you say all? O hell-kite!° All?
What, all my pretty chickens and their dam
At one fell swoop?

Malcolm. Dispute° it like a man.

Macduff.   I shall do so;   220
But I must also feel it as a man.
I cannot but remember such things were,
That were most precious to me. Did heaven look on,
And would not take their part? Sinful Macduff,
They were all struck for thee! Naught° that I am,   225
Not for their own demerits but for mine
Fell slaughter on their souls. Heaven rest them now!

Malcolm. Be this the whetstone of your sword. Let
    grief
Convert to anger; blunt not the heart, enrage it.

206 **quarry** heap of slaughtered game   210 **Whispers the o'er-fraught heart**
whispers to the overburdened heart   217 **hell-kite** hellish bird of prey
220 **Dispute** counter   225 **Naught** wicked

230 *Macduff.* O, I could play the woman with mine eyes,
     And braggart with my tongue! But, gentle heavens,
     Cut short all intermission;° front to front°
     Bring thou this fiend of Scotland and myself;
     Within my sword's length set him. If he 'scape,
     Heaven forgive him too!

235 *Malcolm.*   This time goes manly.
     Come, go we to the King. Our power is ready;
     Our lack is nothing but our leave.° Macbeth
     Is ripe for shaking, and the pow'rs above
     Put on their instruments.° Receive what cheer you
          may.
240 The night is long that never finds the day.   *Exeunt.*

---

232 **intermission** interval   232 **front to front** forehead to forehead i.e.,
face to face   237 **Our lack is nothing but our leave** i.e., we need only
to take our leave   239 **Put on their instruments** arm themselves (?)
urge us, their agents, onward (?)

ACT 5

Scene 1.   [*Dunsinane. In the castle.*]

Enter a Doctor of Physic and a
Waiting-Gentlewoman.

Doctor. I have two nights watched with you, but can
perceive no truth in your report. When was it she
last walked?

Gentlewoman. Since his Majesty went into the field, I
have seen her rise from her bed, throw her night-   5
gown upon her, unlock her closet,° take forth
paper, fold it, write upon 't, read it, afterwards seal
it, and again return to bed; yet all this while in a
most fast sleep.

Doctor. A great perturbation in nature, to receive at   10
once the benefit of sleep and do the effects of
watching!° In this slumb'ry agitation, besides her
walking and other actual performances,° what, at
any time, have you heard her say?

Gentlewoman. That, sir, which I will not report after   15
her.

Doctor. You may to me, and 'tis most meet° you
should.

Gentlewoman. Neither to you nor anyone, having no
witness to confirm my speech.   20

Enter Lady [Macbeth], with a taper.

5.1.   6 **closet** chest   11–12 **effects of watching** deeds of one awake
13 **actual performance** deeds   17 **meet** suitable

Lo you, here she comes! This is her very guise,°
and, upon my life, fast asleep! Observe her; stand
close.°

Doctor. How came she by that light?

25 *Gentlewoman.* Why, it stood by her. She has light by
her continually. 'Tis her command.

Doctor. You see, her eyes are open.

Gentlewoman. Ay, but their sense° are shut.

Doctor. What is it she does now? Look, how she rubs
30 her hands.

Gentlewoman. It is an accustomed action with her, to
seem thus washing her hands: I have known her
continue in this a quarter of an hour.

Lady Macbeth. Yet here's a spot.

35 *Doctor.* Hark! she speaks. I will set down what comes
from her, to satisfy° my remembrance the more
strongly.

Lady Macbeth. Out, damned spot! Out, I say! One:
two: why, then 'tis time to do 't. Hell is murky.
40 Fie, my lord, fie! A soldier, and afeard? What need
we fear who knows it, when none can call our
pow'r to accompt?° Yet who would have thought
the old man to have had so much blood in him?

Doctor. Do you mark that?

45 *Lady Macbeth.* The Thane of Fife had a wife. Where is
she now? What, will these hands ne'er be clean? No
more o' that, my lord, no more o' that! You mar
all with this starting.

Doctor. Go to,° go to! You have known what you
50 should not.

Gentlewoman. She has spoke what she should not, I

21 **guise** custom 23 **close** hidden 28 **sense** i.e., powers of sight 36 **satisfy** confirm 42 **to accompt** into account 49 **Go to** (an exclamation)

am sure of that. Heaven knows what she has known.

Lady Macbeth. Here's the smell of the blood still. All
the perfumes of Arabia will not sweeten this little
hand. Oh, oh, oh!   55

Doctor. What a sigh is there! The heart is sorely
charged.°

Gentlewoman. I would not have such a heart in my
bosom for the dignity° of the whole body.

Doctor. Well, well, well——   60

Gentlewoman. Pray God it be, sir.

Doctor. This disease is beyond my practice.° Yet I
have known those which have walked in their sleep
who have died holily in their beds.

Lady Macbeth. Wash your hands; put on your night-   65
gown; look not so pale! I tell you yet again, Banquo's buried. He cannot come out on 's° grave.

Doctor. Even so?

Lady Macbeth. To bed, to bed! There's knocking at
the gate. Come, come, come, come, give me your   70
hand! What's done cannot be undone. To bed, to
bed, to bed!   *Exit Lady [Macbeth].*

Doctor. Will she go now to bed?

Gentlewoman. Directly.

Doctor. Foul whisp'rings are abroad. Unnatural deeds   75
Do breed unnatural troubles. Infected minds
To their deaf pillows will discharge their secrets.
More needs she the divine than the physician.
God, God forgive us all! Look after her;
Remove from her the means of all annoyance,°   80
And still° keep eyes upon her. So good night.

---

57 **charged** burdened   59 **dignity** worth, rank   62 **practice** professional skill   67 **on 's** of his   80 **annoyance** injury   81 **still** continuously

My mind she has mated° and amazed my sight:
I think, but dare not speak.

Gentlewoman.   Good night, good doctor.

                                                        Exeunt.

Scene 2.   [*The country near Dunsinane.*]

Drum and colors. Enter Menteith, Caithness,
Angus, Lennox, Soldiers.

Menteith. The English pow'r° is near, led on by
    Malcolm,
    His uncle Siward and the good Macduff.
    Revenges burn in them; for their dear° causes
    Would to the bleeding and the grim alarm
    Excite the mortified man.°

5 *Angus.*   Near Birnam Wood
    Shall we well meet them; that way are they coming.

Caithness. Who knows if Donalbain be with his
    brother?

Lennox. For certain, sir, he is not. I have a file°
    Of all the gentry: there is Siward's son,
10 And many unrough° youths that even now
    Protest° their first of manhood.

Menteith.   What does the tyrant?

Caithness. Great Dunsinane he strongly fortifies.
    Some say he's mad; others, that lesser hate him,
    Do call it valiant fury: but, for certain,

82 **mated** baffled   5.2.   1 **pow'r** army   3 **dear** heartfelt   4–5 **Would . . .
man** i.e., would incite a dead man (or "a paralyzed man") to join the
bloody and grim call to battle   8 **file** list   10 **unrough** i.e., beardless
11 **Protest** assert

He cannot buckle his distempered° cause   *15*
Within the belt of rule.°

Angus.   Now does he feel
His secret murders sticking on his hands;
Now minutely revolts upbraid° his faith-breach.
Those he commands move only in command,
Nothing in love. Now does he feel his title   *20*
Hang loose about him, like a giant's robe
Upon a dwarfish thief.

Menteith.   Who then shall blame
His pestered° senses to recoil and start,
When all that is within him does condemn
Itself for being there?

Caithness.   Well, march we on,   *25*
To give obedience where 'tis truly owed.
Meet we the med'cine° of the sickly weal,°
And with him pour we, in our country's purge,
Each drop of us.°

Lennox.   Or so much as it needs
To dew° the sovereign° flower and drown the
     weeds.   *30*
Make we our march towards Birnam.

                           Exeunt, marching.

Scene 3.   [*Dunsinane. In the castle.*]

Enter Macbeth, Doctor, and Attendants.

Overconfident

Macbeth. Bring me no more reports; let them fly all!
    Till Birnam Wood remove to Dunsinane
    I cannot taint° with fear. What's the boy Malcolm?

---

15 **distempered** swollen by dropsy   16 **rule** self-control   18 **minutely revolts upbraid** rebellions every minute rebuke   23 **pestered** tormented 27 **med'cine** i.e., Malcolm   27 **weal** commonwealth   29 **Each drop of us** i.e., every last drop of our blood (?)   30 **dew** bedew, water (and thus make grow)   30 **sovereign** (1) royal (2) remedial   5.3.   3 **taint** become infected

Was he not born of woman? The spirits that know
All mortal consequences° have pronounced me
5   thus:
"Fear not, Macbeth; no man that's born of woman
Shall e'er have power upon thee." Then fly, false
     thanes,
And mingle with the English epicures.
The mind I sway° by and the heart I bear
10 Shall never sag with doubt nor shake with fear.

Enter Servant.

The devil damn thee black, thou cream-faced loon!°
Where got'st thou that goose look?

Servant. There is ten thousand——

Macbeth.   Geese, villain?

Servant.   Soldiers, sir.

Macbeth. Go prick thy face and over-red° thy fear,
15 Thou lily-livered boy. What soldiers, patch?°
Death of° thy soul! Those linen° cheeks of thine
Are counselors to fear. What soldiers, whey-face?

Servant. The English force, so please you.

Macbeth. Take thy face hence.   [*Exit Servant.*]
               Seyton!—I am sick at heart,
20 When I behold—Seyton, I say!—This push°
Will cheer me ever, or disseat° me now.
I have lived long enough. My way of life
Is fall'n into the sear,° the yellow leaf,
And that which should accompany old age,
25 As honor, love, obedience, troops of friends,
I must not look to have; but, in their stead,
Curses not loud but deep, mouth-honor, breath,
Which the poor heart would fain deny, and dare not.
Seyton!

5 **mortal consequences** future human events 9 **sway** move 11 **loon**
fool 14 **over-red** cover with red 15 **patch** fool 16 **of** upon 16 **linen**
i.e., pale 20 **push** effort 21 **disseat** i.e., unthrone (with wordplay on
"cheer," pronounced "chair") 23 **sear** withered

Enter Seyton.

Seyton. What's your gracious pleasure?

Macbeth. 　　　　　　　　　What news more? 　30

Seyton. All is confirmed, my lord, which was reported.

Macbeth. I'll fight, till from my bones my flesh be
　　hacked.
　Give me my armor.

Seyton. 　　　　　　'Tis not needed yet.

Macbeth. I'll put it on.
　Send out moe° horses, skirr° the country round. 　35
　Hang those that talk of fear. Give me mine armor.
　How does your patient, doctor?

Doctor. 　　　　　　　Not so sick, my lord,
　As she is troubled with thick-coming fancies
　That keep her from her rest.

Macbeth. 　　　　　　　Cure her of that.
　Canst thou not minister to a mind diseased, 　40
　Pluck from the memory a rooted sorrow,
　Raze out° the written troubles of the brain,
　And with some sweet oblivious° antidote
　Cleanse the stuffed bosom of that perilous stuff
　Which weighs upon the heart?

Doctor. 　　　　　　　Therein the patient 　45
　Must minister to himself.

Macbeth. Throw physic° to the dogs, I'll none of it.
　Come, put mine armor on. Give me my staff.
　Seyton, send out.—Doctor, the thanes fly from
　　me.—
　Come, sir, dispatch.° If thou couldst, doctor, cast 　50
　The water° of my land, find her disease
　And purge it to a sound and pristine health,
　I would applaud thee to the very echo,

---

35 **moe** more　35 **skirr** scour　42 **Raze out** erase　43 **oblivious** causing
forgetfulness　47 **physic** medical science　50 **dispatch** hurry　50–51 **cast/
The water** analyze the urine

That should applaud again.—Pull 't off, I say.—
55 What rhubarb, senna, or what purgative drug,
    Would scour these English hence? Hear'st thou of
        them?

Doctor. Ay, my good lord; your royal preparation
    Makes us hear something.

Macbeth.   Bring it° after me.
    I will not be afraid of death and bane°
60 Till Birnam Forest come to Dunsinane.

Doctor. [*Aside*] Were I from Dunsinane away
        and clear,
    Profit again should hardly draw me here.   *Exeunt.*

Scene 4.   [*Country near Birnam Wood.*]

*Drum and colors. Enter Malcolm, Siward, Mac-
duff, Siward's Son, Menteith, Caithness, Angus,
and Soldiers, marching.*

Malcolm. Cousins, I hope the days are near at hand
    That chambers will be safe.°

Menteith.   We doubt it nothing.°

Siward. What wood is this before us?

Menteith.   The Wood of Birnam.

Malcolm. Let every soldier hew him down a bough
5   And bear 't before him. Thereby shall we shadow
    The numbers of our host, and make discovery°
    Err in report of us.

Soldiers.   It shall be done.

58 **it** i.e., the armor   59 **bane** destruction   5.4.   2 **That chambers will
be safe** i.e., that a man will be safe in his bedroom   2 **nothing** not at
all   6 **discovery** reconnaissance

Siward. We learn no other but° the confident tyrant
    Keeps still in Dunsinane, and will endure°
    Our setting down before 't.

Malcolm.   'Tis his main hope,   10
    For where there is advantage to be given°
    Both more and less° have given him the revolt,
    And none serve with him but constrainèd things
    Whose hearts are absent too.

Macduff.   Let our just censures
    Attend the true event,° and put we on   15
    Industrious soldiership.

Siward.   The time approaches,
    That will with due decision make us know
    What we shall say we have and what we owe.°
    Thoughts speculative their unsure hopes relate,
    But certain issue strokes must arbitrate:°   20
    Towards which advance the war.°

                        Exeunt, marching.

Scene 5.   [*Dunsinane. Within the castle.*]

*Enter Macbeth, Seyton, and Soldiers, with drum
and colors.*

Macbeth. Hang out our banners on the outward walls.
    The cry is still "They come!" Our castle's strength
    Will laugh a siege to scorn. Here let them lie
    Till famine and the ague° eat them up.
    Were they not forced° with those that should be
        ours,   5

8 **no other but** nothing but that   9 **endure** allow   11 **advantage to
be given** afforded an opportunity   12 **more and less** high and low
14–15 **just censures/Attend the true event** true judgment await the actual
outcome   18 **owe** own (the contrast is between "what we shall say we
have" and "what we shall really have")   20 **certain issue strokes must
arbitrate** the definite outcome must be decided by battle   21 **war** army
5.5.   4 **ague** fever   5 **forced** reinforced

We might have met them dareful,° beard to beard,
And beat them backward home.

A cry within of women.

What is that noise?

Seyton. It is the cry of women, my good lord.   [*Exit.*]

Macbeth. I have almost forgot the taste of fears:
10   The time has been, my senses would have cooled
    To hear a night-shriek, and my fell° of hair
    Would at a dismal treatise° rouse and stir
    As life were in 't. I have supped full with horrors.
    Direness, familiar to my slaughterous thoughts,
    Cannot once start° me.

[Enter Seyton.]

15   Wherefore was that cry?

Seyton. The Queen, my lord, is dead.

Macbeth. She should° have died hereafter;
    There would have been a time for such a word.°
    Tomorrow, and tomorrow, and tomorrow
20   Creeps in this petty pace from day to day,
    To the last syllable of recorded time;
    And all our yesterdays have lighted fools
    The way to dusty death. Out, out, brief candle!
    Life's but a walking shadow, a poor player
25   That struts and frets his hour upon the stage
    And then is heard no more. It is a tale
    Told by an idiot, full of sound and fury
    Signifying nothing.

Enter a Messenger.

Thou com'st to use thy tongue; thy story quickly!

30 *Messenger.* Gracious my lord,
    I should report that which I say I saw,
    But know not how to do 't.

Macbeth.   Well, say, sir.

6 **met them dareful** i.e., met them in the battlefield boldly   11 **fell** pelt
12 **treatise** story   15 **start** startle   17 **should** inevitably   would   (?)
18 **word** message

Messenger. As I did stand my watch upon the hill,
　I looked toward Birnam, and anon, methought,
　The wood began to move.

Macbeth.　　　　　　　　　Liar and slave!　　　　　*35*

Messenger. Let me endure your wrath, if 't be not so.
　Within this three mile may you see it coming;
　I say a moving grove.

Macbeth.　　　　　　　　If thou speak'st false,
　Upon the next tree shalt thou hang alive,
　Till famine cling° thee. If thy speech be sooth,°　*40*
　I care not if thou dost for me as much.
　I pull in resolution,° and begin
　To doubt° th' equivocation of the fiend
　That lies like truth: "Fear not, till Birnam Wood
　Do come to Dunsinane!" And now a wood　　　*45*
　Comes toward Dunsinane. Arm, arm, and out!
　If this which he avouches° does appear,
　There is nor flying hence nor tarrying here.
　I 'gin to be aweary of the sun,
　And wish th' estate° o' th' world were now undone.　*50*
　Ring the alarum bell! Blow wind, come wrack!
　At least we'll die with harness° on our back.

　　　　　　　　　　　　　　　　　　Exeunt.

Scene 6.　　[*Dunsinane. Before the castle.*]

　　　Drum and colors. Enter Malcolm, Siward,
　　　　　Macduff, and their army, with boughs.

Malcolm. Now near enough. Your leavy° screens
　　throw down,
　And show like those you are. You, worthy uncle,

---

40 **cling** wither　40 **sooth** truth　42 **pull in resolution** restrain confidence
43 **doubt** suspect　47 **avouches** asserts　50 **th' estate** the orderly condition　52 **harness** armor　5.6.　1 **leavy** leafy

Shall, with my cousin, your right noble son,
Lead our first battle.° Worthy Macduff and we°
5   Shall take upon 's what else remains to do,
According to our order.°

Siward.   Fare you well.
Do we° but find the tyrant's power° tonight,
Let us be beaten, if we cannot fight.

Macduff. Make all our trumpets speak; give them all
        breath.
10   Those clamorous harbingers of blood and death.

                    Exeunt. Alarums continued.

Scene 7.   [*Another part of the field.*]

                Enter Macbeth.

Macbeth. They have tied me to a stake; I cannot fly,
    But bearlike I must fight the course.° What's he
    That was not born of woman? Such a one
    Am I to fear, or none.

                Enter Young Siward.

Young Siward. What is thy name?

5   *Macbeth.*   Thou'lt be afraid to hear it.

Young Siward. No; though thou call'st thyself a hotter
        name
    Than any is in hell.

    Macbeth.   My name's Macbeth.

4 **battle** battalion   4 **we** (Malcolm uses the royal "we")   6 **order** plan
7 **Do we** if we do   7 **power** forces   5.7.   2 **course** bout, round (he has
in mind an attack of dogs or men upon a bear chained to a stake)

Young Siward. The devil himself could not pronounce
    a title
  More hateful to mine ear.

Macbeth.   No, nor more fearful.

Young Siward. Thou liest, abhorrèd tyrant; with my
    sword   *10*
  I'll prove the lie thou speak'st.

      Fight, and Young Siward slain.

Macbeth.   Thou wast born of woman.
  But swords I smile at, weapons laugh to scorn,
  Brandished by man that's of a woman born.

                              Exit.

      Alarums. Enter Macduff.

Macduff. That way the noise is. Tyrant, show thy face!
  If thou be'st slain and with no stroke of mine,   *15*
  My wife and children's ghosts will haunt me still.
  I cannot strike at wretched kerns,° whose arms
  Are hired to bear their staves.° Either thou,
    Macbeth,
  Or else my sword, with an unbattered edge,
  I sheathe again undeeded.° There thou shouldst
    be;   *20*
  By this great clatter, one of greatest note
  Seems bruited.° Let me find him, Fortune!
  And more I beg not.   *Exit. Alarums.*

      Enter Malcolm and Siward.

Siward. This way, my lord. The castle's gently
    rend'red:°
  The tyrant's people on both sides do fight;   *25*
  The noble thanes do bravely in the war;
  The day almost itself professes° yours,
  And little is to do.

---

17 **kerns** foot soldiers (contemptuous) 18 **staves** spears 20 **undeeded**
i.e., having done nothing 22 **bruited** reported 24 **gently rend'red** surrendered without a struggle 27 **itself professes** declares itself

Malcolm.   We have met with foes
   That strike beside us.°

Siward.   Enter, sir, the castle.

                                        Exeunt. Alarum.

            [Scene 8.   *Another part of the field.*]

                    Enter Macbeth.

Macbeth. Why should I play the Roman fool, and die
   On mine own sword? Whiles I see lives,° the gashes
   Do better upon them.

                    Enter Macduff.

Macduff.   Turn, hell-hound, turn!

Macbeth. Of all men else I have avoided thee.
5   But get thee back! My soul is too much charged°
   With blood of thine already.

Macduff.   I have no words:
   My voice is in my sword, thou bloodier villain
   Than terms can give thee out!°

                    Fight. Alarum.

Macbeth.   Thou losest labor:
   As easy mayst thou the intrenchant° air
10   With thy keen sword impress° as make me bleed:
   Let fall thy blade on vulnerable crests;
   I bear a charmèd life, which must not yield
   To one of woman born.

29 **beside us** i.e., deliberately miss us (?) as our comrades (?) 5.8.
2 **Whiles I see lives** so long as I see living men   5 **charged** burdened
8 **terms can give thee out** words can describe you   9 **intrenchant** incapable
of being cut   10 **impress** make an impression on

Macduff.   Despair° thy charm,
   And let the angel° whom thou still hast served
   Tell thee, Macduff was from his mother's womb   *15*
   Untimely ripped.

Macbeth. Accursèd be that tongue that tells me so,
   For it hath cowed my better part of man!°
   And be these juggling fiends no more believed,
   That palter° with us in a double sense;   *20*
   That keep the word of promise to our ear,
   And break it to our hope. I'll not fight with thee.

Macduff. Then yield thee, coward,
   And live to be the show and gaze o' th' time:°
   We'll have thee, as our rarer monsters° are,   *25*
   Painted upon a pole,° and underwrit,
   "Here may you see the tyrant."

Macbeth.   I will not yield,
   To kiss the ground before young Malcolm's feet,
   And to be baited° with the rabble's curse.
   Though Birnam Wood be come to Dunsinane,   *30*
   And thou opposed, being of no woman born,
   Yet I will try the last. Before my body
   I throw my warlike shield. Lay on, Macduff;
   And damned be him that first cries "Hold,
     enough!"   *Exeunt, fighting. Alarums.*

    *[Re-]enter fighting, and Macbeth slain. [Exit
    Macduff, with Macbeth.] Retreat and flour-
    ish.° Enter, with drum and colors, Malcolm,
    Siward, Ross, Thanes, and Soldiers.*

Malcolm. I would the friends we miss were safe
   arrived.   *35*

Siward. Some must go off;° and yet, by these I see,
   So great a day as this is cheaply bought.

---

13 **Despair** despair of   14 **angel** i.e., fallen angel, fiend   18 **better part of man** manly spirit   20 **palter** equivocate   24 **gaze o' th' time** spectacle of the age   25 **monsters** freaks   26 **Painted upon a pole** i.e., pictured on a banner set by a showman's booth   29 **baited** assailed (like a bear by dogs)   34s.d. **Retreat and flourish** trumpet call to withdraw, and fanfare   36 **go off** die (theatrical metaphor)

Malcolm. Macduff is missing, and your noble son.

Ross. Your son, my lord, has paid a soldier's debt:
40   He only lived but till he was a man;
        The which no sooner had his prowess confirmed
        In the unshrinking station° where he fought,
        But like a man he died.

Siward.   Then he is dead?

Ross. Ay, and brought off the field. Your cause of
        sorrow
45   Must not be measured by his worth, for then
        It hath no end.

Siward.   Had he his hurts before?

Ross. Ay, on the front.

Siward.   Why then, God's soldier be he!
        Had I as many sons as I have hairs,
        I would not wish them to a fairer death:
        And so his knell is knolled.

50 *Malcolm.*   He's worth more sorrow,
        And that I'll spend for him.

Siward.   He's worth no more:
        They say he parted well and paid his score:°
        And so God be with him! Here comes newer
        comfort.

        Enter Macduff, with Macbeth's head.

Macduff. Hail, King! for so thou art: behold, where
        stands
55   Th' usurper's cursèd head. The time is free.°
        I see thee compassed° with thy kingdom's pearl,
        That speak my salutation in their minds,
        Whose voices I desire aloud with mine:
        Hail, King of Scotland!

All.   Hail, King of Scotland!

---

42 **unshrinking station** i.e., place at which he stood firmly   52 **parted
well and paid his score** departed well and settled his account   55 **The
time is free** the world is liberated   56 **compassed** surrounded

Flourish.

Malcolm. We shall not spend a large expense of time   60
    Before we reckon with your several loves,°
    And make us even with you. My thanes and
      kinsmen,
    Henceforth be earls, the first that ever Scotland
    In such an honor named. What's more to do,
    Which would be planted newly with the time°—   65
    As calling home our exiled friends abroad
    That fled the snares of watchful tyranny,
    Producing forth the cruel ministers°
    Of this dead butcher and his fiendlike queen,
    Who, as 'tis thought, by self and violent° hands   70
    Took off her life—this, and what needful else
    That calls upon us,° by the grace of Grace
    We will perform in measure, time, and place:°
    So thanks to all at once and to each one,
    Whom we invite to see us crowned at Scone.   75

Flourish. Exeunt Omnes.

FINIS

---

61 **reckon with your several loves** reward the devotion of each of you
64–65 **What's more ... time** i.e., what else must be done which should
be newly established in this age 68 **ministers** agents 70 **self and violent** her own violent 72 **calls upon us** demands my attention 73 **in
measure, time, and place** fittingly, at the appropriate time and place

Textual Note

Macbeth, never printed during Shakespeare's lifetime, was first printed in the Folio of 1623. The play is remarkably short, and it may be that there has been some cutting. That in 1.5 Lady Macbeth apparently proposes to kill Duncan and that later in the play Macbeth kills him is scarcely evidence that a scene had been lost, but the inconsistent stage directions concerning Macbeth's death (one calls for him to be slain on stage, another suggests he is both slain and decapitated off stage) indicate some sort of revision. Nevertheless, when one reads the account of Macbeth in Holinshed (Shakespeare's source) one does not feel that the play as it has come down to us omits anything of significance. If, as seems likely, the play was presented at court, its brevity may well be due to King James's known aversion to long plays. On the other hand, it is generally believed that Hecate is a non-Shakespearean addition to the play (she dominates 3.5 and has a few lines in 4.1), but the evidence is not conclusive, although the passages (along with 4.1.125–32) sound un-Shakespearean.

The present division into acts and scenes is that of the Folio except for 5.8, a division added by the Globe editors. The present edition silently modernizes spelling and punctuation, regularizes speech prefixes, and translates into English the Folio's Latin designations of act and scene. Other departures from the Folio are listed below. The reading of the present text is given first, in italics, and then the reading of the Folio (F) in roman.

1.1.9 *Second Witch ... Anon* [F attributes to "All," as part of the ensuing speech]

1.2.13 *gallowglasses* gallowgrosses   14 *quarrel* Quarry   26 *thunders break*
Thunders   33–34 *Dismayed . . . Banquo* [one line in F] 33–35 *Dismayed . . .
lion* [three lines in F, ending: Banquoh, Eagles, Lyon]   42 *But . . . faint* [F
gives to previous line]   46 *So . . . look* [F gives to next line]   59 *Sweno . . .
king* [F gives to previous line]

1.3.5 *Give . . . I* [F prints as a separate line]   32 *weïrd* weyward [also at 1.5.9;
2.1.20; "weyard" at 3.1.2; 3.4.134; 4.1.136]   39 *Forres* Soris   78 *Speak . . .
you* [F prints as a separate line]   81–82 *Into . . . stayed* [three lines in F,
ending: corporall, Winde, stay'd]   98 *Came* can   108 *why . . . me* [F gives
to next line]   111–14 *Which . . . not* [five lines in F, ending: loose, Norway,
helpe, labour'd, not]   131 *If ill* [F gives to next line]   140–42 *Shakes . . . not*
[F's lines end: Man, surmise, not]   143 *If . . . crown me* [two lines in F,
ending: King, crown me]   149–53 *Give . . . time* [seven lines in F, ending:
fauour, forgotten, registred, Leafe, them, vpon, time]   156 *Till . . . friends*
[two lines in F, ending: enough, friends]

1.4.1 *Are not* Or not [given in F to next line]   2–8 *My . . . died* [seven lines in
F, ending: back, die, hee, Pardon, Repentance, him, dy'de]   23–27 *In . . .
honor* [six lines in F, ending: selfe, Duties, State, should, Loue, Honor]

1.5.23–24 *And yet . . . have it* [three lines in F, ending: winne, cryes, haue it]

1.6.1 *the air* [F gives to next line]   4 *martlet* Barlet   9 *most* must   17–20
Against . . . hermits [F's lines end: broad, House, Dignities, Ermites]

1.7.6 *shoal* Schoole [variant spelling]   47 *do* no   58 *as you* [F gives to next
line]

2.1.4 *Hold . . . heaven* [two lines in F, ending: Sword, Heauen]   7–9 *And . . .
repose* [F's endings: sleepe, thoughts, repose]   13–17 *He . . . content* [F's
endings: Pleasure, Offices, withall, Hostesse, content]   25 *when 'tis* [F gives
to next line]   55 *strides* sides   56 *sure* sowre   57 *way they* they may

2.2.2–6 *What . . . possets* [6 lines in F, ending: fire, shriek'd, good-night, open,
charge, Possets]   13 s.d. *Enter Macbeth* [F places after "die" in 1.8]   14 *I
. . . noise* [two lines in F, ending: deed, noyse]   18–19 *Hark . . . chamber*
[one line in F]   22–25 *There's . . . sleep* [F's endings: sleepe, other, Prayers,
sleepe]   32 *Stuck . . . throat* [F gives to previous line]   64–65 *To wear . . .
chamber* [three lines in F, ending: white, entry, Chamber]   68 *Hath . . .
knocking* [two lines in F, ending: vnattended, knocking]   72–73 *To . . .
couldst* [four lines in F, ending: deed, my selfe, knocking, could'st. The s.d.
"Knock" appears after "deed"]

2.3.25–27 *Faith . . . things* [two lines of verse in F, the second beginning
"And"]   44 s.d. *Enter Macbeth* [F places after 1.43]   53–54 *I'll . . . service*
[one line of prose in F]   56–63 *The night . . . shake* [10 lines in F, ending:
vnruly, downe, Ayre, Death, terrible, Euents, time, Night, feuorous,
shake]   66 *Tongue nor heart* [F gives to next line]   88–89 *O . . . murdered*

[one line in F]   137–43 *What . . . bloody* [nine lines in F, ending: doe, them, Office, easie, England, I, safer, Smiles, bloody]

2.4.14 *And . . . horses* [F prints as a separate line]   17 *make* [F gives to next line]   19 *They . . . so* [F prints as a separate line]

3.1.34–35 *Craving . . . with you* [three lines in F, ending: Horse, Night, you]   42–43 *The sweeter . . . you* [three lines in F, ending: welcome, alone, you]   72 *Who's there* [F prints as a separate line]   75–82 *Well . . . might* [ten lines in F, ending: then, speeches, past, fortune, selfe, conference, with you, crost, them, might]   85–91 *I . . . ever* [nine lines in F, ending: so, now, meeting, predominant, goe, man, hand, begger'd, euer]   111 *I do* [F gives to previous line]   114–15 *Both . . . enemy* [one line in F]   128 *Your . . . most* [two lines in F, ending: you, most]

3.2.16 *But . . . suffer* [two lines in F, ending: dis-ioynt, suffer]   22 *Duncan . . . grave* [F prints as a separate line]   43 *there . . . done* [F gives to next line]   50 *and . . . crow* [F gives to next line]

3.3.9 *The rest* [F gives to next line]   17 *O . . . fly, fly, fly* [two lines in F, the first ending: Trecherie]   21 *We . . . affair* [two lines in F, ending: lost, Affaire]

3.4.21–22 *Most . . . perfect* [four lines in F, ending: Sir, scap'd, againe, perfect]   49 *Here . . . Highness* [two lines in F, ending: Lord, Highness]   110 *broke . . . meeting* [F gives to next line]   122 s.d. *Exeunt* Exit   123 *blood will have blood* [F prints as a separate line]   145 *in deed* indeed

3.5.36 *back again* [F prints as a separate line]

3.6.1 *My . . . thoughts* [two lines in F, ending: Speeches, Thoughts]   24 *son* Sonnes   38 *the* their

4.1.46–47 *Open . . . knocks* [one line in F]   59 *germens* Germaine   71 *Beware Macduff* [F prints as a separate line]   79 *Laugh to scorn* [F prints as a separate line]   86 *What is this* [F gives to next line]   93 *Dunsinane* Dunsmane   98 *Birnam* Byrnan [this F spelling, or with *i* for *y* or with a final *e*, occurs at 5.2.5, 31; 5.3.2, 60; 5.4.3; 5.5.34, 44; 5.8.30]   119 *eighth* eight   133 *Let . . . hour* [F prints as a separate line]

4.2.27 *Fathered . . . fatherless* [two lines in F, ending: is, Father-lesse]   34 *Poor bird* [F prints as a separate line]   36–43 *Why . . . for thee* [ten lines in F, ending: Mother, for, saying, is dead, Father, Husband, Market, againe, wit, thee]   48–49 *Every . . . hanged* [two lines of verse in F, ending: Traitor, hang'd]   57–58 [two lines of verse in F, ending: Monkie, Father]   77 *What . . . faces* [F prints as a separate line]

4.3.4 *down-fall'n* downfall   15 *deserve* discerne   25 *where . . . doubts* [F prints as a separate line]   102 *Fit to govern* [F gives to next line]   107 *accursed* accust   133 *thy* they   140 *I pray you* [F prints as a separate line]   173 *O relation* [F gives to next line]   211–12 *Wife . . . found* [one line in F]   212–13 *And . . . too* [one line in F]

5.3.39 *Cure her* Cure   55 *senna* Cyme

5.6.1 *Your . . . down* [F prints as a separate line]

5.8.54 *behold . . . stands* [F prints as a separate line]

The Source of *Macbeth*

The selections given below, from the second edition (1587) of Raphael Holinshed's *Chronicles of England, Scotland, and Ireland,* are the materials that furnished Shakespeare his plot. A study of Holinshed's account of Macbeth's usurpation and Donwald's murder of King Duff (which Shakespeare in part transferred to the story of Macbeth) may help a reader to see Shakespeare's play more clearly, for what he added he must have felt necessary, and what he omitted he must have felt undesirable. Some of the changes are examined by E. E. Stoll in an essay printed in this volume, but excellent as his essay is, he has not said the last word on the relation of the play to the historical account. It should be mentioned that scholars have occasionally suggested Shakespeare may have supplemented Holinshed with other accounts, but there is no evidence that he certainly did so. But of course other books gave him hints for phrases. For example, the Porter's comment on those who "go the primrose way to th' everlasting bonfire" (2.3.19–20) is indebted to the Bible's mention of "the wide gate and broad way that leadeth to destruction; and many there be which go in thereat" (Matthew 7:13). But Holinshed alone seems to have provided Shakespeare with the raw material of the story of Macbeth. Presumably Shakespeare read Holinshed's narrative of Macbeth, and in browsing through the adjacent material he hit on the idea of revising this narrative in the light of Donwald's murder of King Duff. Relevant selections from these two portions of Holinshed's chronicle of Scotland are printed below, followed by a brief selection (relevant to 5.8.39–53) from the chronicle of England, telling of Old Siward's response to the news of his son's death. The spelling, except for many proper nouns, has been modernized.

RAPHAEL HOLINSHED

Selections from Chronicles of England, Scotland, and Ireland

[Donwald] conceived such an inward malice towards the king (though he showed it not outwardly at the first) that the same continued still boiling in his stomach, and ceased not, till through setting on of his wife, and in revenge of such unthankfulness, he found means to murder the king within the foresaid castle of Fores where he used to sojourn. For the king being in that country, was accustomed to lie most commonly within the same castle, having a special trust in Donwald, as a man whom he never suspected.

But Donwald, not forgetting the reproach which his lineage had sustained by the execution of those his kinsmen, whom the king for a spectacle to the people had caused to be hanged, could not but show manifest tokens of great grief at home amongst his family: which his wife perceiving, ceased not to travel with him, till she understood what the cause was of his displeasure. Which at length when she had learned by his own relation, she as one that bare no less malice in her heart towards the king, for the like cause on her behalf, than her husband did for his friends, counseled him (sith the king oftentimes used to lodge in his house without any guard about him, other than the garrison of the castle, which was wholly at his commandment) to make him away, and showed him the means whereby he might soonest accomplish it.

Donwald thus being the more kindled in wrath by the words of his wife, determined to follow her advice in the execution of so heinous an act. Whereupon devising with himself for a while, which way he might best accomplish his cursed intent, at length got opportunity, and sped his purpose as followeth. It chanced that the king upon the day before he purposed to depart forth of the castle, was long in his oratory at his prayers, and there continued till it was late in the night. At the last, coming forth, he called such afore him as had faithfully served him in pursuit and apprehension of the rebels, and giving them hearty thanks, he bestowed sundry honorable gifts amongst them, of the which number Donwald was one, as he that had been ever accounted a most faithful servant to the king.

At length, having talked with them a long time, he got him into his privy chamber, only with two of his chamberlains, who having brought him to bed, came forth again, and then fell to banqueting with Donwald and his wife, who had prepared diverse delicate dishes, and sundry sorts of drinks for their rear supper or collation, whereat they sat up so long, till they had charged their stomachs with such full gorges, that their heads were no sooner got to the pillow, but asleep they were so fast, that a man might have removed the chamber over them, sooner than to have awaked them out of their drunken sleep.

Then Donwald, though he abhorred the act greatly in heart, yet through instigation of his wife he called four of his servants unto him (whom he had made privy to his wicked intent before, and framed to his purpose with large gifts) and now declaring unto them, after what sort they should work the feat, they gladly obeyed his instructions, & speedily going about the murder, they enter the chamber (in which the king lay a little before cocks crow, where they secretly cut his throat as he lay sleeping, without any buskling at all: and immediately by a postern gate they carried forth the dead body into the fields. . . .

Donwald, about the time that the murder was in doing, got him amongst them that kept the watch, and so continued in company with them all the residue of the night. But in the morning when the noise was raised in the king's chamber how the king was slain, his body conveyed away, and the bed all berayed with blood; he with the watch ran thither, as though he had known nothing of the matter, and breaking into the chamber, and finding cakes of blood in the bed, and on the floor about the sides of it, he forthwith slew the chamberlains, as guilty of that heinous murder, and then like a mad man running to and fro, he ransacked every corner within the castle, as though it had been to have seen if he might have found either the body, or any of the murderers hid in any privy place: but at length coming to the postern gate, and finding it open, he burdened the chamberlains, whom he had slain, with all the fault, they having the keys of the gates committed to their keeping all the night, and therefore it could not be otherwise (said he) but that they were of counsel in the committing of that most detestable murder.

Finally, such was his overearnest diligence in the severe inquisition and trial of the offenders herein, that some of the lords began to mislike the matter, and to smell forth shrewd tokens, that he should not be altogether clear himself. But for so much as they were in that country, where he had the whole rule, what by reason of his friends and authority together, they doubted to utter what they thought, till time and place should better serve thereunto, and hereupon got them away every man to his home. For the space of six months together, after this heinous murder thus committed, there appeared no sun by day, nor moon by night in any part of the realm, but still was the sky covered with continual clouds, and sometimes, such outrageous winds arose, with lightnings and tempests, that the people were in great fear of present destruction. . . .

Monstrous sights also that were seen within the Scottish kingdom that year were these: horses in Louthian, being of singular beauty and swiftness, did eat their own flesh, and would in no wise taste any other meat. In Angus there was a gentlewoman brought forth a child without eyes, nose, hand, or foot. There was a sparhawk also strangled by an owl. Neither was it any less wonder that the sun, as before is said, was continually covered with clouds for six months' space. But all men understood that the abominable murder of King Duffe was the cause hereof. . . .

Thus might he seem happy to all men, having the love both of his lords and commons: but yet to himself he seemed most unhappy, as he that could not but still live in continual fear, lest his wicked practice concerning the death of Malcolme Duffe should come to light and knowledge of the world. For so cometh it to pass, that such as are pricked in conscience for any secret offense committed, have ever an unquiet mind. And (as the fame goeth) it chanced that a voice was heard as he was in bed in the night time to take his rest, uttering unto him these or the like words in effect: "Think not Kenneth that the wicked slaughter of Malcolme Duffe by thee contrived, is kept secret from the knowledge of the eternal God: thou art he that didst conspire the innocent's death, enterprising by traitorous means to do that to thy neighbor, which thou wouldst have revenged by cruel punishment in any of thy subjects, if it had been offered to thyself. It shall therefore come to pass, that both thou thyself, and thy issue, through the just vengeance of almighty God, shall suffer worthy punishment, to the infamy of thy house and family for evermore. For even at this present are there in hand secret practices to dispatch both thee and thy issue out of the way, that other may enjoy this kingdom which thou dost endeavor to assure unto thine issue."

The king, with this voice being stricken into great dread and terror, passed that night without any sleep coming in his eyes.

[Macbeth's History]

Doada was married unto Sinell the Thane of Glammis, by whom she had issue one Makbeth a valiant gentleman, and one that if he had not been somewhat cruel of nature, might have been thought most worthy the government of a realm. On the other part, Duncane was so soft and gentle of nature, that the people wished the inclinations and manners of these two cousins to have been so tempered and interchangeably bestowed betwixt them, that where the one had too much of clemency, and the other of cruelty, the mean virtue betwixt these two extremities might have reigned by indifferent partition in them both, so should Duncane have proved a worthy king, and Makbeth an excellent captain. The beginning of Duncane's reign was very quiet and peaceable, without any notable trouble; but after it was perceived how negligent he was in punishing offenders, many misruled persons took occasion thereof to trouble the peace and quiet state of the commonwealth, by seditious commotions which first had their beginnings in this wise.

Banquho the Thane of Lochquhaber, of whom the house of the Stewarts is descended, the which by order of lineage hath now for a long time enjoyed the crown of Scotland, even till these our days ... gathered the finances due to the king. ...

Then doubting not but for such contemptuous demeanor against the king's regal authority, they should be invaded with all the power the king could make, Makdowald one of great estimation among them, making first a confederacy with his nearest friends and kinsmen, took upon him to be chief captain of all such rebels as would stand against the king, in maintenance of their grievous offenses lately committed against him. ... He used also such subtle persuasions and forged allurements, that in a small time he had gotten together a mighty power of men: for out of the western Isles there came unto him a great multitude of people ... and out of Ireland ... no small number of *Kerns and Galloglasses*. ...

At length Makbeth speaking much against the king's softness, and overmuch slackness in punishing offenders, ... he promised notwithstanding, if the charge were committed unto him and unto Banquho, so to order the matter, that the rebels should be shortly vanquished & quite put down, and that not so much as one of them should be found to make resistance within the country.

And even so it came to pass: for being sent forth with a new power, at his entering into Lochquhaber, the fame of his coming put the enemies in such fear, that a great number of them stole secretly away from their captain Makdowald, who nevertheless enforced thereto, gave battle unto Makbeth, with the residue which remained with him: but being overcome, and fleeing for refuge into a castle (within the which his wife & children were enclosed) at length when he saw how he could neither defend the hold any longer against his enemies, nor yet upon surrender be suffered to depart with life saved, he first slew his wife and children, and lastly himself, lest if he had yielded simply, he should have been executed in most cruel wise for an example to other. Makbeth entering into the castle by the gates, as then set open, found the carcass of Makdowald lying dead there amongst the residue of the slain bodies, which when he beheld, remitting no piece of his cruel nature with that pitiful sight, he caused the head to be cut off, and set upon a pole's end, and so sent it as present to the king, who as then lay at Bertha. The headless trunk he commanded to be hung up upon a high pair of gallows. . . . Thus was justice and law restored again to the old accustomed course, by the diligent means of Makbeth. Immediately whereupon word came that Sueno king of Norway was arrived in Fife with a puissant army, to subdue the whole realm of Scotland.

. . . Makbeth and Banquho were sent with the king's authority, who having with them a convenient power, encountered the enemies, slew part of them, and chased the other to their ships. They that escaped and got once to their ships, obtained of Makbeth for a great sum of gold, that such of their friends as were slain at this last bickering, might be buried in Saint Colme's Inch. . . .

And these were the wars that Duncane had with foreign enemies, in the seventh year of his reign. Shortly after happened a strange and uncouth wonder, which afterward was the cause of much trouble in the realm of Scotland, as ye shall after hear. It fortuned as Makbeth and Banquho journeyed towards Fores, where the king then lay, they went sporting by the way together without other company, save only themselves, passing through the woods and fields, when suddenly in the midst of a land, there met them three women in strange and wild apparel, resembling creatures of elder world, whom when they attentively beheld, wondering much at the sight, the first of them spoke and said: "All hail Makbeth, Thane of Glammis" (for he had lately entered into that dignity and office by the death of his father Sinell). The second of them said: "Hail Makbeth, Thane of Cawder." But the third said: "All hail Makbeth that hereafter shalt be king of Scotland."

Then Banquho: "What manner of woman (saith he) are you, that seem so little favorable unto me, whereas to my fellow here, besides high offices, ye assign also the kingdom, appointing forth nothing for me at all?" "Yes (saith the first of them) we promise greater benefits unto thee, than unto him, for he shall reign indeed, but with an unlucky end:

neither shall he leave any issue behind him to succeed in his place, where contrarily thou indeed shalt not reign at all, but of thee those shall be born which shall govern the Scottish kingdom by long order of continual descent." Herewith the foresaid women vanished immediately out of their sight. This was reputed at the first but some vain fantastical illusion by Mackbeth and Banquho, insomuch that Banquho would call Mackbeth in jest, king of Scotland; and Mackbeth again would call him in sport likewise, the father of many kings. But afterwards the common opinion was, that these women were either the weird sisters, that is (as ye would say) the goddesses of destiny, or else some nymphs or fairies, endued with knowledge of prophecy by their necromantical science, because everything came to pass as they had spoken. For shortly after, the Thane of Cawder being condemned at Fores of treason against the king committed; his lands, livings, and offices were given of the king's liberality to Mackbeth.

The same night after, at supper, Banquho jested with him and said: "Now Mackbeth thou hast obtained those things which the two former sisters prophesied, there remaineth only for thee to purchase that which the third said should come to pass." Whereupon Mackbeth revolving the thing in his mind, began even then to devise how he might attain to the kingdom: but yet he thought with himself that he must tarry a time, which should advance him thereto (by the divine providence) as it had come to pass in his former preferment. But shortly after it chanced that King Duncane, having two sons by his wife which was the daughter of Siward Earl of Northumberland, he made the elder of them called Malcolme Prince of Cumberland, as it were thereby to appoint him his successor in the kingdom, immediately after his decease. Mackbeth sore troubled herewith, for that he saw by this means his hope sore hindered (where, by the old laws of the realm, the ordinance was, that if he that should succeed were not of able age to take the charge upon himself, he that was next of blood unto him should be admitted) he began to take counsel how he might usurp the kingdom by force, having a just quarrel so to do (as he took the matter) for that Duncane did what in him lay to defraud him of all manner of title and claim, which he might in time to come, pretend unto the crown.

The words of the three weird sisters also (of whom before ye have heard) greatly encouraged him hereunto, but specially his wife lay sore upon him to attempt the thing, as she that was very ambitious, burning in unquenchable desire to bear the name of a queen. At length therefore, communicating his purposed intent with his trusty friends, amongst whom Banquho was the chiefest, upon confidence of their promised aid, he slew the king at Enverns, or (as some say) at Botgosuane, in the sixth year of his reign. Then having a company about him of such as he had made privy to his enterprise, he caused himself to be proclaimed king, and forthwith went into Scone, where (by common consent) he received the investure of the kingdom according to the accustomed manner. The body of Duncane was first conveyed unto Elgine, & there buried in kingly wise; but afterwards it was removed and conveyed unto Colmekill, and there laid in a sepulcher amongst his predecessors, in the year after the birth of our Savior, 1046.

Malcolme Cammore and Donald Bane the sons of King Duncane, for fear of their lives (which they might well know that Mackbeth would seek to bring to end for his more sure confirmation in the estate) fled into Cumberland, where Malcolme remained, till time that Saint Edward the son of Ethelred recovered the dominion of England from the Danish power, the which Edward received Malcolme by way of most friendly entertainment: but Donald passed over into Ireland, where he was tenderly cherished by the king of that land. Mackbeth, after the departure thus of Duncane's sons, used great liberality towards the nobles of the realm, thereby to win their favor, and when he saw that no man went about to trouble him, he set his whole intention to maintain justice, and to punish all enormities and abuses, which had chanced through the feeble and slothful administration of Duncane. . . . He made many wholesome laws and statutes for the public weal of his subjects. [There follows a list of good laws.]

These and the like commendable laws Makbeth caused to be put as then in use, governing the realm for the space of ten years in equal justice. But this was but a counterfeit zeal of equity showed by him, partly against his natural inclination to purchase thereby the favor of the people. Shortly after, he began to show what he was, instead of equity practicing cruelty. For the prick of conscience (as it chanceth ever in tyrants, and such as attain to any estate by unrighteous means) caused him ever to fear, lest he should be served of the same cup, as he had ministered to his predecessor. The words also of the three weird sisters, would not out of his mind, which as they promised him the kingdom, so likewise did they promise it at the same time unto the posterity of Banquho. He willed therefore the same Banquho with his son named Fleance, to come to a supper that he had prepared for them, which was indeed, as he had devised, present death at the hands of certain murderers, whom he hired to execute that deed, appointing them to meet with the same Banquho and his son without the palace, as they returned to their lodgings, and there to slay them, so that he would not have his house slandered, but that in time to come he might clear himself, if anything were laid to his charge upon any suspicion that might arise.

It chanced yet by the benefit of the dark night, that though the father were slain, the son yet by the help of almighty God reserving him to better fortune, escaped that danger: and afterwards having some inkling (by the admonition of some friends which he had in the court) how his life was sought no less than his father's, who was slain not by chance-medley (as by the handling of the matter Makbeth would have had it to appear) but even upon a prepensed device: whereupon to avoid further peril he fled into Wales. . . .

But to return unto Makbeth, in continuing the history, and to begin where I left, ye shall understand that, after the contrived slaughter of Banquho, nothing prospered with the foresaid Makbeth: for in manner every man began to doubt his own life, and durst unneth appear in the king's presence; and even as there were many that stood in fear of him, so likewise stood he in fear of many, in such sort that he began to make those away by one surmised cavillation or other, whom he thought most able to work him any displeasure.

At length he found such sweetness by putting his nobles thus to death, that his earnest thirst after blood in this behalf might in no wise be satisfied: for ye must consider he won double profit (as he thought) hereby: for first they were rid out of the way whom he feared, and then again his coffers were enriched by their goods which were forfeited to his use, whereby he might better maintain a guard of armed men about him to defend his person from injury of them whom he had in any suspicion. Further, to the end he might the more cruelly oppress his subjects with all tyrantlike wrongs, he builded a strong castle on the top of a high hill called Dunsinane, situate in Gowrie, ten miles from Perth, on such a proud height, that, standing there aloft, a man might behold well near all the countries of Angus, Fife, Stermond, and Ernedale, as it were lying underneath him. This castle, then, being founded on the top of that high hill, put the realm to great charges before it was finished, for all the stuff necessary to the building could not be brought up without much toil and business. But Makbeth, being once determined to have the work go forward, caused the thanes of each shire within the realm, to come and help towards that building, each man his course about.

At the last, when the turn fell unto Makduffe, Thane of Fife, to build his part, he sent workmen with all needful provision, and commanded them to show such diligence in every behalf, that no occasion might be given for the king to find fault with him, in that he came not himself as other had done, which he refused to do, for doubt lest the king, bearing him (as he partly understood) no great good will, would lay violent hands upon him, as he had done upon diverse other. Shortly after, Makbeth coming to behold how the work went forward, and because he found not Makduffe there, he was sore offended, and said: "I perceive this man will never obey my commandments, till he be ridden with a snaffle; but I shall provide well enough for him." . . .

Neither could he afterwards abide to look upon the said Makduffe, either for that he thought his puissance overgreat; either else for that he had learned of certain wizards, in whose words he put great confidence (for that the prophecy had happened so right, which the three fairies or weird sisters had declared unto him) how that he ought to take heed of Makduffe, who in time to come should seek to destroy him.

And surely hereupon had he put Makduffe to death, but

that a certain witch, whom he had in great trust, had told that he should never be slain with man born of any woman, nor vanquished till the wood of Bernane came to the castle of Dunsinane. By this prophecy Makbeth put all fear out of his heart, supposing he might do what he would, without any fear to be punished for the same, for by the one prophecy he believed it was unpossible for any man to vanquish him, and by the other unpossible to slay him. This vain hope caused him to do many outrageous things, to the grievous oppression of his subjects. At length Makduffe, to avoid peril of life, purposed with himself to pass into England, to procure Malcolme Cammore to claim the crown of Scotland, But this was not so secretly devised by Makduffe, but that Makbeth had knowledge given him therefore: for kings (as is said) have sharp sight like unto Lynx, and long ears like unto Midas. For Makbeth had in every nobleman's house one sly fellow or other in fee with him, to reveal all that was said or done within the same, by which sleight he oppressed the most part of the nobles of his realm.

Immediately then, being advertised whereabout Makduffe went, he came hastily with a great power into Fife, and forthwith besieged the castle where Makduffe dwelled, trusting to have found him therein. They that kept the house, without any resistance opened the gates, and suffered him to enter, mistrusting none evil. But nevertheless Makbeth most cruelly caused the wife and children of Makduffe, with all other whom he found in that castle, to be slain. Also he confiscated the goods of Makduffe, proclaimed him traitor, and confined him out of all the parts of his realm; but Makduffe was already escaped out of danger, and gotten into England unto Malcolme Cammore, to try what purchase he might make by means of his support, to revenge the slaughter so cruelly executed on his wife, his children, and other friends. At his coming unto Malcolme, he declared into what great misery the estate of Scotland was brought, by the detestable cruelties exercised by the tyrant Makbeth, having committed many horrible slaughters and murders, both as well of the nobels as commons, for the which he was hated right mortally of all his liege people, desiring nothing more than to be delivered of that intolerable and most heavy yoke of thralldom, which they sustained at such a caitiff's hands.

Malcolme hearing Makduffe's words, which he uttered in very lamentable sort, for mere compassion and very ruth that pierced his sorrowful heart, bewailing the miserable state of his country, he fetched a deep sigh; which Makduffe perceiving, began to fall most earnestly in hand with him, to enterprise the delivering of the Scottish people out of the hands of so cruel and bloody a tyrant, as Makbeth by too many plain experiments did show himself to be: which was an easy matter for him to bring to pass, considering not only the good title he had, but also the earnest desire of the people to have some occasion ministered, whereby they might be revenged of those notable injuries, which they daily sustained by the outrageous cruelty of Makbeth's misgovernance. Though Malcolme was very sorrowful for the oppression of his countrymen the Scots, in manner as Makduffe had declared; yet doubting whether he were come as one that meant unfeignedly as he spoke, or else as sent from Makbeth to betray him, he thought to have some further trial, and thereupon dissembling his mind at the first, he answered as followeth.

"I am truly very sorry for the misery chanced to my country of Scotland, but though I have never so great affection to relieve the same, yet by reason of certain incurable vices, which reign in me, I am nothing meet thereto. First, such immoderate lust and voluptuous sensuality (the abominable fountain of all vices) followeth me, that if I were made king of Scots, I should seek to deflower your maids and matrons, in such wise that mine intemperancy should be more importable unto you than the bloody tyranny of Makbeth now is." Hereunto Makduffe answered: "This surely is a very evil fault, for many noble princes and kings have lost both lives and kingdoms for the same; nevertheless there are women enow in Scotland, and therefore follow my counsel. Make thyself king, and I shall convey the matter so wisely, that thou shalt be so satisfied at thy pleasure in such secret wise, that no man shall be aware thereof."

Then said Malcolme, "I am also the most avaricious creature on the earth, so that if I were king, I should seek so many ways to get lands and goods, that I would slay the most part of all the nobles of Scotland by surmised accusations, to the end I might enjoy their lands, goods, and possessions; and therefore to show you what mischief may ensue on you through mine unsatiable covetousness, I will rehearse unto you a fable. There was a fox having a sore place on her overset with a swarm of flies, that continually sucked out her blood: and when one that came by and saw this manner, demanded whether she would have the flies driven beside her, she answered no: for if these flies that are already full, and by reason thereof suck not very eagerly, should be chased away, other that are empty and fellie and hungered, should light in their places, and suck out the residue of my blood far more to my grievance than these, which now being satisfied do not much annoy me. Therefore," saith Malcolme, "suffer me to remain where I am, lest if I attain to the regiment of your realm, mine unquenchable avarice may prove such; that ye would think the displeasures which now grieve you, should seem easy in respect of the unmeasurable outrage, which might ensure through my coming amongst you."

Makduffe to this made answer, how it was a far worse fault than the other: "for avarice is the root of all mischief, and for that crime the most part of our kings have been slain and brought to their final end. Yet notwithstanding follow my counsel, and take upon thee the crown. There is gold and riches enough in Scotland to satisfy thy greedy desire." Then said Malcolme again, "I am furthermore inclined to dissimulation, telling of leasings, and all other kinds of deceit, so that I naturally rejoice in nothing so much, as to betray & deceive such as put any trust or confidence in my words. Then sith there is nothing that more becometh a prince than constancy, verity, truth, and justice, with the other laudable fellowship of those fair and noble virtues which are comprehended only in soothfastness, and that lying utterly over throweth the same; you see how unable I am to govern any province or region: and therefore sith you have remedies to cloak and hide all the rest of my other vices, I pray you find shift to cloak this vice amongst the residue."

Then said Makduffe: "This yet is the worst of all, and there I leave thee, and therefore say: Oh ye unhappy and miserable Scottishmen, which are thus scourged with so many and sundry calamities, each one above other! Ye have one cursed and wicked tyrant that now reigneth over you, without any right or title, oppressing you with his most bloody cruelty. This other that hath the right to the crown, is so replete with the inconstant behavior and manifest vices of Englishmen, that he is nothing worthy to enjoy it: for by his own confession he is not only avaricious, and given to unsatiable lust, but so false a traitor withal, that no trust is to be had unto any word he speaketh. Adieu Scotland, for now I account myself a banished man forever, without comfort or consolation": and with those words the brackish tears trickled down his cheeks very abundantly.

At the last, when he was ready to depart, Malcolme took him by the sleeve, and said: "Be of good comfort Makduffe, for I have none of these vices before remembered, but have jested with thee in this manner, only to prove thy mind: for diverse times heretofore hath Makbeth sought by this manner of means to bring me into his hands, but the more slow I have showed myself to condescend to thy motion and request, the more diligence shall I use in accomplishing the same." Incontinently hereupon they embraced each other, and promising to be faithful the one to the other, they fell in consultation how they might best provide for all their business, to bring the same to good effect. Soon after, Makduffe repairing to the borders of Scotland, addressed his letters with secret dispatch unto the nobles of the realm, declaring how Malcolme was confederate with him, to come hastily into Scotland to claim the crown, and therefore he required them, sith he was right inheritor thereto, to assist him with their powers to recover the same out of the hands of the wrongful usurper.

In the meantime, Malcolme purchased such favor at King Edward's hands, that old Siward Earl of Northumberland was appointed with ten thousand men to go with him into Scotland, to support him in this enterprise, for recovery of his right. After these news were spread abroad in Scotland, the nobles drew into two several factions, the one taking part with Makbeth, and the other with Malcolme. Hereupon ensued oftentimes sundry bickerings, & diverse light skirmishes: for those that were of Malcolme's side, would not jeopard to join with their enemies in a pight field, till his coming out of England to their support. But after that Makbeth perceived his enemy's power to increase, by such aid as came to them forth of England with his adversary Malcolme, he recoiled back into Fife, there purposing to abide in camp fortified, at the castle of Dunsinane, and to fight with his enemies, if they meant to pursue him; howbeit some of his friends advised him, that it should be best for him, either to make some agreement with Malcolme, or else to flee with all speed into the Isles, and to take his treasure with him, to the end he might wage sundry great princes of the realm to take his part, & retain strangers, in whom he might better trust than in his own subjects, which stole daily from him: but he had such confidence in his prophecies, that he believed he should never be vanquished, till Brinane wood were brought to Dunsinane; nor yet to be slain with any man, that should be or was born of any woman.

Malcolme following hastily after Makbeth, came the night before the battle unto Brinane wood, and when his army had rested a while there to refresh them, he commanded every man to get a bough of some tree or other of that wood in his hand, as big as he might bear, and to march forth therewith in such wise, that on the next morrow they might come closely and without sight in this manner within view of his enemies. On the morrow when Makbeth beheld them coming in this sort, he first marveled what the matter meant, but in the end remembered himself that the prophecy which he had heard along before that time, of the coming of Birnane wood to Dunsinane castle, was like to be now fulfilled. Nevertheless, he brought his men in order of battle, and exhorted them to do valiantly, howbeit his enemies had scarcely cast from them their boughs, when Makbeth perceiving their numbers, betook him straight to flight, whom Makduffe pursued with great hatred even till he came unto Lunfannaine, where Makbeth perceiving that Makduffe was hard at his back, leaped beside his horse, saying: "Thou traitor, what meaneth it that thou shouldest thus in vain follow me that am not appointed to be slain by any creature that is born of a woman, come on therefore, and receive thy reward which thou hast deserved for thy pains," and therewithal he lifted up his sword thinking to have slain him.

But Makduffe quickly avoiding from his horse, ere he came at him, answered (with his naked sword in his hand) saying: "It is true Makbeth, and now shall thine insatiable cruelty have an end, for I am even he that thy wizards have told thee of, who was never born of my mother, but ripped out of her womb": therewithal he stepped unto him, and slew him in the place. Then cutting his head from his shoulders, he set it upon a pole, and brought it unto Malcolme. This was the end of Makbeth, after he had reigned 17 years over the Scottishmen. In the beginning of his reign he accomplished many worthy acts, very profitable to the commonwealth (as ye have heard), but afterward by illusion of the devil, he defamed the same with most terrible cruelty. He was slain in the year of the incarnation 1057, and in the 16 year of King Edward's reign over the Englishmen.

Malcolme Cammore thus recovering the realm (as ye have heard) by support of King Edward, in the 16 year of the same Edward's reign, he was crowned at Scone, the 25 day of April, in the year of our Lord 1057. Immediately after his coronation he called a parliament at Forfair, in the which he rewarded them with lands and livings that had assisted him against Makbeth, advancing them to fees and offices as he saw cause, & commanded that specially those, that bare the surname of any offices or lands, should have and enjoy the same. He created many earls, lords, barons, and knights. Many of them, that before were thanes, were at this time made earls, as Fife, Menteth ... Leuenox ... Cathnes, Rosse, and Angus. These were the first earls that have been heard of amongst the Scottishmen as their histories do make mention. Many new surnames were taken up at this time amongst them, as Cauder ... Seiton ... with many other that had possessions given them, which gave names to the owners for the time. ...

[Siward and his Son]

About the thirteenth year of King Edward his reign (as some write) or rather about the nineteenth or twentieth year, as should appear by the Scottish writers, Siward the noble Earl of Northumberland with a great power of horsemen went into Scotland, and in battle put to flight Makbeth that had usurped the crown of Scotland, and, that done, placed Malcolme surnamed Camoir, the son of Duncane, sometime king of Scotland, in the government of that realm, who after-ward slew the said Mackbeth, and then reigned in quiet. . . .

It is recorded also, that, in the foresaid battle, in which Earl Siward vanquished the Scots, one of Siward's sons chanced to be slain, whereof although the father had good cause to be sorrowful, yet, when he heard that he died of a wound which he had received in fighting stoutly, in the forepart of his body, and that with his face towards the enemy, he greatly rejoiced thereat, to hear that he died so manfully. But here is to be noted, that not now, but a little before (as *Henry Hunt* saith) that Earl Siward went into Scotland himself in person, he sent his son with an army to conquer the land, whose hap was there to be slain: and when his father heard the news, he demanded whether he received the wound whereof he died, in the forepart of the body, or in the hinder part: and when it was told him that he received it in the forepart: "I rejoice (saith he) even with all my heart, for *I would not wish* either to my son nor to myself any other kind of *death*."

Commentaries

SAMUEL JOHNSON

Macbeth

Most of the notes which the present editor has subjoined to this play were published by him in a small pamphlet in 1745.

1.1. "*Enter three* Witches." In order to make a true estimate of the abilities and merit of a writer, it is always necessary to examine the genius of his age and the opinions of his contemporaries. A poet who should now make the whole action of his tragedy depend upon enchantment and produce the chief events by the assistance of supernatural agents, would be censured as transgressing the bounds of probability, be banished from the theater to the nursery, and condemned to write fairy tales instead of tragedies; but a survey of the notions that prevailed at the time when this play was written will prove that Shakespeare was in no danger of such censures, since he only turned the system that was then universally admitted to his advantage and was far from overburdening the credulity of his audience.

The reality of witchcraft or enchantment, which, though not strictly the same, are confounded in this play, has in all ages and countries been credited by the common people, and in most, by the learned themselves. These phantoms have indeed appeared more frequently in proportion as the darkness of ignorance has been more gross; but it cannot be

From *The Plays of William Shakespeare* (1765).

shown that the brightest gleams of knowledge have at any time been sufficient to drive them out of the world. The time in which this kind of credulity was at its height seems to have been that of the holy war, in which the Christians imputed all their defeats to enchantments or diabolical opposition, as they ascribed their success to the assistance of their military saints; and the learned Dr. Warburton appears to believe (*Supplement to the Introduction to "Don Quixote"*) that the first accounts of enchantments were brought into this part of the world by those who returned from their eastern expeditions. But there is always some distance between the birth and maturity of folly as of wickedness; this opinion had long existed, though perhaps application of it had in no foregoing age been so frequent, nor the reception so general. Olympiodorus, in Photius's extracts, tells us of one Libanius, who practiced this kind of military magic and having promised χωρὶς ὁπλιτῶν κατὰ βαρβάρων ἐνεργεῖν, *to perform great things against the barbarians without soldiers,* was, at the instances of the empress Placidia, put to death, when he was about to have given proof of his abilities. The empress showed some kindness in her anger by cutting him off at a time so convenient for his reputation.

But a more remarkable proof of the antiquity of this notion may be found in St. Chrysostom's book *de Sacerdotio,* which exhibits a scene of enchantments not exceeded by any romance of the Middle Age: he supposes a spectator overlooking a field of battle attended by one that points out all the various objects of horror, the engines of destruction, and the arts of slaughter. Δεικνύτο δὲ ἔτι παρὰ τοῖς ἐναντίοις καὶ πετομένους ἵππους διά τινος μαγγανείας, καὶ ὁπλίτας δι᾽ ἀέρος φερομένους, καὶ πάσην γοητείας δυναμιν καὶ ἰδέαν. "Let him then proceed to show him in the opposite armies horses flying by enchantment, armed men transported through the air, and every tower and form of magic." Whether St. Chrysostom believed that such performances were really to be seen in a day of battle, or only endeavored to enliven his description by adopting the notions of the vulgar, it is equally certain that such notions were in his time received, and that therefore they were not imported from the Saracens in a later age; the wars with the Saracens, however, gave occasion to their propagation, not only as bigotry naturally discovers prodigies, but as the scene of action was removed to a great distance.

The Reformation did not immediately arrive at its meridian, and though day was gradually increasing upon us, the goblins of witchcraft still continued to hover in the twilight. In the time of Queen Elizabeth was the remarkable trial of the witches of Warbois, whose conviction is still commemorated in an annual sermon at Huntingdon. But in the reign of King James, in which this tragedy was written, many circumstances concurred to propagate and confirm this opinion. The king, who was much celebrated for his knowledge, had, before his arrival in England, not only examined in person a woman accused of witchcraft but had given a very formal account of the practices and illusions of evil spirits, the compacts of witches, the ceremonies used by them, the manner of detecting them, and the justice of punishing them, in his dialogues of *Daemonologie*, written in the Scottish dialect, and published at Edinburgh. This book was, soon after his accession, reprinted in London, and as the ready way to gain King James's favor was to flatter his speculations, the system of *Daemonologie* was immediately adopted by all who desired either to gain preferment or not to lose it. Thus the doctrine of witchcraft was very powerfully inculcated; and as the greatest part of mankind have no other reason for their opinions than that they are in fashion, it cannot be doubted but this persuasion made a rapid progress, since vanity and credulity cooperated in its favor. The infection soon reached the Parliament, who, in the first year of King James, made a law, by which it was enacted, Chapter XII: That "if any person shall use any invocation or conjuration of any evil or wicked spirit; 2. or shall consult, covenant with, entertain, employ, feed or reward any evil or cursed spirit to or for any intent or purpose; 3. or take up any dead man, woman or child out of the grave,—or the skin, bone, or any part of the dead person, to be employed or used in any manner of witchcraft, sorcery, charm, or enchantment; 4. or shall use, practice, or exercise any sort of witchcraft, sorcery, charm, or enchantment; 5. whereby any person shall be destroyed, killed, wasted, consumed, pined, or lamed in any part of the body; 6. that every such person being convicted shall suffer death." This law was repealed in our own time.

Thus, in the time of Shakespeare, was the doctrine of witchcraft at once established by law and by the fashion, and it became not only unpolite, but criminal, to doubt it; and as prodigies are always seen in proportion as they are expected, witches were every day discovered and multiplied so fast in some places that Bishop Hall mentions a village in Lancashire where their number was greater than that of the houses. The Jesuits and sectaries took advantage of this universal error and endeavored to promote the interest of their parties by pretended cures of persons afflicted by evil spirits; but they were detected and exposed by the clergy of the Established Church.

Upon this general infatuation Shakespeare might be easily allowed to found a play, especially since he has followed with great exactness such histories as were then thought true; nor can it be doubted that the scenes of enchantment, however they may now be ridiculed, were both by himself and his audience thought awful and affecting.

1.7.28. "*Enter* Lady Macbeth." The arguments by which Lady Macbeth persuades her husband to commit the murder afford a proof of Shakespeare's knowledge of human nature. She urges the excellence and dignity of courage, a glittering idea which has dazzled mankind from age to age and animated sometimes the housebreaker and sometimes the conqueror; but this sophism Macbeth has forever destroyed, by distinguishing true from false fortitude, in a line and a half; of which it may almost be said that they ought to bestow immortality on the author, though all his other productions had been lost;

> I dare do all that may become a man,
> Who dares do more, is none.

This topic, which has been always employed with too much success, is used in this scene with peculiar propriety, to a soldier by a woman. Courage is the distinguishing virtue of a soldier, and the reproach of cowardice cannot be borne by any man from a woman, without great impatience.

She then urges the oaths by which he had bound himself

to murder Duncan, another art of sophistry by which men have sometimes deluded their consciences and persuaded themselves that what would be criminal in others is virtuous in them; this argument Shakespeare, whose plan obliged him to make Macbeth yield, has not confuted, though he might easily have shown that a former obligation could not be vacated by a latter; that obligations laid on us by a higher power could not be overruled by obligations which we lay upon ourselves.

2.1.49. "*Macbeth.* Now o'er the one half-world / Nature seems dead." This is, *over our hemisphere all action and motion seem to have ceased.* This image, which is perhaps the most striking that poetry can produce, has been adopted by Dryden in his *Conquest of Mexico*:

> All things are hush'd as Nature's self lay dead,
> The mountains seem to nod their drowsy head;
> The little birds in dreams their songs repeat,
> And sleeping flow'rs beneath the night dews sweat.
> Even lust and envy sleep!

These lines, though so well known, I have transcribed, that the contrast between them and this passage of Shakespeare may be more accurately observed.

Night is described by two great poets, but one describes a night of quiet, the other of perturbation. In the night of Dryden, all the disturbers of the world are laid asleep; in that of Shakespeare, nothing but sorcery, lust, and murder is awake. He that reads Dryden finds himself lulled with serenity and disposed to solitude and contemplation. He that peruses Shakespeare looks round alarmed and starts to find himself alone. One is the night of a lover, the other, of a murderer.

2.2.55. "*Lady Macbeth.* Gild the faces of the grooms withal; / For it must seem their guilt." Could Shakespeare possibly mean to play upon the similitude of *gild* and *guilt*?

2.3.113–14. "*Macbeth.* Here lay Duncan, / His silver skin lac'd with his golden blood." Mr. Pope has endeavored to improve one of these lines by substituting *gory blood* for *golden blood*; but it may easily be admitted that he who could on such occasion talk of *lacing the silver skin* would *lace it* with *golden blood.* No amendment can be made to this line, of which every word is equally faulty, but by a general blot.

It is not improbable that Shakespeare put these forced and unnatural metaphors into the mouth of Macbeth as a mark of artifice and dissimulation, to show the difference between the studied language of hypocrisy and the natural outcries of sudden passion. This whole speech so considered is a remarkable instance of judgment, as it consists entirely of antithesis and metaphor.

3.1.68–69. "Mine eternal jewel / Giv'n to the common enemy of man." It is always an entertainment to an inquisitive reader, to trace a sentiment to its original source, and therefore though the term "enemy of man," applied to the devil, is in itself natural and obvious, yet some may be pleased with being informed, that Shakespeare probably borrowed it from the first lines of the destruction of Troy, a book which he is known to have read.

That this remark may not appear too trivial, I shall take occasion from it to point out a beautiful passage of Milton evidently copied from a book of no greater authority, in describing the gates of hell. Book 2. v. 879. he says,

> . . . On a sudden open fly,
> With impetuous recoil and jarring sound,
> Th' infernal doors, and on their hinges grate
> Harsh thunder.

In the history of Don Bellianis, when one of the knights approaches, as I remember, the castle of Brandezar, the gates are said to open "grating harsh thunder upon their brazen hinges."

4.1. As this is the chief scene of enchantment in the play, it is proper in this place to observe, with how much judgment Shakespeare has selected all the circumstances of his infernal ceremonies, and how exactly he has conformed to common opinions and traditions.

> Thrice the brinded cat hath mew'd.

The usual form in which familiar spirits are reported to converse with witches, is that of a cat. A witch, who was tried about half a century before the time of Shakespeare, had a cat named Rutterkin, as the spirit of one of those witches was Grimalkin; and when any mischief was to be done she used to bid Rutterkin "go and fly," but once when she would have sent Rutterkin to torment a daughter of the countess of Rutland, instead of "going" or "flying," he only cried "mew," from whence she discovered that the lady was out of his power, the power of witches not being universal, but limited, as Shakespeare has taken care to inculcate.

> Though his bark cannot be lost,
> Yet it shall be tempest tost.

The common afflictions which the malice of witches produced were melancholy, fits, and loss of flesh, which are threatened by one of Shakespeare's witches.

> Weary sev'n-nights, nine times nine,
> Shall he dwindle, peak and pine.

It was likewise their practice to destroy the cattle of their neighbors, and the farmers have to this day many ceremonies to secure their cows and other cattle from witchcraft; but they seem to have been most suspected of malice against swine. Shakespeare has accordingly made one of his witches declare that she has been "killing swine," and Dr. Harsenet observes, that about that time, "a sow could not be ill of the measles, nor a girl of the sullens, but some old woman was charged with witchcraft."

> Toad, that under the cold stone,
> Days and nights has, thirty-one,
> Swelter'd venom sleeping got;
> Boil thou first i' th' charmed pot.

Toads have likewise long lain under the reproach of being by some means accessory to witchcraft, for which reason Shakespeare, in the first scene of this play, calls one of the spirits Padock or toad, and now takes care to put a toad first into the pot. When Vaninus was seized at Tholouse, there was found at his lodgings *ingens Bufo Vitro inclusus,* "a great Toad shut in a Vial," upon which those that prosecuted him *Veneficium exprobrabant,* "charged him," I suppose, "with witchcraft."

> Fillet of a fenny snake,
> In the cauldron boil and bake;
> Eye of newt, and toe of frog . . .
> For a charm, &c.

The propriety of these ingredients may be known by consulting the books *de Viribus Animalium* and *de Mirabilibus Mundi,* ascribed to Albertus Magnus, in which the reader, who has time and credulity, may discover wonderful secrets.

> Finger of birth-strangled babe,
> Ditch-deliver'd by a drab. . . .

It has been already mentioned in the law against witches, that they are supposed to take up dead bodies to use in enchantments, which was confessed by the woman whom King James examined, and who had of a dead body that was divided in one of their assemblies, two fingers for her share. It is observable that Shakespeare, on this great occasion, which involves the fate of a king, multiplies all the circumstances of horror. The babe, whose finger is used, must be strangled in its birth; the grease must not only be human but must have dropped from a gibbet, the gibbet of a murderer; and even the sow, whose blood is used, must have offended nature by devouring her own farrow. These are touches of judgment and genius.

> And now about the cauldron sing . . .
> Black spirits and white,
>   Blue spirits and grey,
> Mingle, mingle, mingle,
>   You that mingle may.

And in a former part,

> . . . weyward sisters, hand in hand, . . .
> Thus do go about, about,

Thrice to thine, and thrice to mine,
And thrice again to make up nine!

These two passages I have brought together, because they both seem subject to the objection of too much levity for the solemnity of enchantment, and may both be shown, by one quotation from Camden's account of Ireland, to be founded upon a practice really observed by the uncivilized natives of that country. "When any one gets a fall," says the informer of Camden, "he starts up, and *turning three times to the right* digs a hole in the earth; for they imagine that there is a spirit in the ground, and if he falls sick in two or three days, they send one of their women that is skilled in that way to the place, where she says, I call thee from the east, west, north and south, from the groves, the woods, the rivers, and the fens, from the *fairies red, black, white.*" There was likewise a book written before the time of Shakespeare, describing amongst other properties, the colors of spirits.

Many other circumstances might be particularized, in which Shakespeare has shown his judgment and his knowledge.

General Observation. This play is deservedly celebrated for the propriety of its fictions, and solemnity, grandeur, and variety of its action; but it has no nice discriminations of character, the events are too great to admit the influence of particular dispositions, and the course of the action necessarily determines the conduct of the agents.

The danger of ambition is well described; and I know not whether it may not be said in defense of some parts which now seem improbable, that, in Shakespeare's time, it was necessary to warn credulity against vain and illusive predictions.

The passions are directed to their true end. Lady Macbeth is merely detested; and though the courage of Macbeth preserves some esteem, yet every reader rejoices at his fall.

A. C. BRADLEY

From Shakespearean Tragedy

From this murky background stand out the two great terrible figures who dwarf all the remaining characters of the drama. Both are sublime, and both inspire, far more than the other tragic heroes, the feeling of awe. They are never detached in imagination from the atmosphere which surrounds them and adds to their grandeur and terror. It is, as it were, continued into their souls. For within them is all that we felt without—the darkness of night, lit with the flame of tempest and the hues of blood, and haunted by wild and direful shapes, "murdering ministers," spirits of remorse, and maddening visions of peace lost and judgment to come. The way to be untrue by Shakespeare here, as always, is to relax the tension of imagination, to conventionalize, to conceive Macbeth, for example, as a halfhearted cowardly criminal, and Lady Macbeth as a wholehearted fiend.

These two characters are fired by one and the same passion of ambition; and to a considerable extent they are alike. The disposition of each is high, proud, and commanding. They are born to rule, if not to reign. They are peremptory or contemptuous to their inferiors. They are not children of light, like Brutus and Hamlet; they are of the world. We observe in them no love of country, and no interest in the welfare of anyone outside their family. Their habitual thoughts and aims are, and, we imagine, long have been, all

From *Shakespearean Tragedy* A. C. Bradley (London: Macmillan, 1904). Reprinted by permission of Macmillan & Company, Ltd. (London), St. Martin's Press, Inc. (New York), and The Macmillan Company of Canada, Ltd. (Toronto).

of station and power. And though in both there is something, and in one much, of what is higher—honor, conscience, humanity—they do not live consciously in the light of these things or speak their language. Not that they are egoists, like Iago; or, if they are egoists, theirs is an *egoïsme à deux*. They have no separate ambitions.[1] They support and love one another. They suffer together. And if, as time goes on, they drift a little apart, they are not vulgar souls, to be alienated and recriminate when they experience the fruitlessness of their ambition. They remain to the end tragic, even grand.

So far there is much likeness between them. Otherwise they are contrasted, and the action is built upon this contrast. Their attitudes towards the projected murder of Duncan are quite different; and it produces in them equally different effects. In consequence, they appear in the earlier part of the play as of equal importance, if indeed Lady Macbeth does not overshadow her husband; but afterwards she retires more and more into the background, and he becomes unmistakably the leading figure. His is indeed far the more complex character: and I will speak of it first.

Macbeth, the cousin of a King mild, just, and beloved, but now too old to lead his army, is introduced to us as a general of extraordinary prowess, who has covered himself with glory in putting down a rebellion and repelling the invasion of a foreign army. In these conflicts he showed great personal courage, a quality which he continues to display throughout the drama in regard to all plain dangers. It is difficult to be sure of his customary demeanor, for in the play we see him either in what appears to be an exceptional relation to his wife, or else in the throes of remorse and desperation; but from his behavior during his journey home after the war, from his *later* conversations with Lady Macbeth, and from his language to the murderers of Banquo and to others, we imagine him as a great warrior, somewhat masterful, rough, and abrupt, a man to inspire some fear and much admiration. He was thought "honest," or honorable; he was trusted apparently, by everyone; Macduff, a man of

[1] The assertion that Lady Macbeth sought a crown for herself, or sought anything for herself, apart from her husband, is absolutely unjustified by anything in the play. It is based on a sentence of Holinshed's which Shakespeare did *not* use.

the highest integrity, "loved him well." And there was, in fact, much good in him. We have no warrant, I think, for describing him, with many writers, as of a "noble" nature, like Hamlet or Othello;[2] but he had a keen sense both of honor and of the worth of a good name. The phrase, again, "too full of the milk of human kindness," is applied to him in impatience by his wife, who did not fully understand him; but certainly he was far from devoid of humanity and pity.

At the same time he was exceedingly ambitious. He must have been so by temper. The tendency must have been greatly strengthened by his marriage. When we see him, it has been further stimulated by his remarkable success and by the consciousness of exceptional powers and merit. It becomes a passion. The course of action suggested by it is extremely perilous: it sets his good name, his position, and even his life on the hazard. It is also abhorrent to his better feelings. Their defeat in the struggle with ambition leaves him utterly wretched, and would have kept him so, however complete had been his outward success and security. On the other hand, his passion for power and his instinct of self-assertion are so vehement that no inward misery could persuade him to relinquish the fruits of crime, or to advance from remorse to repentance.

In the character as so far sketched there is nothing very peculiar, though the strength of the forces contending in it is unusual. But there is in Macbeth one marked peculiarity, the true apprehension of which is the key to Shakespeare's conception.[3] This bold ambitious man of action has, within certain limits, the imagination of a poet—an imagination on the one hand extremely sensitive to impressions of a certain kind, and, on the other, productive of violent disturbance both of mind and body. Through it he is kept in contact with supernatural impressions and is liable to supernatural fears. And through it, especially, come to him the intimations of conscience and honor. Macbeth's better nature—to put the matter for clearness' sake too broadly—instead of speaking to him in the overt language of moral ideas, commands, and

---

[2]The word is used of him (1.2.67), but not in a way that decides this question or even bears on it.

[3]This view, thus generally stated, is not original, but I cannot say who first stated it.

prohibitions, incorporates itself in images which alarm and horrify. His imagination is thus the best of him, something usually deeper and higher than his conscious thoughts; and if he had obeyed it he would have been safe. But his wife quite misunderstands it, and he himself understands it only in part. The terrifying images which deter him from crime and follow its commission, and which are really the protest of his deepest self, seem to his wife the creations of mere nervous fear, and are sometimes referred by himself to the dread of vengeance or the restlessness of insecurity.[4] His conscious or reflective mind, that is, moves chiefly among considerations of outward success and failure, while his inner being is convulsed by conscience. And his inability to understand himself is repeated and exaggerated in the interpretations of actors and critics, who represent him as a coward, cold-blooded, calculating, and pitiless, who shrinks from crime simply because it is dangerous, and suffers afterwards simply because he is not safe. In reality his courage is frightful. He strides from crime to crime, though his soul never ceases to bar his advance with shapes of terror, or to clamor in his ears that he is murdering his peace and casting away his "eternal jewel."

It is of the first importance to realize the strength, and also (what has not been so clearly recognized) the limits, of Macbeth's imagination. It is not the universal meditative imagination of Hamlet. He came to see in man, as Hamlet sometimes did, the "quintessence of dust"; but he must always have been incapable of Hamlet's reflections on man's noble reason and infinite faculty, or of seeing with Hamlet's eyes "this brave o'erhanging firmament, this majestical roof fretted with golden fire." Nor could he feel, like Othello, the romance of war or the infinity of love. He shows no sign of any unusual sensitiveness to the glory or beauty in the world or the soul; and it is partly for this reason that we have no inclination to love him, and that we regard him with more of awe than of pity. His imagination is excitable and intense, but narrow. That which stimulates it is, almost solely, that which thrills with sudden, startling, and often supernatural fear.[5] There is a

---

[4]The latter, and more important, point was put quite clearly by Coleridge.
[5]It is the consequent insistence on the idea of fear, and the frequent repetition of the word, that have principally led to misinterpretation.

famous passage late in the play (5.5.10) which is here very significant, because it refers to a time before his conscience was burdened, and so shows his native deposition:

> The time has been, my senses would have cool'd
> To hear a night-shriek; and my fell of hair
> Would at a dismal treatise rise and stir
> As life were in't.

This "time" must have been in his youth, or at least before we see him. And, in the drama, everything which terrifies him is of this character, only it has now a deeper and a moral significance. Palpable dangers leave him unmoved or fill him with fire. He does himself mere justice when he asserts he "dare do all that may become a man," or when he exclaims to Banquo's ghost,

> What man dare, I dare:
> Approach thou like the rugged Russian bear,
> The arm'd rhinoceros, or the Hyrcan tiger;
> Take any shape but that, and my firm nerves
> Shall never tremble.

What appalls him is always the image of his own guilty heart or bloody deed, or some image which derives from them its terror or gloom. These, when they arise, hold him spell-bound and possess him wholly, like a hypnotic trance which is at the same time the ecstasy of a poet. As the first "horrid image" of Duncan's murder—of himself murdering Duncan—rises from unconsciousness and confronts him, his hair stands on end and the outward scene vanishes from his eyes. Why? For fear of "consequences"? The idea is ridiculous. Or because the deed is bloody? The man who with his "smoking" steel "carved out his passage" to the rebel leader, and "unseam'd him from the nave to the chops," would hardly be frightened by blood. How could fear of consequences make the dagger he is to use hang suddenly glittering before him in the air, and then as suddenly dash it with gouts of blood? Even when he *talks* of consequences, and declares that if he were safe against them he would "jump the life to come," his imagination bears witness against him, and shows us that what really holds him back is the hideous vileness of the deed:

> He's here in double trust;
> First, as I am his kinsman and his subject,
> Strong both against the deed; then, as his host,
> Who should against his murderer shut the door,
> Not bear the knife myself. Besides, this Duncan
> Hath borne his faculties so meek, hath been
> So clear in his great office, that his virtues
> Will plead like angels, trumpet-tongued, against
> The deep damnation of his taking-off;
> And pity, like a naked new-born babe,
> Striding the blast, or heaven's cherubim, horsed
> Upon the sightless couriers of the air,
> Shall blow the horrid deed in every eye,
> That tears shall drown the wind.

It may be said that he is here thinking of the horror that others will feel at the deed—thinking therefore of consequences. Yes, but could he realize thus how horrible the deed would look to others if it were not equally horrible to himself?

It is the same when the murder is done. He is well-nigh mad with horror, but it is not the horror of detection. It is not he who thinks of washing his hands or getting his nightgown on. He has brought away the daggers he should have left on the pillows of the grooms, but what does he care for that? What *he* thinks of is that, when he heard one of the men awaked from sleep say "God bless us," he could not say "Amen"; for his imagination presents to him the parching of his throat as an immediate judgment from heaven. His wife heard the owl scream and the crickets cry; but what *he* heard was the voice that first cried "Macbeth doth murder sleep," and then, a minute later, with a change of tense, denounced on him, as if his three names gave him three personalities to suffer in, the doom of sleeplessness:

> Glamis hath murdered sleep, and therefore Cawdor
> Shall sleep no more, Macbeth shall sleep no more.

There comes a sound of knocking. It should be perfectly familiar to him; but he knows not whence, or from what world, it comes. He looks down at his hands, and starts violently: "What hands are here?" For they seem alive, they move, they mean to pluck out his eyes. He looks at one of them again; it does not move; but the blood upon it is enough to dye the whole ocean red. What has all this to do with fear of "consequences"? It is his soul speaking in the only shape in which it can speak freely, that of imagination.

So long as Macbeth's imagination is active, we watch him fascinated; we feel suspense, horror, awe; in which are latent, also, admiration and sympathy. But so soon as it is quiescent these feelings vanish. He is no longer "infirm of purpose": he becomes domineering, even brutal, or he becomes a cool pitiless hypocrite. He is generally said to be a very bad actor, but this is not wholly true. Whenever his imagination stirs, he acts badly. It so possesses him, and is so much stronger than his reason, that his face betrays him, and his voice utters the most improbable untruths[6] or the most artificial rhetoric.[7] But when it is asleep he is firm, self-controlled and practical, as in the conversation where he skillfully elicits from Banquo that information about his movements which is required for the successful arrangement of his murder.[8] Here he is hateful; and so he is in the conversation with the murderers, who are not professional cutthroats but old soldiers, and whom, without a vestige of remorse, he beguiles with calumnies against Banquo and with such appeals as his wife had used to him.[9] On the other

[6]E.g., 1.3.149, where he excuses his abstraction by saying that his "dull brain was wrought with things forgotten," when nothing could be more natural than that he should be thinking of his new honor.

[7]E.g., in 1.4. This is so also in 2.3.110 ff., though here there is some real imaginative excitement mingled with the rhetorical antitheses and balanced clauses and forced bombast.

[8]3.1. Lady Macbeth herself could not more naturally have introduced at intervals the questions. "Ride you this afternoon?" (19), "Is't far you ride?" (23), "Goes Fleance with you?" (35).

[9]We feel here, however, an underlying subdued frenzy which awakes some sympathy. There is an almost unendurable impatience expressed even in the rhythm of many of the lines; e.g.:

> Well then, now
> Have you consider'd of my speeches? Know
> That it was he in the times past which held you

hand, we feel much pity as well as anxiety in the scene (1.7) where she overcomes his opposition to the murder; and we feel it (though his imagination is not specially active) because this scene shows us how little he understands himself. This is his great misfortune here. Not that he fails to realize in reflection the baseness of the deed (the soliloquy with which the scene opens shows that he does not). But he has never, to put it pedantically, accepted as the principle of his conduct the morality which takes shape in his imaginative fears. Had he done so, and said plainly to his wife, "The thing is vile, and, however much I have sworn to do it, I will not," she would have been helpless; for all her arguments proceed on the assumption that there is for them no such point of view. Macbeth does approach this position once, when, resenting the accusation of cowardice, he answers,

> I dare do all that may become a man;
> Who dares do more is none.

She feels in an instant that everything is at stake, and ignoring the point, overwhelms him with indignant and contemptuous personal reproach. But he yields to it because he is himself half-ashamed of that answer of his, and because, for want of habit, the simple idea which it expresses has no hold on him comparable to the force it acquires when it becomes incarnate in visionary fears and warnings.

Yet these were so insistent, and they offered to his ambition a resistance so strong, that it is impossible to regard him

> So under fortune, which you thought had been
> Our innocent self: this I made good to you
> In our last conference, pass'd in probation with you,
> How you were borne in hand, how cross'd, the instruments,
> Who wrought with them, and all things else that might
> To half a soul and to a notion crazed
> Say, "Thus did Banquo."

This effect is heard to the end of the play in Macbeth's less poetic speeches, and leaves the same impression of burning energy, though not of imaginative exaltation, as his great speeches. In these we find either violent, huge, sublime imagery, or a torrent of figurative expressions (as in the famous lines about "the innocent sleep"). Our impressions as to the diction of the play are largely derived from these speeches of the hero, but not wholly so. The writing almost throughout leaves an impression of intense, almost feverish, activity.

as falling through the blindness or delusion of passion. On the contrary, he himself feels with such intensity the enormity of his purpose that, it seems clear, neither his ambition nor yet the prophecy of the Witches would ever without the aid of Lady Macbeth have overcome this feeling. As it is, the deed is done in horror and without the faintest desire or sense of glory—done, one may almost say, as if it were an appalling duty; and, the instant it is finished, its futility is revealed to Macbeth as clearly as its vileness had been revealed beforehand. As he staggers from the scene he mutters in despair,

> Wake Duncan with thy knocking! I would thou could'st.

When, half an hour later, he returns with Lennox from the room of the murder, he breaks out:

> Had I but died an hour before this chance,
> I had lived a blessed time; for from this instant
> There's nothing serious in mortality:
> All is but toys: renown and grace is dead;
> The wine of life is drawn, and the mere lees
> Is left this vault to brag of.

This is no mere acting. The language here has none of the false rhetoric of his merely hypocritical speeches. It is meant to deceive, but it utters at the same time his profoundest feeling. And this he can henceforth never hide from himself for long. However he may try to drown it in further enormities, he hears it murmuring,

> Duncan is in his grave:
> After life's fitful fever he sleeps well:

or,

> better be with the dead:

or,

> I have lived long enough:

and it speaks its last words on the last day of his life:

> Out, out, brief candle!
> Life's but a walking shadow, a poor player
> That struts and frets his hour upon the stage
> And then is heard no more: it is a tale
> Told by an idiot, full of sound and fury,
> Signifying nothing.

How strange that this judgment on life, the despair of a man who had knowingly made mortal war on his own soul, should be frequently quoted as Shakespeare's own judgment, and should even be adduced, in serious criticism, as a proof of his pessimism!

It remains to look a little more fully at the history of Macbeth after the murder of Duncan. Unlike his first struggle this history excites little suspense or anxiety on his account: we have now no hope for him. But it is an engrossing spectacle, and psychologically it is perhaps the most remarkable exhibition of the *development* of a character to be found in Shakespeare's tragedies.

That heartsickness which comes from Macbeth's perception of the futility of his crime, and which never leaves him for long, is not, however, his habitual state. It could not be so, for two reasons. In the first place the consciousness of guilt is stronger in him than the consciousness of failure; and it keeps him in a perpetual agony of restlessness, and forbids him simply to droop and pine. His mind is "full of scorpions." He cannot sleep. He "keeps alone," moody and savage. "All that is within him does condemn itself for being there." There is a fever in his blood which urges him to ceaseless action in the search for oblivion. And, in the second place, ambition, the love of power, the instinct of self-assertion, are much too potent in Macbeth to permit him to resign, even in spirit, the prize for which he has put rancors in the vessel of his peace. The "will to live" is mighty in him. The forces which impelled him to aim at the crown reassert themselves. He faces the world, and his own conscience, desperate, but never dreaming of acknowledging defeat. He will see "the frame of things disjoint" first. He challenges fate into the lists.

The result is frightful. He speaks no more, as before

Duncan's murder, of honor or pity. That sleepless torture, he tells himself, is nothing but the sense of insecurity and the fear of retaliation. If only he were safe, it would vanish. And he looks about for the cause of his fear; and his eye falls on Banquo. Banquo, who cannot fail to suspect him, has not fled or turned against him: Banquo has become his chief counselor. Why? Because, he answers, the kingdom was promised to Banquo's children. Banquo, then, is waiting to attack him, to make a way for them. The "bloody instructions" he himself taught when he murdered Duncan, are about to return, as he said they would, to plague the inventor. *This* then, he tells himself, is the fear that will not let him sleep; and it will die with Banquo. There is no hesitation now, and no remorse: he has nearly learned his lesson. He hastens feverishly, not to murder Banquo, but to procure his murder: some strange idea is in his mind that the thought of the dead man will not haunt him, like the memory of Duncan, if the deed is done by other hands.[10] The deed is done: but, instead of peace descending on him, from the depths of his nature his half-murdered conscience rises; his deed confronts him in the apparition of Banquo's Ghost, and the horror of the night of his first murder returns. But, alas, *it* has less power, and *he* has more will. Agonized and trembling, he still faces this rebel image, and it yields:

> Why, so: being gone,
>   I am a man again.

Yes, but his secret is in the hands of the assembled lords. And, worse, this deed is as futile as the first. For, though Banquo is dead and even his Ghost is conquered, that inner torture is unassuaged. But he will not bear it. His guests have hardly left him when he turns roughly to his wife:

> How say'st thou, that Macduff denies his person
>   At our great bidding?

Macduff it is that spoils his sleep. He shall perish,—he and aught else that bars the road to peace.

[10]See his first words to the Ghost: "Thou canst not say I did it."

> For mine own good
> All causes shall give way: I am in blood
> Stepp'd in so far that, should I wade no more,
> Returning were as tedious as go o'er:
> Strange things I have in head that will to hand,
> Which must be acted ere they may be scann'd.

She answers, sick at heart,

> You lack the season of all natures, sleep.

No doubt: but he has found the way to it now:

> Come, we'll to sleep. My strange and self abuse
> Is the initiate fear that wants hard use:
> We are yet but young in deed.

What a change from the man who thought of Duncan's virtues, and of pity like a naked newborn babe! What a frightful clearness of self-consciousness in this descent to hell, and yet what a furious force in the instinct of life and self-assertion that drives him on!

He goes to seek the Witches. He will know, by the worst means, the worst. He has no longer any awe of them.

> How now, you secret, black and midnight hags!

—so he greets them, and at once he demands and threatens. They tell him he is right to fear Macduff. They tell him to fear nothing, for none of woman born can harm him. He feels that the two statements are at variance; infatuated, suspects no double meaning; but, that he may "sleep in spite of thunder," determines not to spare Macduff. But his heart throbs to know one thing, and he forces from the Witches the vision of Banquo's children crowned. The old intolerable thought returns, "for Banquo's issue have I filed my mind"; and with it, for all the absolute security apparently promised him, there returns that inward fever. Will nothing quiet it?

Nothing but destruction. Macduff, one comes to tell him, has escaped him; but that does not matter: he can still destroy:[11]

> And even now,
> To crown my thoughts with acts, be it thought and done:
> The castle of Macduff I will surprise;
> Seize upon Fife; give to the edge o' the sword
> His wife, his babes, and all unfortunate souls
> That trace him in's line. No boasting like a fool;
> This deed I'll do before this purpose cool.
> But no more sights!

No, he need fear no more "sights." The Witches have done their work, and after this purposeless butchery his own imagination will trouble him no more.[12] He has dealt his last blow at the conscience and pity which spoke through it.

The whole flood of evil in his nature is now let loose. He becomes an open tyrant, dreaded by everyone about him, and a terror to his country. She "sinks beneath the yoke."

> Each new morn
> New widows howl, new orphans cry, new sorrows
> Strike heaven on the face.

[11]For only in destroying I find ease
To my relentless thoughts.—*Paradise Lost,* 9.129.

Milton's portrait of Satan's misery here, and at the beginning of Book 4, might well have been suggested by *Macbeth.* Coleridge, after quoting Duncan's speech, 1.4.35ff., says: "It is a fancy; but I can never read this, and the following speeches of Macbeth, without involuntarily thinking of the Miltonic Messiah and Satan." I doubt if it was a mere fancy. (It will be remembered that Milton thought at one time of writing a tragedy on Macbeth.)

[12]The immediate reference in "But no more sights" is doubtless to the visions called up by the Witches; but one of these, the "blood-bolter'd Banquo," recalls to him the vision of the preceding night, of which he had said,

> You make me strange
> Even to the disposition that I owe,
> When now I think you can behold such *sights,*
> And keep the natural ruby of your cheeks,
> When mine is blanch'd with fear.

She weeps, she bleeds, "and each new day a gash is added to her wounds." She is not the mother of her children, but their grave;

> where nothing,
> But who knows nothing, is once seen to smile:
> Where sighs and groans and shrieks that rend the air
> Are made, not mark'd.

For this wild rage and furious cruelty we are prepared; but vices of another kind start up as he plunges on his downward way.

> I grant him bloody,
> Luxurious, avaricious, false, deceitful,
> Sudden, malicious,

says Malcolm; and two of these epithets surprise us. Who would have expected avarice or lechery[13] in Macbeth? His ruin seems complete.

Yet it is never complete. To the end he never totally loses our sympathy; we never feel towards him as we do to those who appear the born children of darkness. There remains something sublime in the defiance with which, even when cheated of his last hope, he faces earth and hell and heaven. Nor would any soul to whom evil was congenial be capable of that heartsickness which overcomes him when he thinks of the "honor, love, obedience, troops of friends" which "he must not look to have" (and which Iago would never have cared to have), and contrasts with them

> Curses, not loud but deep, mouth-honor, breath,
> Which the poor heart would fain deny, and dare not,

(and which Iago would have accepted with indifference). Neither can I agree with those who find in his reception of the news of his wife's death proof of alienation or utter carelessness. There is no proof of these in the words,

---

[13]"Luxurious" and "luxury" are used by Shakespeare only in this older sense. It must be remembered that these lines are spoken by Malcolm, but it seems likely that they are meant to be taken as true throughout.

> She should have died hereafter;
> There would have been a time for such a word,

spoken as they are by a man already in some measure prepared for such news, and now transported by the frenzy of
his last fight for life. He has no time now to feel.[14] Only,
as he thinks of the morrow when time to feel will come—
if anything comes, the vanity of all hopes and forward-
lookings sinks deep into his soul with an infinite weariness,
and he murmurs,

> Tomorrow, and tomorrow, and tomorrow,
> Creeps in this petty pace from day to day
> To the last syllable of recorded time,
> And all our yesterdays have lighted fools
> The way to dusty death.

In the very depths a gleam of his native love of goodness,
and with it a touch of tragic grandeur, rests upon him. The
evil he has desperately embraced continues to madden or to
wither his inmost heart. No experience in the world could
bring him to glory in it or make his peace with it, or to forget
what he once was and Iago and Goneril never were.

---

[14]I do not at all suggest that his love for his wife remains what it was when
he greeted her with the words "My dearest love, Duncan comes here tonight."
He has greatly changed; she has ceased to help him, sunk in her own despair;
and there is no intensity of anxiety in the questions he puts to the doctor about
her. But his love for her was probably never unselfish, never the love of
Brutus, who, in somewhat similar circumstances, uses, on the death of Cas-
sius, words which remind us of Macbeth's:

> I shall find time, Cassius, I shall find time.

For the opposite strain of feeling cf. Sonnet 90:

> Then hate me if thou wilt; if ever, now,
> Now while the world is bent my deeds to cross.

ELMER EDGAR STOLL

Source and Motive in *Macbeth* and *Othello*

The best tragedy—highest tragedy in short—is that of the worthy encompassed by the inevitable.

— THOMAS HARDY

Shakespeare, of course, has, like the Greeks—unlike the Bourbon French—no *règles,* neither rule nor formula. But for all that, why in *Othello* and *Macbeth,* two of the great tragedies that are not histories and that apparently are not in any measure *rifacimenti* of previous plays, does he, in the matter of motivation, deviate so widely and so similarly from his source?

I

What in *Macbeth* he has omitted and what substituted Sir Arthur Quiller-Couch has made admirably clear, but has not considered the reasons for this or the similarity of procedure in *Othello.* In Holinshed's chronicle there is the suggestion that, cut off by the nomination of Malcolm as successor to the throne from his own expectations, Macbeth had for his usurpation "a juste quarell so to do (as he tooke the matter)." The crown was then not strictly hereditary, and "by the old lawes of the realme, if he that should succeed were not of able age to take the charge upon himselfe, he that was next

From *From Shakespeare to Joyce* by Elmer Edgar Stoll (New York: Doubleday, 1944). Copyright 1944 by Elmer Edgar Stoll. Reprinted by permission of Doubleday and Company, Inc.

of blood should be admitted."[1] "Did Shakespeare use that one hint, enlarge that loophole?" asks Sir Arthur. "He did not."

> Instead of using a paltry chance to condone Macbeth's guilt, he seized on it and plunged it threefold deeper. . . .
>
> He made this man, a sworn soldier, murder Duncan, his liege-lord.
>
> He made this man, a host, murder Duncan, a guest within his gates.
>
> He made this man, strong and hale, murder Duncan, old, weak, asleep and defenceless.
>
> He made this man commit murder for nothing but his own advancement.
>
> He made this man murder Duncan, who had steadily advanced him hitherto, who had never been aught but trustful, and who (that no detail of reproach might be wanting) had that very night, as he retired, sent, in most kindly thought, the gift of a diamond to his hostess.
>
> To sum up: instead of extenuating Macbeth's criminality, Shakespeare doubles and redoubles it. (*Shakespeare's Workmanship* [New York: Holt, 1930], pp. 19–20.)

And yet Macbeth is the protagonist, the hero, with whom as such, for the right tragic effect, there must, naturally, be some large measure of sympathy. So, having thus put him much farther beyond the reach of our sympathy than in the original, what does the dramatist then do but (indirectly) bring him back within it—in general, by the power of poetry, in particular, by the exhibition of the hero's bravery and virtue at the beginning, by emphasizing the influence of the supernatural presented, and of his wife's inordinate ambition distinctly mentioned, in the source.

There are additional devices which Sir Arthur dwells upon, such as the flattening of the other characters—that the hero and heroine may stand out in high relief, to absorb our interest and (presumably on the principle considered in the

---

[1] *Boswell-Stone's Holinshed* (1896), p. 25. Sir Arthur's quotation, preceding, is curtailed: "for that Duncane did what in him lay to defraud him of all maner of title and claime, which he might, in time to come, pretend unto the crowne."

preceding chapter) our sympathy also; and such as the keeping of the murders, as the ancients do, in the background, off the stage. "There is some deep law in imaginative illusion," says Watts-Dunton,[2] "whereby the identification of the spectator's personality is with the active character in most dramatic actions rather than the passive." We share the emotions, the perturbations, of Macbeth and his Lady, as even of Clytemnestra and Phaedra, because they are the impassioned doers and speakers, constantly in the foreground; and it is with their ears that we hear the owl and the cricket, the voices in the castle and the knocking at the gate. And still more clearly than in the veiling of the horrors the method is that of the ancients. The central complication—the contrast—is that recommended by Aristotle,[3] the *good* man doing the dreadful deed, though not unwittingly, nor quite unwillingly either. As with the ancients, again, he is under the sway of fate; for the Weird Sisters and his Lady—"burning in unquenchable desire to beare the name of a queene"[4] —together amount to that.

This, of course, is not what we ordinarily call motivation, not psychology. For both—the narrative or external motivation and the internal—there was, positively and negatively, better provision in Holinshed—not only the "juste quarell (as he tooke the matter)" but also "the feeble and slouthfull administration of Duncane,"[5] no treachery or violation of the laws of hospitality in the killing, and the just and efficient rule (for ten years) in the sequel.[6] *La carrière ouverte aux talents,* and Macbeth had the justification of Napoleon, of Cromwell. But not Shakespeare's Macbeth.

Nor is this what we call drama, either, as it is ordinarily practiced today. It is as in Aristotle—situation first and motivation or psychology afterwards, if at all. The effect is emotional, with which psychology or even simple narrative coherence often considerably interferes. To Schiller's

[2]*Harper's* (November, 1906), p. 818.
[3]*Poetics, cap.* 13, 14.
[4]*Boswell-Stone's Holinshed*, p.25.
[5]*Ibid.,* p. 32. Cf. p. 20: "At length, Macbeth speaking much against the kings softnes and overmuch slacknesse in punishing offenders."
[6]*Ibid.,* p. 32: "he set his whole intention to maintaine justice and to punish all enormities and abuses which had chanced," etc. "made manie holesome laws and statutes for the publike weale."

neglect of careful motivation, and in a day of psychology and philosophy both, Goethe even attributes his superiority on the stage.[7] Shakespeare sometimes neglects it because it can be counted upon as familiar; sometimes, as with Hamlet's feigning of lunacy and Lear's dividing of the kingdom, because, the motive in the old play not being a good one, it is better that it should be omitted or only hinted at; but in *Macbeth* the omission is for a positive purpose, and the contravention of psychological probability is so as well. Here, as generally in Shakespeare, *Coriolanus* being only a partial exception, character is not its own destiny, the action is not exclusively derived from it. For Shakespeare "a human being" is *not,* as in Galsworthy's words or as in his own and his fellows' practice, "the best plot there is." To his minor characters the words better apply. The hero's conduct, at the heart of the action, is often not in keeping with his essential nature but in contrast with it.

Manifestly, and, if not forthwith, certainly upon a moment's consideration, by all the motives prompting or circumstances attending the murder of Duncan that have been omitted, the big, sharply outlined, highly emotional contrast in the situation of a good man doing the deed of horror would be broken or obscured. If Macbeth had been thwarted or (to use Holinshed's word) "defrauded," as having, at this juncture, a better title to the throne than Malcolm, or had thought himself better fitted to rule; or, again, if Duncan had not borne his faculties so meek and been so clear in his great office, as in the tragedy but not the chronicle he is; why, then, Macbeth's conduct in killing him would have been more reasonable and more psychologically in keeping, to be sure, but less terrible, less truly tragic. Even if Duncan had been less affectionate and generous, less admiring and confiding, still the hero's conduct would have been less truly tragic! There is positive need of "the deep damnation of his taking-off" (1.7.20). For the tragedy is of the brave and honorable man suddenly and squarely—fatally, too—turned against the moral order. Sir Arthur compares him to Satan about to engage in the temptation: "Evil, be thou my good."

[7]Eckermann (Castle), I, 400.

Or "Fair is foul and foul is fair" (1.1.10) as the Weird Sisters
have it, which Macbeth on his first appearance echoes—

> So foul and fair a day I have not seen.   (1.3.38)

And that situation, no question, is a contrast big and sharp
enough.

Sir Arthur does not, indeed, pause to take notice how
unpsychological the change here is. Others besides fallen
archangels have so turned about, but evil they do not continue to call evil. Macbeth so does. He has scarcely a word
of ambition beforehand, not a word of delight in the power
when attained. As Mr. Firkins and even Mr. Bradley have
noticed, it is the deterrents that he dwells upon, not the
incentives; it is the spectral bloody dagger that he sees, not
a glittering crown; it is "withered murder" that he follows to
the chamber, not the call to sovereign sway and masterdom.
In horror he commits the crime, even as he is to remember
it. There is no satisfaction but only torment in the thought
of it. The conscience in him, before and after, is that of a
good man, not that of the man who can do such wickedness;
first the voice of God, then either that or else—"accuser of
mankind"!—the devil's. It is Macbeth himself that considers the "deep damnation," and neither before nor after
does he deceive himself, as the good turning to wickedness
necessarily do. But the contrast is kept clear and distinct;
and the emotional effect—that the whole world has
acknowledged.

If, on the other hand, Shakespeare had kept to history, to
reality and psychology! If he had followed Holinshed—
made more of Macbeth's grievances, dilated on Duncan's
unfitness and his own fitness to rule, without bringing on his
head the blood of an old man, asleep, his benefactor and
guest! If he had dwelt on reasons for committing instead of
not committing the crime! And if afterwards he had expressed the psychologically natural or appropriate opinions
upon his own conduct, excusing or palliating it, perhaps
even justifying it! If in short Macbeth (and his Lady, too,
who invokes the powers of evil at the outset and is tormented
by conscience at the end) had acted more like the human

beings we know of; why, then we should have had decidedly less of contrast and excitement, of imaginative and emotional power generated and discharged, of poetry and drama.

II

The treatment of the material in *Othello*, probably an earlier play, is somewhat the same. In Cinthio there is no warrant for introducing the supernatural; but in Shakespeare's hands the villain takes the place of Fate—of the Weird Sisters and the Lady—and more completely than is usual in the tragedy of the Renaissance. He is a devil in the flesh, as Booth played him, as Coleridge and Lamb implied, and George Woodberry, J. J. Chapman, Lytton Strachey, John Palmer, not to mention others, have put it explicitly.[8] Iago himself practically acknowledges it in the soliloquies— "Hell and night," "Divinity of hell! When devils will the blackest sins put on" (1.3.394; 2.3.350–51)—and on that point apparently he and Othello at the end are agreed:

> *Othello.* If that thou be'st a devil, I cannot kill thee.
>
> [*Wounds Iago.*]
>
> *Iago.*   I bleed, sir, but not kill'd.
>
> (5.2.283–84)

Before that, to be sure, the Ancient is misapprehended by everybody; yet as Fate, as master of the show, he is holding nearly all the strings of the action in hand, and leading both heroine and hero to destruction. In the victim now, not the victimizer, is the great change; but from good to evil only under a complete delusion—"be thou my good" he neither says nor thinks, and the prince of villains himself has no need to say it. For again, as in *Macbeth*, the motives are dispensed with. The Ensign of the *novella* is deprived of the internal incentives to his wickedness, and the Moor relieved of the traits which might have provoked or somewhat warranted it.

As Professor Wolfgang Keller notices, the villainy is "better motived" in the source. That is, more plausibly, more

---

[8]For their opinions see my *Shakespeare and Other Masters*, pp. 233, 238, 243–44.

realistically. Not a devil in the flesh, a "black angel," as Mr. Chapman calls him, Cinthio's Ensign is still of "the most depraved nature in the world" (*della più scelerata natura che mai fosse huomo del mondo*). But as such he has provocation enough. He is rejected suitor, and really suspects the Captain (Shakespeare's Cassio) of being the favored one. Against both him and the lady he has a grudge; his love for her is turned to the "bitterest hate"; whereas in the tragedy his love for Desdemona and her intrigue with Cassio are, like Cassio's and Othello's with Emilia, pretexts and afterthoughts. There he has need of these. His genuine reason for resentment is against Othello, but only for promoting Cassio above him, and against Cassio (incidentally) for being promoted. In soliloquy, as always in drama, the truth will out. "I hate the Moor," he mutters,

> *And it is thought* abroad that 'twixt my sheets
> H'as done my office. (1.3.377–79)

And the next moment the pretext is made still plainer: "I know not if't be true, but I, for mere suspicion in that kind, will do, as if for surety."[9]

So the Ensign is deprived of his motive as much as the Thane of Glamis—as much as Richard III of his, which was ambition, or as Goneril and Regan of theirs, which was envy,[10]—but without an external Fate to relieve him of the burden of his iniquity. He carries it indeed, like the Weird Sisters, lightly enough; and the Aristotelian contrast of the good man doing the deed of horror is presented in his victim, who, however, unlike Macbeth, is guilty only of a mistake in judgment—the *hamartia*—and is far from uttering Satan's cry. Othello never loses our sympathy, as Macbeth, despite the poignant presentation of his sufferings, cannot but in some measure do.

What is almost quite as important to the emotional effect—to the steep tragic contrast—as the apparently un-

---

[9]Cf. *Shakespeare and Other Masters*, pp. 236–38, for the way that his suspicions become convictions.

[10]In the old *King Leir*, envy of Cordelia's beauty, cf. E. E. Kellett, *Suggestions* (1923), p. 38. For Richard, cf. Brandl, *Shakespeare* (1937), p. 120.

mitigated wickedness of Iago, is, as in the Caledonian tragedy, the nature of the victim and the circumstances of the crime. As we have seen, Shakespeare's Moor has changed places with his wife in the villain's enmity. Love turned to hatred is too ambiguous and appealing a passion—it is that, moreover, into which the Moor himself is precipitated, and, as Strachey observes, the villain's must not be anything of a parallel. For the contrast, again, it must not be. Moreover, though Cinthio's Moor is given some noble and attractive traits, especially at the outset, Shakespeare's is both there and throughout on a far higher level of intelligence and feeling. He is not a stupid dupe or a vulgarly vindictive cuckold. He is not the man to call the informer in to do the killing, or the concealing of it afterwards. For his own safety, Shakespeare's, unlike Cinthio's Moor, shows no concern. Nor is there, for that matter, the slightest evidence in his conduct or his utterance, nor in the woman's either, of the love Iago suspects between him and Emilia—no more than there is in Iago's own conduct or utterance, indeed, of his own love for Desdemona—though of late there has been a fairly prominent critic to say there is.[11] That would be like thinking, with some Germans, that Hamlet had betrayed Ophelia, for which, to be sure, there is a little evidence, though far from enough; or with some Frenchmen, that Lady Macbeth as, re-enacting in memory the deed of blood, she whispers, "To bed, to bed! There's knocking at the gate . . . to bed, to bed, to bed" (5.1.69–72), she, having enticed her husband, is now for rewarding him. On the contrary, the black man is made the grandest and noblest of Shakespeare's lovers; and it is only through Iago's overwhelming reputation for honesty and sagacity, the impenetrableness of his mask together with the potency of his seductive arts, that he is led astray and succumbs. For the highest tragic effect it is the great and good man that succumbs. Like other

[11]It is of course not enough to urge the probabilities upon us—that a healthy and vigorous soldier of the time would lead "a *man's* life," and that Emilia was none too good for taking up with him. As I have repeatedly reminded my readers, no character in fiction has a private life, beyond the reach of the writer, which a character in a biography or history, on the other hand, has, not being the writer's own creation. And in Shakespearean drama, as in the ancient or the classical French, none has the "past" or the "love life" that is more readily expected, and so more easily suggested, today.

supreme artists, Shakespeare has here created his own world, which holds together. Like Corneille (*les grands sujets de la tragédie doivent toujours aller au delà du vraisemblable*) Goethe holds that *in den höheren Regionen des künstlerischen Verfahrens, hat der Künstler ein freieres Spiel, und er darf sogar zu Fiktionen schreiten.*[12] This Shakespeare boldly does. No one else sees through Iago, including his own wife; so Othello, for not seeing, is no gull or dupe. In the matter of the Ancient's cleverness in maneuver and also of his success in hypocrisy the English is a little indebted to the Italian writer; but the Ensign's wife does see through him and only for fear of him holds her tongue.

III

In both *Macbeth* and *Othello,* then, it is the whole situation that is mainly important, not the character; it is the reciprocal matter of motivation (whether present or missing), of defects or qualities in both victim and victimizer together. Here lies the chief point of the present discussion. What if Shakespeare's Macbeth and Duncan had been like Holinshed's, or like Henry IV and Richard II, or like Cromwell and Charles I? And as I have elsewhere said, "How the scope and stature of Iago's wickedness (and of Othello's virtue) would be limited by any adequate grudge!"[13] How they would be also by a credulous or suspicious nature—a predisposition or a psychology—in the hero! Against that Shakespeare has guarded not only by Iago's impregnable reputation and by his all-prevailing arts but also by Othello's own reputation for capability and for virtue. (A world of reputation and circumstance here, not of motive!) Before the temptation begins, as in *Macbeth*, but much more fully and felicitously, the Moor has not only in his own right but through the admiration of everybody (and here even of the villain) been firmly established in our good opinion and our sympathies. So with Desdemona, too, and she is not deceitful or supersubtle as Mr. Shaw would have her, not enough so "to strengthen the case for Othello's jealousy"; the

---

[12]Eckermann, April 18, 1827.—I hope Corneille here does not go beyond the endurable.

[13]*Shakespeare and Other Masters*, p. 245.

dramatic preparations are emotional, not analytical and psychological, primarily for the situation, not the character. And both women, Emilia at the last and Desdemona once the action is well started, are shocked at the discoveries they make in their husbands. But she is justified, when hers gives signs of jealousy, in being unable to believe it; "not easily jealous" (5.2.341) he himself says (where a Shakespearean hero, or his best friend, is expected to know and everything comes to light) at the end. Even Iago, hearing that Othello is angry, exclaims,

> and is he angry?
> Something of moment then. I will go meet him.
> There's matter in't indeed if he be angry.   (3.4.137–39)

And in the fourth act, when the jealous rage is fully upon him, Lodovico, newly come from Venice, is moved to wonder and to grief.

> Is this the nature
> Whom passion could not shake? whose solid virtue
> The shot of accident nor dart of chance
> Could neither graze nor pierce?   (4.1.265–68)

"He is much changed," Iago coolly, and still not superfluously, replies. So he is, until, in the last scene, by Emilia's disclosures and Iago's self-betraying resentment, he recovers something of his old stately and generous self.

Macbeth too is changed, but for once and all. Othello had suffered from an overpowering delusion, and has just now, he thinks, performed an act of justice. Macbeth, not deluded, has come under the dominion of evil, his "eternal jewel given to the common enemy of man." Neither change is probable. In neither is there much of what can be called psychology. In life neither person would really have done what he did. In both tragedy and comedy, however, that is not exactly what is to be expected: for a Henry IV, a Cromwell, we should turn to history, not the stage. What is expected is what from life we do not get—enlargement, excitement, another world, not a copy of this. And that airy edifice, an imaginative structure, is the emotionally consistent story or situation as a whole—the conduct of characters both active and passive, perhaps also a motiving both external and internal, but in any case an interplay of relations or circumstances as important as the motives themselves; not to mention the apportionment of emphasis or relief whether in the framework or the expression, the poetry that informs both, and the individuality of the speech, which, real, though poetical, leads one to accept and delight in the improbable things said or done. "It is when their minds [those of the audience] are preoccupied with his personality," says Dr. Bridges of Macbeth, "that the actions follow as unquestionable realities."[14] Not merely, that is, when the actions proceed from the character; and the convincing quality of the speech is only a participating element in the consistent overpowering imaginative and emotional effect of the whole.

IV

"In tragedy and comedy both," I have said elsewhere, "life must be, as it has ever been, piled on life, or we have visited the theater in vain." It is not primarily to present characters in their convincing reality that Shakespeare and the Greeks have written, nor in an action strictly and wholly of their doing, but to set them in a state of high commotion, and thus to move and elevate the audience in turn. And here I fall back upon the authority of Mr. Santayana, a philosopher (but also a poet and critic) who, without my knowledge until of late,[15] expressed, though from a different point of view, similar opinions before me:

> Aristotle was justified in making the plot the chief element in fiction; for it is by virtue of the plot that the characters live, or, rather, that we live in them, and by virtue of the plot accordingly that our soul rises to the imaginative activity by which we tend at once to escape from the personal life and to realise its ideal. . . .

[14]*The Influence of the Audience on Shakespeare's Drama.*
[15]*Poetry and Religion* (1900). Cf. my *Shakespeare and Other Masters*, p. 369. The passage here quoted is as in the *Works* (New York: Scribner, 1936) ii. Cf. my "Plot and Character," to appear.

And as the eminent critic proceeds, he maintains that poetry is not

> at its best when it depicts a further possible experience, but when it initiates us, by feigning something which as an experience is impossible, into the meaning of the experience which we have actually had.

And that is partly because "in the theater," as the producer Mr. Robert Edmond Jones has assured us, "the actual thing is never the exciting thing. Unless life is turned into art on the stage it stops being alive and goes dead."[16] It is by the excitement that the meaning is brought home to us. And that is true ... even without a stage or without poetry, as in Dickens, who, according to Chesterton, "could only make his characters probable if he was allowed to make them impossible."

[16]*The Dramatic Imagination* (1941), p. 82 (quoted by W. W. Lawrence, *Modern Language Review* [October, 1942] 424).

General Macbeth

He is a general and has just won a battle; he enters the scene making a remark about the weather. "So fair and foul a day I have not seen." On this flat note Macbeth's character tone is set. "Terrible weather we're having." "The sun can't seem to make up its mind." "Is it hot/cold/wet enough for you?" A commonplace man who talks in commonplaces, a golfer, one might guess, on the Scottish fairways, Macbeth is the only Shakespeare hero who corresponds to a bourgeois type: a murderous Babbitt, let us say.

You might argue just the opposite, that Macbeth is over-imaginative, the prey of visions. It is true that he is impressionable. Banquo, when they come upon the witches, amuses himself at their expense, like a man of parts idly chaffing a fortune-teller. Macbeth, though, is deeply impressed. "Thane of Cawdor and King." He thinks this over aloud. "How can I be Thane of Cawdor when the Thane of Cawdor is alive?" When this mental stumbling block has been cleared away for him (the Thane of Cawdor has received a death sentence), he turns his thoughts *sotto voce* to the next question. "How can I be king when Duncan is alive?" The answer comes back, "Kill him." It does fleetingly occur to Macbeth, as it would to most people, to leave matters alone and let destiny work it out. "If chance will have me king, why, chance may crown me, without my stir." But this goes against his grain. A reflective man might wonder how fate would spin her plot, as the Virgin Mary

From *Harper's Magazine* (June, 1962). Copyright © 1962 by Mary Mc-Carthy. Reprinted by permission of Mary McCarthy.

wondered after the Angel Gabriel's visit. But Macbeth does not trust to fate, that is, to the unknown, the mystery of things; he trusts only to a known quantity—himself—to put the prophecy into action. In short, he has no faith, which requires imagination. He is literal-minded; that, in a word, is his "tragedy" and his tragedy.

It was not *his* idea, he could plead in self-defense, but the witches', that he should have the throne. *They* said it first. But the witches only voiced a thought that was already in his mind; after all, he was Duncan's cousin and close to the crown. And once the thought has been put into *words*, he is in a scrambling hurry. He cannot wait to get home to tell his wife about the promise; in his excitement, he puts it in a letter, which he sends on ahead, like a businessman briefing an associate on a piece of good news for the firm.

Lady Macbeth—has this been noted?—takes very little stock in the witches. She never pesters her husband, as most wives would, with questions about the Weird Sisters: "What did they say, exactly?" "How did they look?" "Are you sure?" She is less interested in "fate and metaphysical aid" than in the business at hand—how to nerve her husband to do what he wants to do. And later, when Macbeth announces that he is going out to consult the Weird Sisters again, she refrains from comment. As though she were keeping her opinion—"O proper stuff!"—to herself. Lady Macbeth is not superstitious. Macbeth is. This makes her repeatedly impatient with him, for Macbeth, like many men of his sort, is an old story to his wife. A tale full of sound and fury signifying nothing. Her contempt for him perhaps extends even to his ambition. "Wouldst not play false, And yet wouldst wrongly win." As though to say, "All right, if that's what you want, have the courage to get it." Lady Macbeth does not so much give the impression of coveting the crown herself as of being weary of watching Macbeth covet it. Macbeth, by the way, is surely her second husband (she has "given suck" and Macbeth "has no children"), and either her first husband was a better man than he, which galls her, or he was just another general, another superstitious golfer, which would gall her too.

Superstition here is the opposite of reason on the one hand

and of imagination on the other. Macbeth is credulous, in contrast to Lady Macbeth, to Banquo, and, later, to Malcolm, who sets the audience an example of the right way by mistrusting Macduff until he has submitted him to an empirical test. Believing and knowing are paired in Malcolm's mind; what he *knows* he believes. Macbeth's eagerness to believe is the companion of his lack of faith. If all works out right for him in this world, Macbeth says, he can skip the next ("We'd jump the life to come"). Superstition whispers when true religion has been silenced, and Macbeth becomes the butt of his own know-nothing materialism incarnate in the jeering witches on the heath.

As in his first interview with them he is too quick to act literally on a dark saying, in the second he is too easily reassured. He will not be conquered till "Great Birnam Wood to High Dunsinane shall come against him." "Why, that can never happen!" he cries out in immediate relief, his brow clearing.

It never enters his mind to examine the saying more closely, test it, so to speak, for a double bottom, as was common in those days (Banquo even points this out to him) with prophetic utterances, which were known to be ambiguous and tricky. Any child knew that a prophecy often meant the reverse of what it seemed to say, and any man of imagination would ask himself how Birnam Wood *might* come to Dunsinane and take measures to prevent it, as King Laius took measures to prevent his own death by arranging to have the baby Oedipus killed. If Macbeth had thought it out, he could have had Birnam Wood chopped down and burned on the spot and the ashes dumped into the sea. True, the prophecy might still have turned against him (since destiny cannot be avoided and the appointment will be kept at Samarra), but that would have been another story, another tragedy, the tragedy of a clever man not clever enough to circumvent fate. Macbeth is not clever; he is taken in by surfaces, by appearance. He cannot think beyond the usual course of things. As with "No man of woman born." All men, he says to himself, sagely, are born of women; Malcolm and Macduff are men; therefore I am safe. This logic leaves out of account the extraordinary: the man brought into the world by Caesarean section. In the same way, it

leaves out of account the supernatural—the very forces he is
trafficking with. He might be overcome by an angel or a
demon, as well as by Macduff.

Yet this pedestrian general sees ghosts and imaginary
daggers in the air. Lady Macbeth does not, and this tendency
in her husband grates on her nerves; she is sick of his terrors
and fancies. A practical woman, Lady Macbeth, more a
partner than a wife, though Macbeth treats her with a
trite domestic fondness—"Love," "Dearest love," "Dearest
chuck," "Sweet remembrancer." These endearments, this
middle-aged, middle-class cuddliness, as though he called
her "Honeybunch" or "Sweetheart," as well as the obliga-
tory "Dear," are a master stroke of Shakespeare's and perfectly in keeping with the prosing about the weather, the
heavy credulousness.

Naturally Macbeth is dominated by his wife. He is old
Iron Pants in the field (as she bitterly reminds him), but at
home she has to wear the pants; she has to unsex herself. No
"chucks" or "dearests" escape her tightened lips, and yet she
is more feeling, more human at bottom than Macbeth. She
thinks of her father when she sees the old King asleep, and
this natural thought will not let her kill him. Macbeth has to
do it, just as the quailing husband of any modern virago is
sent down to the basement to kill a rat or drown a set of kit-
tens. An image of her father, irrelevant to her purpose,
softens this monster woman; sleepwalking, she thinks of
Lady Macduff. "The Thane of Fife had a wife. Where is she
now?" Stronger than Macbeth, less suggestible, she is nevertheless imaginative, where he is not. She does not see ghosts
and daggers; when she sleepwalks, it is simple reality that
haunts her—the crime relived. "Who would have thought
the old man to have had so much blood in him?" Over and
over, the details of the crime repeat themselves on the screen
of her consciousness. This nightly reliving is not penitence
but more terrible—remorse, the agenbite of the restless
deed. Lady Macbeth's uncontrollable imagination drives her
to put herself in the place of others—the wife of the Thane
of Fife—and to recognize a kinship between all human kind:
the pathos of old age in Duncan makes her think, "Why, he
might be my father!" This sense of a natural bond among
men opens her to contrition—sorrowing with. To ask whe-

ther, waking, she is "sorry" for what she has done is imper-
tinent. She lives with it and it kills her.

Macbeth has absolutely no feeling for others, except
envy, a common middle-class trait. He *envies* the murdered
Duncan his rest, which is a strange way of looking at your
victim. What he suffers on his own account after the crimes
is simple panic. He is never contrite or remorseful; it is not
the deed but a shadow of it, Banquo's spook, that appears
to him. The "scruples" that agitate him before Duncan's
murder are mere echoes of conventional opinion, of what
might be *said* about his deed: that Duncan was his king, his
cousin, and a guest under his roof. "I have bought golden
opinions," he says to himself (note the verb), "from all sorts
of people"; now these people may ask for their opinions
back if they suspect him of the murder. It is like a business
firm's being reluctant to part with its "goodwill"—an asset.
The fact that Duncan was such a good king bothers him, and
why? Because there will be universal grief at his death. But
his chief "scruple" is even simpler. "If we should fail?" he
says timidly to Lady Macbeth. Sweet chuck tells him that
they will not. Yet once she has ceased to be effectual as a
partner, Dearest love is an embarrassment. He has no time
for her; she should have died hereafter. That is, when he was
not so busy. Again the general is speaking.

The idea of Macbeth as a conscience-tormented man is a
platitude as false as Macbeth himself. Macbeth has no conscience. His main concern throughout the play is that most
selfish of all concerns: to get a good night's sleep. His invocation to sleep, while heartfelt, is perfectly conventional;
sleep builds you up, enables you to start the day fresh. Thus
the virtue of having a good conscience is seen by him in
terms of bodily hygiene, as if it were a Simmons mattress or
an electric blanket. Lady Macbeth shares these preoccupa-
tions. When he tells her he is going to see the witches, she
remarks that he needs sleep.

Her wifely concern is mechanical and far from real solici-
tude. She is aware of Macbeth; she *knows* him (he does not
know her at all, apparently), but she regards him coldly as a
thing, a tool that must be oiled and polished. His soul-states
do not interest her; her attention is narrowed on his morale,
his public conduct, the shifting expressions of his face. But

in a sense she is right, for there is nothing to Macbeth but fear and ambition, both of which he tries to hide, except from her. This naturally gives her a poor opinion of the inner man.

Why is it, though, that Lady Macbeth seems to us a monster while Macbeth does not? Partly because she is a woman and has "unsexed" herself, which makes her a monster by definition. Also because the very prospect of murder quickens an hysterical excitement in her, like the discovery of some object in a shop—a set of emeralds or a sable stole—which Macbeth can give her and which will be an "outlet" for all the repressed desires he cannot satisfy. She behaves as though Macbeth, through his weakness, will deprive her of self-realization; the unimpeded exercise of her will is the voluptuous end she seeks. That is why she makes naught of scruples, as inner brakes on her throbbing engines. Unlike Macbeth, she does not pretend to harbor a conscience, though this, on her part, by a curious turn, *is* a pretense, as the sleepwalking scene reveals. After the first crime, her will subsides, spent; the devil has brought her to climax and left her.

Macbeth is not a monster, like Richard III or Iago or Iachimo, though in the catalogue he might go for one because of the blackness of his deeds. But his deeds are only the wishes and fears of the average, undistinguished man translated halfheartedly into action. Pure evil is a kind of transcendence that he does not aspire to. He only wants to be king and sleep the sleep of the just, undisturbed. He could never have been a good man, even if he had not met the witches; hence we cannot see him as a devil incarnate, for the devil is a fallen angel. Macbeth does not fall; if anything, he somewhat improves as the result of his career of crime. He throws off his dependency and thus achieves the "greatness" he mistakenly sought in worldly symbols.

The isolation of Macbeth, which is at once a punishment and a tragic dignity or honor, takes place by stages and by deliberate choice; it begins when he does not tell Lady Macbeth that he has decided to kill Banquo and reaches its height in the final action. Up to this time, though he has cut himself off from all human contacts, he is relying on the witches as a substitute. When he first hears the news that Macduff is not "of woman born," he is unmanned; everything he trusted (the literal word) has betrayed him, and he screams in terror, "I'll not fight with thee!" But Macduff's taunts make a man of him; he cannot die like this, shamed. His death is his first act of courage, though even here he has had to be pricked to it by mockery, Lady Macbeth's old spur. Nevertheless, weaned by his very crimes from dependency, nursed in a tyrant's solitude, he meets death on his own, without metaphysical aid. "Lay on, Macduff."

What is modern and bourgeois in Macbeth's character is his wholly *social* outlook. He has no feeling for others, and yet until the end he is a vicarious creature, existing in his own eyes through others, through what they may say of him, through what they tell him or promise him. This paradox is typical of the social being—at once a wolf out for himself, and a sheep. Macbeth, moreover, is an expert buckpasser; he sees how others can be used. It is he, not Lady Macbeth, who thinks of smearing the drunken chamberlains with blood, so that they shall be caught "red-handed" the next morning when Duncan's murder is discovered. At this idea he brightens; suddenly, he sees his way clear. It is the moment when at last he decides. The eternal executive, ready to fix responsibility on a subordinate, has seen the deed finally take a *recognizable* form. Now he can do it. And the crackerjack thought of killing the grooms afterwards (dead men tell no tales—old adage) is again purely his own on-the-spot inspiration; no credit to Lady Macbeth.

It is the sort of thought that would have come to Claudius in *Hamlet*, another trepidant executive. Indeed, Macbeth is more like Claudius than like any other character in Shakespeare. Both are doting husbands; both rose to power by betraying their superior's trust; both are easily frightened and have difficulty saying their prayers. Macbeth's "Amen" sticks in his throat, he complains, and Claudius, on his knees, sighs that he cannot make what priests call a "good act of contrition." The desire to say his prayers like any pewholder, quite regardless of his horrible crime, is merely a longing for respectability. Macbeth "repents" killing the grooms, but this is strictly for public consumption. "O, yet I do repent me of my fury, That I did kill them." In fact, it is the one deed he does *not* repent (i.e., doubt the wisdom of) either before or after. This hypocritical self-accusation, which is his sidelong way of announcing the embarrassing fact that he has just done away with the grooms, and his simulated grief at Duncan's murder ("All is but toys. Renown and grace is dead, The wine of life is drawn," etc.) are his basest moments in the play, as well as his boldest; here is nearly a magnificent monster.

The dramatic effect, too, is one of great boldness on Shakespeare's part. Macbeth is speaking pure Shakespearean poetry, but in his mouth, since we know he is lying, it turns into facile verse, Shakespearean poetry parodied. The same with "Here lay Duncan, his silver skin laced with his golden blood. . . ." If the image were given to Macduff, it would be uncontaminated poetry; from Macbeth it is "proper stuff"—fustian. This opens the perilous question of sincerity in the arts: is a line of verse altered for us by the sincerity of the poet (or speaker)? In short, is poetry relative to the circumstances or absolute? Or, more particularly, are Macbeth's soliloquies poetry, which they sound like, or something else? Did Shakespeare intend to make Macbeth a poet, like Hamlet, Lear, and Othello? In that case, how can Macbeth be an unimaginative mediocrity? My opinion is that Macbeth's soliloquies are not poetry but rhetoric. They are tirades. That is, they do not trace any pensive motion of the soul or heart but are a volley of words discharged. Macbeth is neither thinking nor feeling aloud; he is declaiming. Like so many unfeeling men, he has a facile emotionalism, which he turns on and off. Not that his fear is insincere, but his loss of control provides him with an excuse for histrionics.

These gibberings exasperate Lady Macbeth. "What do you mean?" she says coldly after she has listened to a short harangue on "Methought I heard a voice cry 'Sleep no more.' " It is an allowable question—what *does* he mean? And his funeral oration on *her*, if she could have heard it, would have brought her back to life to protest. "She should have died hereafter"—fine, that was the real Macbeth. But then, as if conscious of the proprieties, he at once begins on a series of bromides ("Tomorrow and tomorrow . . .") that he seems to have had ready to hand for the occasion like a black mourning suit. All Macbeth's soliloquies have that ready-to-hand, if not hand-me-down, air, which is perhaps why they are given to schoolchildren to memorize, often with the result of making them hate Shakespeare. What children resent in these soliloquies is precisely their sententiousness—the sound they have of being already memorized from a copybook.

Macbeth's speeches often recall the Player's speech in *Hamlet*—Shakespeare's example of how-not-to-do-it. He tears a passion to tatters. He has a rather Senecan rhetoric, the fustian of the time; in the dagger speech, for example, he works in Hecate, Tarquin, and the wolf—recherché embellishment for a man who is about to commit a real murder. His taste for hyperbole goes with a habit of euphuism, as when he calls the sea "the green one." And what of the remarkable line just preceding, "the multitudinous seas incarnadine," with its onomatopoeia of the crested waves rising in the *t*'s and *d*'s of "multitudinous" and subsiding in the long swell of the verb? This is sometimes cited as an example of pure poetry, which it would be in an anthology of isolated lines, but in the context, dramatically, it is bombast, a kind of stuffing or padding.

The play between poetry and rhetoric, the *conversion* of poetry to rhetoric, is subtle and horrible in *Macbeth*, being itself a subversive process or treasonous manipulation. The suggestion seems to be that poetry used for an ulterior purpose (as Macbeth uses it) turns into rhetoric. Macbeth is the perfect utilitarian. If an explanation is needed, you might say he learned to *use* words through long practice in haranguing his troops, whipping them and himself into battle frenzy. Up to recent times a fighting general, like a football coach, was an orator.

But it must be noted that it is not only Macbeth who rants. Nor is it only Macbeth who talks about the weather. The play is stormy with atmosphere—the screaming and shrieking of owls, the howling of winds. Nature herself is ranting, like the witches, and Night, black Hecate, is queen of the scene. Bats are flitting about; ravens and crows are hoarse; the house-martin's nests on the battlements of Macbeth's castle give a misleading promise of peace and gentle domesticity. "It will be rain tonight," says Banquo simply, looking at the sky (note the difference between this and Macbeth's pompous generality), and the First Murderer growls at him, striking, "Let it come down." The disorder of Nature, as so often in Shakespeare, presages and reflects the disorder of the body politic. Guilty Macbeth cannot sleep, but the night of Duncan's murder, the whole house, as if guilty too, is restless; Malcolm and Donalbain talk and laugh in their sleep; the drunken porter, roused, plays that he is gatekeeper of hell.

Indeed, the whole action takes place in a kind of hell and is pitched to the demons' shriek of hyperbole. This would appear to be a peculiar setting for a study of the commonplace. But only at first sight. The fact that an ordinary philistine like Macbeth goes on the rampage and commits a series of murders is a sign that human nature, like Nature, is capable of any mischief if left to its "natural" self. The witches, unnatural beings, are Nature spirits, stirring their snake-filet and owl's wing, newt's eye and frog toe in a camp stew: earthy ingredients boil down to an unearthly broil. It is the same with the man Macbeth. Ordinary ambition, fear, and a kind of stupidity make a deadly combination. Macbeth, a self-made king, is not kingly, but simply the original Adam, the social animal, and Lady Macbeth is Mother Eve.

There is no play of Shakespeare's (I think) that contains the words *Nature* and *natural* so many times, and the word *Nature* within the same speech can mean first something good and then something evil, as though it were a pun. Nature is two-sided, double-talking, like the witches. "Fair is foul and foul is fair," they cry, and Macbeth enters the play unconsciously echoing them, for he is never original but chock-full of the "milk of human kindness," which does not mean kindness in the modern sense but simply human "nature," human kind. The play is about Nature, and its blind echo, human nature.

Macbeth, in short, shows life in the cave. Without religion, animism rules the outer world, and without faith, the human soul is beset by hobgoblins. This at any rate was Shakespeare's opinion, to which modern history, with the return of the irrational in the Fascist nightmare and its new specters of Communism, Socialism, etc., lends support. It is a troubling thought that Macbeth, of all Shakespeare's characters, should seem the most "modern," the only one you could transpose into contemporary battle dress or a sport shirt and slacks.

The contemporary Macbeth, a churchgoer, is indifferent to religion, to the categorical imperative or any group of principles that may be held to stand above and govern human behavior. Like the old Macbeth, he'd gladly skip the future life, not only for himself but for the rest of humanity. He listens to soothsayers and prophets and has been out on the heath and in the desert, interfering with Nature on a grand scale, lest his rivals for power get ahead of him and Banquo's stock, instead of his, inherit the earth—why this should have seemed such a catastrophe to the real Macbeth, who had no children, is a mystery the scholars never mention. Unloosing the potential destructiveness that was always there in Nature, as Shakespeare understood, the contemporary Macbeth, like the old one, is not even a monster, though he may breed monsters, thanks to his activities on the heath; he is timorous, unimaginative, and the prayer he would like to say most fervently is simply "Amen."

JOAN LARSEN KLEIN

Lady Macbeth: "Infirm of Purpose"

In the Elizabethan marriage service, in the Elizabethan homily on marriage, in books like Vives's *Instruction of a Christen Woman* and Tilney's discourse on marriage, women were said to be weaker than men in reason and physical strength, prone to fears and subject to the vagaries of their imaginations. The second account of the creation in Genesis even suggests that the perfect woman was an afterthought, created later than the perfect man, shaped from his rib in order to forestall his loneliness and to be a "helpe meet for him" (Chapter 2, verse 20). The serpent was able to seduce Eve, many theologians said, because she was the weaker vessel. When she seduced Adam, they concluded she reversed the order and denied the purpose of her own creation. On account of the original created estate of woman and the curse of the Fall, therefore, it was said that women were bound by nature and laws to obey their husbands as well as their God. Only when husbands acted in opposition to divine law, said all the treatises, could their wives disobey them, however, the chief duty of good wives was to try lovingly to bring their errant husbands back into virtuous ways.

Lady Macbeth violates her chief duty to her husband and her God when she urges Macbeth to murder his king. For these and other reasons, most critics believe that Lady Macbeth, the "fiend-like queen" (5.8.69), lapses from womanli-

Joan Larsen Klein, "Lady Macbeth: 'Infirm of Purpose,' " in *The Woman's Part: Feminist Criticism of Shakespeare*, eds. Carol Ruth Swift Lenz, Gayle Greene, and Carol Thomas Neely (Urbana: University of Illinois Press, 1980), pp. 240–51.

ness. I want to suggest, however, that Shakespeare intended us to think that Lady Macbeth, despite her attempt to unsex herself, is never able to separate herself completely from womankind—unlike her husband, who ultimately becomes less and worse than a man. At the beginning Lady Macbeth embodies certain Renaissance notions about women. But when she wills actions that are opposed to the dictates of charity and fails in her chief duty, her wifely roles of hostess and helpmate are perverted. She is deprived of even those perverted roles in the banquet scene as Macbeth abandons his roles of host and husband. Her occupation gone, Lady Macbeth is left anguished, alone, and guilty in ways which are particularly "feminine."

Lady Macbeth embodies in extremity, I think, the Renaissance commonplace that women reflect God's image less clearly than men and that consequently women are less reasonable than men. Right reason enables mankind to choose between good and evil and thus to know right from wrong. Lady Macbeth, however, seems to have repudiated whatever glimmerings of right reason she might once have possessed. She does not consider the ethical or the religious aspects of murder. She seems to believe, for instance, that ambition is attended with "illness" (1.5.21). That which one craves "highly," she says, cannot be got "holily" (21–22). The dying grooms' prayers for blessing and Macbeth's inability to say "Amen," she insists, must not be considered "so deeply" (2.2.26–29). She refuses, in fact, to think of "These deeds . . . After these ways" (32–33). Thus she seems to have forgotten or repudiated the dictates of reason and her own conscience. Shakespeare may even intend us to conclude that she has renounced her God.

Having put away the knowledge of good, Lady Macbeth is without charity. She is without, in other words, the virtue enjoined on mankind by Christ when He told man to love his neighbor as himself, the virtue which gave man the will to act upon his knowledge of good. Macbeth himself appears to be imperfectly rational and infected in will. That the witches wait for no other purpose than to meet him suggests that he has long since opened his mind to demonic temptation, for "that olde and craftie enemie of ours, assailes none . . . except he first finde an entresse reddy for him." In fact, it is

Macbeth who seems originally to have thought of murdering Duncan (see 1.7.47–48). Yet Macbeth, unlike Lady Macbeth, can at first perceive goodness. He knows that "Duncan . . . hath been / So clear in his great office" (16–18) and that Banquo is royal "of nature" (3.1.50). He also, for one short moment, seems to understand that charity, not cruelty, ought to motivate human action and that pity, not cruelty, is strong—that pity strides the blast and tears drown the wind. His momentary vision of pity as a newborn babe, furthermore, evokes not only the image of Christ triumphant but also the emblem of charity—a naked babe sucking the breast. We should remember, however, that charity was associated more often with woman than it was with men because women, like children, were thought to be physically weak: "hit is natural for women to be kynde and gentyll / bicause they be feble / and nede the ayde of other," said Vives (sig. M^v). But the woman who denies her nature and is consumed with "outragious ire and cruelte," said Vives, "hit is jeoperdye / leest she be distroyed / and have everlastynge payne / bothe in this lyfe / and in an other" (sig. M^v–Mii). Portia argues for mercy; Cordelia practices it. It is Macbeth, however, not Lady Macbeth, who has right reason enough to glimpse both the strength of pity and its chief resting place. But he never acts upon his vision and she never sees it.

Having apparently denied her God, Lady Macbeth puts her trust in the murdering ministers of Hell. Thus she disobeys the first rule of marriage as it was formulated in the sixteenth century. A wife, said Tilney in the language of natural fruition common to *Macbeth,* must trust wholly in God: a wife "must being of hir selfe weake, and unable besides hir owne diligence, put hir whole trust in the first . . . author thereof, whome if she serve faythfullye, wyll no doubt, make thys Flower [of Friendship in holye Matrimonie] to spring up in hir aboundantly" (sig. E[7]). Nothing in life can prosper, say all the authorities, when faith is dead, and the commandments of Christ denied. Thus, despite her wish to aid her husband, Lady Macbeth cannot give him that lasting companionship under God which the *Homilies* saw as true marriage. Furthermore, although Lady Macbeth may once have had a child, its absence from her life and her willingness to contemplate its destruction contradict the *Homilies'* view that children are an end of marriage, a blessing upon their parents, and a means of enlarging God's kingdom. Macbeth at first tries crookedly to keep the ways of faith even as he dwells on the prospect of damnation and feels the loss of grace: "Wherefore could not I pronounce 'Amen'?" he asks (2.2.30). But Lady Macbeth refuses from the outset to consider the first author of her being, the last judge of her actions, and the life to come.

Perhaps because of her separation from God, Lady Macbeth is as mistaken about her own nature as she is about her marriage. She says she could dash out the brains of her suckling child. She thinks of wounding with her keen knife. But she has no child and can not murder the sleeping Duncan. She begs to be unsexed, but is never able to assume in fact what she wrongly believes is the masculine attribute of "direst cruelty" (1.5.41). Lady Macbeth, therefore, cannot act out of cruelty. But she refuses to act out of what Latimer called "charitable" love. As she forfeits the power for good which derives from the practice of pity, she is left only with loss and weakness. She is further enfeebled to the point of madness by what Bright called the awareness of sin. Along this path to despair, she does not even seem to notice that she also loses her husband. But Macbeth loses too. He exchanges the fellowship of his badly founded marriage to Lady Macbeth for union with the weird sisters. He exchanges his hopes for men-children born to his wife for the grisly finger of a birth-strangled babe and tormenting visions of the crowned children of other men.

Despite Lady Macbeth's heavy ignorance of Christian marriage, she conceives of herself almost exclusively as a wife, a helpmate. Thus she epitomizes at the same time that she perverts Renaissance views of the woman's role. Macbeth, she says, shall be what he is "promised" (1.5.17). "Great Glamis" must have the "golden round" (23, 29). When Lady Macbeth reads Macbeth's letter, she speaks not to herself but to her husband: "Thou wouldst be great . . . wouldst not play false, / And yet wouldst wrongly win" (16–20). (Macbeth, on the contrary, absents himself in soliloquy even in company.) Lady Macbeth will "chastise" Macbeth with the "valor" of her tongue so that he, not she,

might have what he wants (28). Nowhere does she mention
Macbeth's implied bribe—that she, too, has been promised
"greatness" (14). When Lady Macbeth later speaks to Macbeth in person, she measures what she takes to be his love for
her by his willingness to murder. But love for Lady Macbeth
never figures in Macbeth's stated desires for the kingdom or
for an heir. Nor does he give in to her persuasions out of
love. On the contrary, he responds to her only when she
impeaches his manliness and arouses his fear. "If we should
fail?" (1.7.59), he asks. In a grim perversion of married companionship, Lady Macbeth responds by assuming the feminine role of comforter and helper: "we'll not fail" (61). But
Macbeth never includes Lady Macbeth in any of his visions
of the deed successfully done.

Although Lady Macbeth always thinks of herself as a
wife, Macbeth thinks of himself as a husband only when
she forces him to do so. Otherwise he is concerned solely
for himself: "I am Thane of Cawdor ... My thought ...
Shakes ... my single state of man" (1.3.133–40). (The
witches recognize Macbeth's self-interest better than Lady
Macbeth does; they never discuss her with him.) In his soliloquy during the first banquet, Macbeth uses the royal *we*
proleptically when he describes his readiness to jump the life
to come and the first person singular when he thinks about
his own ambition and his present relationship to a loving
king. Nowhere in this soliloquy does he speak of a wife or
future queen. When Macbeth goes to murder Duncan, it is
the fatal vision of his own mind that materializes before him.
The "I" sees the dagger of his own fantasy and the "I" draws
the dagger of steel. After the murder of Duncan, there is almost no husband to talk to a wife, for Lady Macbeth can
scarcely reach Macbeth. "What do you mean?" (2.2.39), she
asks him. "Be not lost / So poorly in your thoughts" (70–71),
she begs him, quite uselessly. After the murder of Banquo, Macbeth is wholly dominated by self: "For mine own
good / All causes shall give way" (3.4.136–37).

In spite of the view of some critics that Lady Macbeth is
the evil force behind Macbeth's unwilling villainy, she
seems to epitomize the sixteenth-century belief that women
are passive, men active: "nature made man more strong and
couragiouse, the woman more weake fearefull and scrupu-

louse, to the intente that she for her feblenesse shulde be more circumspecte, the man for his strengthe moche more adventurouse." It is Macbeth, the man, who must be the "same in [his] own act and valor / As [he is] in desire" (1.7.40–41), Macbeth, who must "screw [his] courage to the sticking-place" (60). Lady Macbeth's threats of violence, for all their force and cruelty, are empty fantasies. It is Macbeth who converts them to hard reality. He does so in terms of his single self and his singular act: "I am settled, and bend up / Each corporal agent to this terrible feat" (79–80).

One can suggest, I think, that the virtues which Lady Macbeth sees as defects in Macbeth's character and obstacles to his success are in fact the better parts of her own being—which she determines to suppress. She says that she fears Macbeth's nature because "It is too full o' th' milk of human kindness" (1.5.18), but we have never seen Macbeth "kind." On the contrary, we were told about a man whose sword "smoked with bloody execution" and were shown a man whose thought was taken over by murderous "imaginings" (1.2.18; 1.3.138). It is Lady Macbeth who knows "How tender 'tis to love the babe that milks" her (1.7.55). It is Lady Macbeth who could not kill because she remembered her father as he slept. Thus it is Lady Macbeth, not Macbeth, who feels the bonds of kind, Lady Macbeth who has, as women were supposed to have, something of the milk of human kindness in her, and who, to rid herself of it, begs murdering ministers to come to her woman's breasts and take that milk "for gall" (1.5.59). She also begs those demonic ministers to stop up in her "th' access and passage to remorse" and thus forestall the "compunctious visitings of nature" which result when bonds of kind are violated (45–46; "compunction" = the stings of conscience, *OED*, 1). But Lady Macbeth's prayers are never granted by any of the murdering ministers we see waiting on nature's mischief. Unlike Macbeth and until her own suicide, Lady Macbeth does not succeed in breaking that great bond which keeps him pale and ties her to her kind.

Remorse and guilt finally overtake Lady Macbeth. But she manages for a short time to slow their advent by occupying herself with the practical details of murder. Indeed, Lady Macbeth's preparations for the clearing up after

Duncan's murder become a frightening perversion of Renaissance woman's domestic activity. As Vives said, "the busynes and charge within the house lyeth upon the woman's hande" (sig. Kiiv). Unlike Goneril, Regan, Cordelia, and Desdemona—all of whom take to the field of battle— Lady Macbeth waits for Macbeth at home, where good-conduct books told her to stay: "whan her husbande is forth a dores, then kepe her house moche more diligently shutte" (Vives, sig. Kiiv). At home, Lady Macbeth remembers to give "tending" to the messenger who comes with the news of Duncan's arrival (1.5.32). She remembers that the king "that's coming / Must be provided for" (67–69). She is called "hostess," "Fair and noble hostess" (1.6.10, 24, 31). As she connives at murder, she thinks to assail the grooms with "wine and wassail" (1.7.64). Even the images she uses to describe her domestic battleground evoke the limbeck and fumes of home-brewed liquor (66–67). Before Duncan's murder, it is Lady Macbeth who unlocks the king's doors and lays the daggers ready—although Macbeth draws one of his own. After the murder, it is Lady Macbeth who smears the grooms with blood. In her last act as housekeeper, Lady Macbeth remembers to wash Duncan's blood off their hands and to put on nightgowns.

As soon as Duncan's murder is a public fact, Lady Macbeth begins to lose her place in society and her position at home. She does so because there is no room for her in the exclusively male world of treason and revenge. Therefore, her true weakness and lack of consequence are first revealed in the discovery scene. Lady Macbeth's feeble and domestic response, for instance, to the news she expected to hear— "What, in our house?" (2.3.89)—is very different from the cries and clamors she said she would raise. When she asks Macduff the domestic question, "What's the business" that wakes the "sleepers of the house?" (83–85), he refuses to answer a "gentle lady": " 'Tis not for you to hear what I can speak" (86). It is apparent, therefore, that Lady Macbeth has as little place in the male world of revenge as she had in the male world of war. Thus it may be that her faint is genuine, a confirmation of her debility. On the other hand, if her faint is only pretended in order to shield Macbeth, it is still a particularly feminine ploy. True or false, it dramatically symbolizes weakness. It has the further effect of removing her from the center of events to the periphery, from whence she never returns. It is characteristic that Macbeth, busy defending himself, ignores his lady's fall. Only Banquo and Macduff in the midst of genuine grief take time to "Look to the lady" (121, 128).

After Macbeth becomes king, he, the man, so fully commands Lady Macbeth that he allows her no share in his new business. No longer his accomplice, she loses her role as housekeeper. Macbeth plans the next feast, not Lady Macbeth. It is Macbeth who invites Banquo to it, not Lady Macbeth, who had welcomed Duncan to Inverness by herself. When Macbeth commands his nobles to leave him alone, Lady Macbeth withdraws silently and unnoticed along with them (3.1.39–43). Macbeth does not tell Lady Macbeth that he plans to murder Banquo before his feast or even that he wanted Macduff to attend it. Although Macbeth needed Lady Macbeth to keep house during Duncan's murder, he disposes of Banquo well outside the castle walls. Thus Lady Macbeth is now neither companion nor helpmate. Finally, in the great banquet scene, she loses even her faltering role as hostess. Because Macbeth is there beyond her reach and her comprehension, she is powerless. Ross, not Lady Macbeth, gives the first command to rise. When Lady Macbeth twice tries to tell the nobles that Macbeth has been thus since his youth, no one pretends to believe her. When she attempts to preserve the "good meeting" (3.4.110), even Macbeth ignores her. As soon as she is forced by Macbeth's actions to give over her last role, she dissolves in confusion the very society upon whose continuance that role depends. With her husband out of her reach and society in shambles, Lady Macbeth no longer has any reason for being.

As soon as Macbeth abandons her company for that of the witches, Lady Macbeth is totally alone. In fact, Macbeth's union with the witches symbolizes the culmination of Lady Macbeth's loss of womanly social roles as well as her loss of home and family. But her growing isolation had been apparent from the moment her husband became king. Unlike Portia or Desdemona or even Macbeth himself, Lady Macbeth was never seen with friends or woman-servants in whose presence she could take comfort. Even when she appeared in company, she was the only woman there. Consequently, once she begins to lose her husband, she has neither person nor occupation to stave off the visitings of nature. All she has is time, time to succumb to that human kindness which, said Bright, no one could forget and remain human. Thus, in Lady Macbeth's short soliloquy before Macbeth's feast, even though she still talks in terms of "we," she seems to be speaking only of herself. Alone and unoccupied, she is visited by the remorse and sorrow she had hoped to banish:

> Nought's had, all's spent,
> Where our desire is got without content.
> 'Tis safer to be that which we destroy
> Than by destruction dwell in doubtful joy.   (3.2.4–7)

Lady Macbeth's existence now is circumscribed by the present memory of past loss. Absent from her mind is the sense of future promise she had anticipated before Duncan's murder when she thought herself transported beyond the "ignorant present" and felt "The future in the instant" (1.5.58–59). In her words we also hear, I think, what Bright calls the afflictions of a guilt-ridden conscience, that "internal anguish [which] bereve[s] us of all delight" in "outward benefits." Even after Macbeth joins Lady Macbeth, her words seem to continue her own thoughts, not to describe his: "Why do you keep alone, / Of sorriest fancies your companions making" (3.2.8–9). For we know, as Lady Macbeth does not, that Macbeth is thinking of the coming murder of Banquo, not the past murder of Duncan. We know his recent companions have been murderers, not "fancies." Only Lady Macbeth suffers now the "repetition" of the "horror" of Duncan's death which Macduff had feared "in a woman's ear / Would murder as it fell" (2.3.82, 87–88). When Lady Macbeth thinks to quiet her husband, she does so with advice she has already revealed she cannot herself take: "Things without all remedy / Should be without regard" (3.2.11–12). But Macbeth no longer needs her advice: "Duncan is in his grave," he says, "nothing, / Can touch him further" (22–26). Thus Shakespeare shows us that the differences between husband and wife are extreme. Macbeth wades deeper and deeper in blood in order to stifle the tortures of a mind which fears only the future: Banquo's increasing kingliness, Fleance and his unborn children, all living things and their seed. Lady Macbeth, her husband's "Sweet remembrancer" (3.4.38), does little else but think of horrors past: of the "air drawn" dagger which led Macbeth to Duncan (63), of the king slaughtered and her hands bloodied, of Banquo dead and Lady Macduff in realms unknown.

In the banquet scene, Lady Macbeth's words reveal an increase in weakness, emphasize the loss of her womanly roles, and lay bare her present isolation. Her scolding, for instance, is no more than a weak, futile imitation of the cruelty of her earlier goading. Her images, correspondingly, are more obviously feminine: "these flaws and starts," she tells Macbeth, "would well become / A woman's story at a winter's fire, / Authorized by her grandam" (64–67). But her images also evoke a kind of homeliness and comfort she can never know: the security that other women feel when they sit at their warm hearths and tell tales to their children. In fact, Lady Macbeth's words describe the comforts of a home she so little knows that she uses the picture her words evoke to castigate a man who will soon destroy the only real home we see in the play. Thus it is not surprising that Lady Macbeth at the end of the banquet scene does not seem to realize that Macbeth is leaving her as well as the community of men in order to join the unsexed witches in an unholy union—one wherein they joy to "grieve his heart" (4.1.110). As soon as Macbeth joins the witches, Lady Macbeth no longer has any place anywhere. Offstage, she is neither wife, queen, housekeeper, nor hostess. When we see her next, she will have lost the memories of motherhood and childhood she remembered so imperfectly and used so cruelly at the beginning of the play. She will also have lost that fragmented glimpse of womanly life she repudiates during her last banquet.

In her sleepwalking scene, Lady Macbeth exists (for she cannot be said to *live*) in the perpetual darkness of the soul which no candle can enlighten, although she has a taper by her continually. This is the darkness of the soul which, said Bright, "is above measure unhappy and most miserable."

Cut off from grace, Lady Macbeth is without hope. Like the damned in the *Inferno,* she exists solely within the present memory of past horrors. In fact, her existence seems to exemplify—but only in relation to herself—medieval definitions of eternal time as the everlasting "now," the present during which all things that have happened or will happen are happening. For she relives outside of any temporal sequence all Macbeth's murders and senses, as if damnation were an already accomplished fact, that "Hell is murky" (5.1.39). Without grace, Lady Macbeth cannot envision a world outside her own where Lady Macduff might possess another kind of being. Nor can she conceive of a power greater than that which she still seems to think she and Macbeth possess, a power which might call theirs "to accompt" (42). In the prison of her own anguish, she is ignorant of good and the God she long ago renounced. This is the illness that Bright said no physic could cure: "Here no medicine, no purgation, no cordiall, no tryacle or balme are able to assure the afflicted soule and trembling heart." This is the infection of the mind which the physician hired by Macbeth says only a divine can cure—although Shakespeare shows us no priest in Scotland.

It is painfully ironic that Lady Macbeth, who had once thought that drink could make "memory, the warder of the brain," into a fume and sleep into something "swinish" (1.7.65–67), can now neither forget her guilt nor sleep the sleep of oblivion. Unlike Macbeth, however, who revealed his guilt before the assembled nobility of Scotland, Lady Macbeth confesses hers when she is alone. She does so because she has always been, as women were supposed to be, a private figure, living behind closed doors. She also reveals her anguish in sleep partly because she has no purposeful waking existence and partly, as Banquo said, because in repose the fallen, unblessed nature "gives way" to "cursèd thoughts" (2.1.8–9; see also 5.1.69–72). Macbeth's guilty soul is as public as his acts. Lady Macbeth's is as private as memory, tormented by a self whose function is only to remember in isolation and unwillingly the deeds done by another. So tormented is Lady Macbeth that the gentlewoman—the first we ever see tending her—says she would not have the heart in her "bosom for the dignity of the whole body" (5.1.59).

Our final glimpse into the afflicted and brainsick mind of Lady Macbeth reveals that her doctor is either mistaken or lying when he says she is troubled with "thick-coming fancies" (5.3.38). Her madness is not that melancholy which springs from delusion, but rather that which stems from true and substantial causes. Her mind, like her being as mother, child, wife, and hostess, has also been twisted by her destructive longing for Macbeth to murder cruelly and deliberately. When we see Lady Macbeth at the end, therefore, she is "womanly" only in that she is sick and weak. All the valor of her tongue is gone, as is her illusion of its power. The hands which she cannot sweeten with the perfumes of Arabia are the little hands of a woman. As long as she lives, Lady Macbeth is never unsexed in the only way she wanted to be unsexed—able to act with the cruelty she ignorantly and perversely identified with male strength. But she has lost that true strength which Shakespeare says elsewhere is based on pity and fostered by love.

She is not now—perhaps she never was—of real concern to her lord, whom she remembers and speaks to even as she sleepwalks. Macbeth does not think of her as he prepares himself for war. When her doctor forces Macbeth to speak about her troubled mind, Macbeth renounces physic on his own account, not hers. "I'll none of it," he says (5.3.47). It is ironic, therefore, that Lady Macbeth, offstage and neglected, is able at the last to unsex herself only through the act of self-murder—in contrast to her husband, whose single attribute now is the "direst cruelty" she begged for, who wills himself to murder others tomorrow after tomorrow so long as he sees "lives" (5.8.2). The cry of women which rises at his wife's death is no more than another proof to him that he is fearless, that no "horrors" can move him (5.5.13). Even her death to him is only a "word," a word for which he has no "time" (18).

ALAN SINFIELD

Macbeth: History, Ideology, and Intellectuals

It is often said that *Macbeth* is about "evil," but we might draw a more careful distinction: between the violence the state considers legitimate and that which it does not. Macbeth, we may agree, is a dreadful murderer when he kills Duncan. But when he kills Macdonwald—"a rebel" (1.2.10)—he has Duncan's approval:

> *Captain.* For brave Macbeth—well he deserves that name—
> Disdaining Fortune, with his brandished steel,
> Which smoked with bloody execution,
> Like Valor's minion carved out his passage,
> Till he faced the slave;
> Which nev'r shook hands, nor bade farewell to him
> Till he unseamed him from the nave to th' chops,
> And fix'd his head upon our battlements.
> *King [Duncan].* O valiant cousin! worthy gentleman!
>
> (1.2.16–24)[1]

This material is an abridgment of a chapter in Alan Sinfield, *Faultlines: Cultural Materialism and the Politics of Dissident Reading* (Berkeley: University of California Press, 1992), pp. 95–108. Copyright © 1992 The Regents of the University of California.

[1]Since this chapter was written, I have become aware of two important essays that anticipate aspects of its argument. Harry Berger, Jr., "The Early Scenes of *Macbeth*: Preface to a New Interpretation," *English Literary History* 47 (1980): 1–31, shows how Duncan's Scotland is already subject to major structural political disturbance. David Norbrook, "*Macbeth* and the Politics of Historiography," in Kevin Sharpe and Steven N. Zwicker, eds., *Politics of Discourse: The Literature and History of Seventeenth-Century England* (Berkeley: Univ. of California Press, 1987), shows the significance of George Buchanan's account of Macbeth and Scottish history, and argues that Shakespeare follows neither Buchanan's hostility to unreasoning submission to hierarchy and tradition, nor King James's line.

Violence is good, in this view, when it is in the service of the prevailing dispositions of power; when it disrupts them, it is evil. A claim to a monopoly of legitimate violence is fundamental in the development of the modern state; when that claim is successful, most citizens learn to regard state violence as qualitatively different from other violence, and perhaps they don't think of state violence as violence at all (consider the actions of police, army, and judiciary as opposed to those of pickets, protesters, criminals, and terrorists). *Macbeth* focuses major strategies by which the state asserted its claim at one conjuncture. . . .

Putting the issue succinctly in relation to Shakespeare's play, what is the difference between Macbeth's rule and that of contemporary European monarchs?

In *Basilikon Doron* (1599), King James tried to protect the absolutist state from such pertinent questions by asserting an utter distinction between "a lawful good King" and "an usurping Tyran":

> The one acknowledgeth himself ordained for his people, having received from God a burthen of government, whereof he must be countable: the other thinketh his people ordained for him, a prey to his passions and inordinate appetites, as the fruits of his magnanimity: And therefore, as their ends are directly contrary, so are their whole actions, as means whereby they press to attain to their ends.[2]

Evidently James means to deny that the absolutist monarch has anything significant in common with someone like Macbeth. Three aspects of James's strategy in this passage are particularly revealing. First, he depends upon an utter polarization between the two kinds of ruler. Such antitheses are characteristic of the ideology of absolutism: they were called upon to tidy the uneven apparatus of feudal power into a far neater structure of the monarch versus the rest, and protestantism tended to see "spiritual" identities in similarly polarized terms. James himself explained the function of

[2]*The Political Works of James I*, ed. Charles Howard McIlwain (New York: Russell & Russell, 1965), p.18.

demons like this: "Since the Devil is the very contrary opposite to God, there can be no better way to know God, than by the contrary."[3] So it is with the two kinds of rulers: the badness of one seems to guarantee the goodness of the other. Second, by defining the lawful good king against the usurping tyrant, James refuses to admit the possibility that a ruler who has *not* usurped will be tyrannical. Thus he seems to cope with potential splits between legitimacy and actual power by insisting on the unique status of the lawful good king, and to head off questions about the violence committed by such a ruler by suggesting that all his actions will be uniquely legitimate. Third, we may notice that the whole distinction, as James develops it, is cast in terms, not of the *behavior* of the lawful good king and the usurping tyrant, respectively, but of their *motives*. This seems to render vain any assessment of the actual manner of rule of the absolute monarch. On these arguments, any disturbance of the current structure of power relations is against God and the people, and consequently any violence in the interest of the status quo is acceptable. . . .

Like other kinds of cultural production, literary criticism helps to influence the way people think about the world; that is why the present study seeks to make space for an oppositional understanding of the text and the state. It is plain that most criticism has not only reproduced but also endorsed Jamesian ideology, so discouraging scrutiny, which *Macbeth* may promote, of the legitimacy of state violence. That we are dealing with live issues is shown by the almost uncanny resemblances between the Gunpowder Plot and the bombing in 1984 by the Irish Republican Army of the Brighton hotel where leading members of the British government were staying, and in the comparable questions about state and other violence that they raise. My concluding thoughts are about the politics of the prevailing readings of *Macbeth*. I distinguish conservative and liberal positions; both tend to dignify their accounts with the honorific term *tragedy*.

The conservative position insists that the play is about

[3]James I, *Daemonologie* (1597), *Newes from Scotland* (1591) (London: Bodley Head, 1924), p. 55.

"evil." Kenneth Muir offers a string of quotations to this effect: it is Shakespeare's "most profound and mature vision of evil"; "the whole play may be writ down as a wrestling of destruction with creation"; it is "a statement of evil"; "it is a picture of a special battle in a universal war"; and it "contains the decisive orientation of Shakespearean good and evil."[4] This is little more than Jamesian ideology writ large: killing Macdonwald is "good" and killing Duncan is "evil," and the hierarchical society envisaged in absolutist ideology is identified with the requirements of nature, supernature, and the "human condition." Often this view is elaborated as a sociopolitical program, allegedly expounded by Shakespeare, implicitly endorsed by the critic. So Muir writes of "an orderly and close-knit society, in contrast to the disorder consequent upon Macbeth's initial crime [i.e., killing Duncan, not Macdonwald]. The naturalness of that order, and the unnaturalness of its violation by Macbeth, is emphasized" (New Arden *Macbeth*, p. li). Irving Ribner says Fleance, Banquo's son, is "symbolic of a future rooted in the acceptance of natural law, which inevitably must return to reassert God's harmonious order when evil has worked itself out."[5]

This conservative endorsement of Jamesian ideology is not intended to ratify the modern state. Rather, like much twentieth-century literary criticism, it is backward-looking, appealing to an imagined earlier condition of society. Roger Scruton comments: "If a conservative is also a restorationist, this is because he lives close to society, and feels in himself the sickness which infects the common order. How, then, can he fail to direct his eyes towards that state of health from which things have declined?"[6] This quotation is close to the terms in which many critics write of *Macbeth*, and their evocation of the Jamesian order allegedly restored at the end of the play constitutes a wistful gesture towards what they

[4]Muir in the New Arden *Macbeth*, p. xlix, quoting G. Wilson Knight, L. C. Knights, F. C. Kolbe, Derek Traversi. See also Irving Ribner, *Patterns in Shakespearean Tragedy* (London: Methuen, 1960), p. 153; Robert Ornstein, *The Moral Vision of Jacobean Tragedy* (Madison: University of Wisconsin Press, 1965), p. 230; Hunter (Penguin ed.), p. 7.

[5]Ribner, *Patterns in Shakespearean Tragedy*, p. 159.

[6]Roger Scruton, *The Meaning of Conservatism* (Harmondsworth: Penguin, 1980), p. 21.

would regard as a happy ending for our troubled society. However, because this conservative approach is based on an inadequate analysis of political and social process, it gains no purchase on the main determinants of state power.

A liberal position hesitates to endorse any state power so directly, finding some saving virtue in Macbeth: "To the end he never totally loses our sympathy"; "we must still not lose our sympathy for the criminal."[7] In this view there is a flaw in the state; it fails to accommodate the particular consciousness of the refined individual. Macbeth's imagination is set against the blandness of normative convention, and for all his transgressions, perhaps because of them, he transcends the laws he breaks. In John Bayley's version: "His superiority consists in a passionate sense for ordinary life, its seasons and priorities, a sense which his fellows in the play ignore in themselves or take for granted. Through the deed which tragedy requires of him he comes to know not only himself but what life is all about."[8] I call this view liberal because it is anxious about a state, absolutist or modern, that can hardly take cognizance of the individual sensibility, and it is prepared to validate to some degree the recalcitrant individual. But it will not undertake the political analysis that would press the case. Hence there is always in such criticism a reservation about Macbeth's revolt and a sense of relief that it ends in defeat: nothing could have been done anyway; it was all inevitable, written in the human condition. This retreat from the possibility of political analysis and action leaves the state virtually unquestioned, almost as fully as the conservative interpretation.

Shakespeare, notoriously, has a way of anticipating all possibilities. The idea of literary intellectuals identifying their own deepest intuitions of the universe in the experience of the "great" tragic hero who defies the limits of the human

[7] A. C. Bradley, *Shakespearean Tragedy*, 2d ed. (London: Macmillan, 1965), p. 305; Wayne Booth, "Macbeth as Tragic Hero," *Journal of General Education* 6 (1951): revised for *Shakespeare's Tragedies*, ed. Laurence Lerner (Harmondsworth: Penguin, 1963), p. 186. See also Hunter (Penguin ed.) pp. 26–29; Wilbur Sanders, *The Dramatist and the Received Idea* (Cambridge: Cambridge University Press, 1968), pp. 282–307.

[8] John Bayley, *Shakespeare and Tragedy* (London: Routledge, 1981), p. 199; see also p. 193. I am grateful for the stimulating comments of Russell Jackson, Tony Inglis, Peter Holland, and Jonathan Dollimore.

condition is surely a little absurd; we may sense delusions of grandeur. *Macbeth* includes much more likely models for its conservative and liberal critics in the characters of the two doctors. The English Doctor has just four and a half lines (4.3.141–45), in which he says that King Edward is coming and that sick people whose malady conquers the greatest efforts of medical skill await him, expecting a heavenly cure for "evil." Malcolm, the king to be, says, "I thank you, Doctor." This doctor is the equivalent of conservative intellectuals who encourage respect for mystificatory images of ideal hierarchy that have served the state in the past, and who invoke "evil," "tragedy," and "the human condition" to produce, in effect, acquiescence to state power.

The Scottish Doctor, in act 5, scenes 1 and 3, is actually invited to cure the sickness of the rulers and by implication the state: "If thou couldst, doctor, cast / The water of my land, find her disease" (5.3.50–51). But this doctor, like the liberal intellectual, hesitates to press an analysis. He says: "This disease is beyond my practice" (5.1.62); "I think, but dare not speak" (83); "Therein the patient / Must minister to himself" (5.3.45–46); "Were I from Dunsinane away and clear, / Profit again should hardly draw me here" (61–62). He wrings his hands at the evidence of state violence and protects his conscience with asides. This is like the liberal intellectual who knows there is something wrong at the heart of the system but will not envisage a radical alternative and, to ratify this attitude, discovers in Shakespeare's plays "tragedy" and "the human condition" as explanations of the supposedly inevitable defeat of the person who steps out of line.

By conventional standards, this chapter is perverse. But an oppositional criticism is bound to appear thus: its task is to work across the grain of customary assumptions and, if necessary, across the grain of the test as it is customarily perceived. Of course, literary intellectuals don't have much influence over state violence; their therapeutic power is very limited. Nevertheless, writing, teaching, and other modes of communicating all contribute to the steady, long-term formation of opinion, to the establishment of legitimacy. This contribution King James himself did not neglect.

SYLVAN BARNET

Macbeth on Stage and Screen

Macbeth is not open to a range of interpretations equal to, say, *King Lear*, *Hamlet*, or *The Merchant of Venice*. There have, of course, been younger and older Macbeths and Lady Macbeths, expressionistic sets (toppling walls, tilted arches) and realistic sets (based on medieval Scottish architecture), and no sets (beyond the bare stage). There have been ugly witches and seductive witches, and highly physical ghosts of Banquo (the man himself), more ethereal ghosts (a shadow, a light, a rustling curtain), and no ghosts (in such productions Macbeth looks, as Lady Macbeth says, "but on a stool"). But on the whole there has been great uniformity as to what the play is about. And because the text is fairly short—it is the shortest of Shakespeare's tragedies, more than half the length of *Hamlet*—it can easily be staged uncut. Not much can be accomplished, in the way of interpretation, by cutting, and, in fact, the cuts are usually limited to the Hecate scenes and the passage on the King's Evil in 4.3, although this passage significantly serves to contrast the power of virtuous kingship with the demise of a wicked king.

We know that Shakespeare's company, the King's Men, was paid to perform a play at court on 7 August 1605, and it is likely that this play was *Macbeth*, but in fact the records do not name the play. The earliest specific reference to *Macbeth* on the stage appears in Simon Forman's *Book of Plays*, which includes his description of a performance at the Globe in 1611. The document, although thought by some to be a forgery, is now widely accepted as genuine. Alas, it is not terribly informative. We would like to know, for instance, what the witches looked like, and how they disappeared—did they disappear through traps, or did they fly on wires?—but Forman does not mention the first two scenes. He begins with Macbeth and Banquo "riding thorowe a wod" and meeting "3 women feiries or Nimphes." But does "riding" really mean that Macbeth and Banquo were mounted on horses? Almost surely not, for in 3.3.11–14 Shakespeare goes out of his way to explain why horses are *not* present on the stage in a scene where we might expect them. Perhaps, then, Macbeth and Banquo were mounted on some sort of hobby-horses? Or perhaps (and this is the most likely) Forman's statement that they were "riding" is merely his way of saying what Macbeth and Banquo were *imagined* to be doing. (By the way, one reason that Forman's account has been suspected of being a nineteenth-century forgery rather than a seventeenth-century document is this very passage. It shows no real knowledge of a performance at all, and it may well be derived from Holinshed, Shakespeare's source, which speaks of "three women . . . nymphs or feiries." But of course Forman may have known his Holinshed, and drawn on it to refresh his memory when he came to write about his visit to the Globe theater.) Forman, then, is of little or no help, but we nevertheless can get a glimpse, from stage directions in the earliest published text (1623) of the play, of what *Macbeth* at the Globe was like. Take, for instance, the first direction in the play: "Thunder and lightning. Enter three Witches." We know, from other sources, that lightning was produced by fireworks and by blowing resin through a candle, thunder by rolling a cannonball in a wooden trough. References to "Banquet prepared" and "Drum and colors" strengthen our impression that the Globe offered realism of a spectacular sort. But aside from what the text of 1623 tells us, or implies, we know nothing further about the staging of *Macbeth* for the next forty years.

Between 1664 and 1669 Samuel Pepys saw the play at least nine times. Here are two samples of entries from his diary. On 5 November 1664 he writes, "Macbeth, a pretty good play"; one 19 April 1667 he writes, "Here we saw Macbeth, which though I have seen it often yet it is one of the best plays for a stage, and variety of dancing and music, that ever I saw." Dancing and music in *Macbeth*? Yes, because Sir William Davenant adapted the play into operatic form in 1663, adding dancing and singing to the roles of the witches, who flew through the air on machines.

Davenant made other changes, as well, of two sorts: (1) he expanded the roles of Macduff and especially of Lady Macduff, making them more evident foils to Macbeth and Lady Macbeth, and (2) he simplified the language. For instance, his witches do not say, "Fair is foul, and foul is fair"; instead, they say, "To us, fair weather's foul, and foul is fair." Davenant thus simplifies a rich, paradoxical statement with thematic implications into a statement about the weather. Here is another example of a simplified speech: In 2.2, in place of Shakespeare's

> Will all great Neptune's ocean wash this blood
> Clean from my hand? No; this my hand will rather
> The multitudinous seas incarnadine,
> Making the green one red,   (59–62)

Davenant gives us this:

> Can the sea afford
> Water enough to wash away the stains?
> No, they would sooner add a tincture to
> The sea, and turn the green into a red.

Davenant's most infamous alteration, in 5.3.11–12, is of Macbeth's nearly hysterical words to the terrified servant who comes to report that Birnam Wood is on the move:

> The devil damn thee black, thou cream-faced loon!
> Where got'st thou that goose look?

becomes, in Davenant's more decorous text,

> Now friend, what means thy change of countenance?

Davenant's adaptation held the stage until 1744, when David Garrick brought back, to great acclaim, what can be thought of as Shakespeare's *Macbeth*. Garrick's claim that he would perform *Macbeth* as Shakespeare wrote it baffled the actor James Quin who had for two decades been performing in Davenant's adaptation: "What does he mean? Don't I play Macbeth as Shakespeare wrote it?" It is said the Quin, especially puzzled by Shakespeare's line about the "goose look," asked Garrick where he got such an odd expression. Although Garrick restored much of the play, he did not restore it all. (In fact, though he kept the goose look, he seems to have omitted the "The devil damn thee black.") The chief changes are these:

1. Following Davenant, he heightened the parts of Macduff and Lady Macduff

2. His witches, like Davenant's, still danced and sang some added songs, and they remained somewhat comic (though unlike Davenant's witches they disappeared through traps, rather than flew through the air)

3. He reduced the dagger scene

4. He eliminated 269 lines of Shakespeare's play (for instance, he eliminated most of the scene showing the murder of Lady Macduff's son, preferring to have Ross report it later, and he altered the drunken porter into a respectable servant

5. He killed Banquo offstage

6. He did not bring on the severed head of Macbeth at the end

7. He added some lines of his own, notably a dying speech for Macbeth:

> 'Tis done! The scene of life will quickly close.
> Ambitions vain, delusive dreams are fled,
> And now I wake to darkness, guilt and horror.
> I cannot bear it! let me shake it off—
> Two' [sic] not be; my soul is clogged with blood—
> I cannot rise! I dare not ask for mercy—
> It is too late, hell drags me down. I sink,

> I sink—Oh!—my soul is lost forever.
> Oh!

Today it is difficult to see the appeal of this speech, but Garrick's contemporaries praised it. Francis Gentleman, a drama critic of the time, gives us some idea of how it was regarded:

> Shakespeare's idea of having [Macbeth's] head brought on by Macduff is either ludicrous or horrid, therefore commendably changed to visible punishment—a dying speech and a very good one has been furnished by Mr. Garrick, to give the actor more éclat.

Garrick's costumes for the play were, as was customary in the period, the costumes of his own age; late in his career he toyed with the idea of doing *Macbeth* in some sort of "ancient dress," but he never put the motion into practice. Apparently the earliest use of Scottish dress in *Macbeth* was in a production in Scotland in 1757; the first use of it on the English stage was in Charles Macklin's production of 1773. But even Macklin's production was only a first step toward historical realism, since he used sixteenth-century dress for Macbeth rather than some pre-Norman Conquest costume, and Lady Macbeth wore fashionable modern attire. The argument in favor of historical realism (as the eighteenth century saw it) was that it made the play more probable; the argument against historical realism was that it endangered the dignity of tragedy and therefore made the play less probable.

In the late eighteenth century and early nineteenth the chief Macbeth was John Philip Kemble, and the chief Lady Macbeth was Kemble's sister, Sarah Siddons. Kemble, who is always characterized (doubtless with some injustice) as a "formal" or "statuesque" or "classical" actor, emphasized Macbeth's greatness as a soldier, and tended to avoid any suggestion that Macbeth degenerates and becomes cowardly. One critic complained that at the sight of Banquo's ghost, Kemble "seemed not to fear while yet he said he 'trembled.' " His text was very close to Shakespeare's, and in costuming he made an effort at what was thought to be historical realism, wearing chain mail, a plaid, and a bonnet with a single feather, in the manner of some clan chieftains. Possibly in accord with his desire to make the play somewhat more rational, Kemble in 1794 dared to break with tradition by not showing the ghost of Banquo, though in 1809 (against his better judgment), he restored the ghost at the request of the public.

Sarah Siddons played Lady Macbeth for forty years, from 1777 to 1817. Like her brother, she is known as a great representative of the late eighteenth-century classical school of acting. In the early nineteenth century, toward the end of her career, when the public taste was changing, and grandeur was less valued, some spectators were unimpressed by her long pauses, her slow delivery, and her solemnity, but somehow all such reports are less impressive than the anecdote telling how she struck terror into the heart of a clerk in a dry-goods shop when, before deciding to buy, she asked, "But will it wash?" Nor, according to the American actor Edwin Forrest, did she seem remote and stagy to James Sheridan Knowles, who had often seen Mrs. Siddons act. Forrest reports a conversation with Knowles:

> We have read all the high-flown descriptions of the critics, and they fall short. I want you to tell me in a plain blunt phrase just what impression she produced on you. Knowles replied, with a sort of shudder, . . . "Well, sir, I smelt blood! I swear that I smelt blood."

Other accounts insist that in the sleepwalking scene she marvelously retained her dignity while conveying her anguish, moving the audience with pity and awe. In her "Remarks on the Character of Lady Macbeth," a longish essay reprinted in Thomas Campbell's *Life of Mrs. Siddons* and elsewhere, Mrs. Siddons emphasizes, Stanislavsky-like, the importance of becoming the character and the importance of careful observation. To this end she observed a real sleepwalker. Curiously, however, reports of her acting often differ from the view of the character that she sets forth in her essay. For instance, she says that Lady Macbeth, like Macbeth, sees the ghost of Banquo, but none of the reports of her performances indicates that she conveyed this to the audience.

If the Kembles represent classical acting, Edmund Kean represents romantic acting. He first performed Macbeth in London in 1814, and immediately established himself as Kemble's rival, though many reviewers found Kean was too given to fits and starts. (One thinks of Coleridge's famous comment that watching Kean act was like reading Shakespeare by lightning.) Kean, perhaps reacting against Kemble's heroic Macbeth, emphasized Macbeth's disintegration, so much so that some reviewers believed he went too far and lost the dignity (and the pathos) of the tragic hero. Interestingly, the difference was not obtained by cutting anything in one version or the other, for Kean's text (like Kemble's) seems to have been very close to Garrick's; certainly he retained the speech Garrick had written for the dying Macbeth. And, like Kemble, he used Highland costumes.

In 1847 Samuel Phelps restored the drunken porter in 2.3, presenting a text whose only noticeable departure from Shakespeare's was the omission of the English doctor in 4.3. Following the Folio, he even killed Macbeth offstage and then brought in the head on a pole. Furthermore, in an effort at historical realism, he abandoned the by then conventional tartans and introduced primitive mantles. But after Kean, the most famous nineteenth-century actor to play the role was not Phelps but Henry Irving, who staged *Macbeth* in 1875, when it ran for eighty performances. Irving revived it in 1888, with Ellen Terry as Lady Macbeth. It is customary to say that Ellen Terry was a softer, frailer, more sympathetic Lady Macbeth than was Sarah Siddons, and there must be something to this view, especially given the difference in their physiques. But when one reads accounts of how heartrending Mrs. Siddons was in the sleepwalking scene, one begins to suspect that Terry's performance was not so much softer as more sentimental.

Irving's 1888 production was, in his usual style, lavishly mounted with three-dimensional illusionistic sets that were as archaeologically accurate as the age could produce. The lighting effects were elaborate, and the costumes were splendid, though Oscar Wilde commented that although Lady Macbeth patronized local manufacturers for the clothes of her husband and the servants, she bought her own clothing in Byzantium. Because the sets took considerable time to assemble and strike, not all of Shakespeare's scenes could be given, and not always in Shakespeare's order. For instance, in Shakespeare, 2.3 and 3.1 are set in Macbeth's household, but between them comes 2.4, the brief scene between Ross and the Old Man, which takes place somewhere outside. One will hardly strike the set of a castle for such a minor scene—so one can either alter its position in the play or delete it. Irving chose to delete it. His cuts amounted to almost one quarter of the play, but it should be mentioned that not all of them were made to enable him to use elaborate scenery. Some cuts, for instance the report of the bleeding soldier in 1.2, were based on current scholarly opinions, which held that the passage was not authentic.

One point about Irving's interpretation of his role must be mentioned. In 1875 he took the view that Macbeth is a good man who is destroyed by the fates, but in his second (1888) production he assumed (and tried to convey in his acting) that the witches initiate nothing. They meet Macbeth, Irving came to believe, because Macbeth's mind has already turned to evil thoughts. Irving's changing conception of Banquo's ghost is also worth mentioning: in 1877 some sort of optical illusion produced a transparent greenish silhouette; in 1888 the ghost was a real man, who rose from a trick chair, and who later emerged from the crowd; in 1895 the ghost was not an actor but simply a shaft of blue limelight.

In 1911 Herbert Beerbohm Tree presented a *Macbeth* that was in the elaborate tradition of Irving. Thus, Duncan was escorted by a train that included a harp player; the singing turned into a hymn as the king blessed the kneeling company, and when the stage was empty after Duncan had gone to bed, the witches entered and cackled with satisfaction. This sort of slow-moving pictorial amplification had been under attack by William Poel, who from the last decade of the nineteenth century argued that Shakespeare's plays should be done on the stage for which they were written— that is, on a stage unencumbered with scenery so that the action could flow continuously from scene to scene. If the plays were done on a Shakespeare-like stage, Poel argued, they would not have to be cut, their scenes would not have to be rearranged, and there would not have to be long pauses when new scenery was being set up. In 1895 he directed the Shakespeare Reading Society in a production of *Macbeth*. Bernard Shaw, an enemy of Irving's method, was then serving as drama critic for *The Saturday Review*. Shaw wrote of the production:

> It is one of my eccentricities to be old-fashioned in my artistic tastes. For instance, I am fond—unaffectedly fond—of Shakespear's plays. I do not mean actor-managers' editions and revivals; I mean the plays as Shakespeare wrote them, played straight through line by line and scene by scene as nearly as possible under the conditions of representation for which they were designed. I have seen the suburban amateurs of the Shakespeare Reading Society, seated like Christy minstrels on the platform of the lecture hall at the London Institution produce, at a moderate computation, about sixty-six times as much effect by reading straight through *Much Ado About Nothing* as Mr. Irving with his expensively mounted and superlatively dull Lyceum version. When these same amateurs invited me to a regular stage performance of *Macbeth* in aid of the Siddons Memorial Fund, I went, not for the sake of Sarah the Respectable, whose great memory can take care of itself, . . . but simply because I wanted to see *Macbeth*.

Although Shaw goes on to say that the acting was, predictably, weak ("As to this performance of *Macbeth* at St George's Hall, of course it was, from the ordinary professional standpoint, a very bad one"), what is important here is the support he offers to a method of production that was antithetical to Irving's and Tree's method. (It is easy to laugh at Irving and Tree, and to approve of Poel, but one should recall that some sensitive students of Shakespeare—G. Wilson Knight, for instance—have believed that the elaborate Victorian style conferred on the plays the "richness and dignity," in Knight's words, which they require.) In 1909 Poel staged the play again, in what he claimed was "the Elizabethan manner." By this he meant not only that it was done on a stage without sets, but also that it was done not in Scottish garb but Elizabethan garb. As we will see in a moment, it required only a small additional step to argue that since the Elizabethans staged their plays in the garb of the performers' day, we should stage the plays in the garb of our own. Against this view, however, it can be argued that modern-dress productions make the play too local, too bound to the present, and rob the play—any play—of its archetypal dimension.

Barry Jackson's modern dress *Macbeth* (1928), in which Macbeth was a general who wore khaki, riding breeches, and boots, and in which Lady Macduff was murdered while taking afternoon tea, can be seen as part of the anti-Victorian movement that Poel began. In 1925 Jackson had staged, with considerable success, a modern-dress *Hamlet*, but the *Macbeth* was widely considered (except for the drunken porter and for the scene in which Macduff received the news of the slaughter of his family) a failure. Why? Any Elizabethan play done in modern dress will present some problems (e.g., why do people engage in sword fights when they have pistols at hand?), but *Macbeth* seemed especially troublesome. First of all, since a murder had been committed in the house, why didn't they call the police? More seriously, what was gained by associating the play with World War I? Further, the witches were a problem, since witches are not a part of modern society. (As we'll see, various solutions have been proposed in other modern versions of *Macbeth*.) Jackson himself said he engaged in the experiment partly to see how it would come out. He had trouble getting an actor to play Macbeth, and finally settled on Eric Maturin, a realistic actor who could not speak verse effectively.

In 1933 Theodore Komisarjevsky, a Russian émigré who served as a visiting director at Stratford-upon-Avon, did another modern-dress version. Macbeth, dressed rather like a German officer of World War I, met the witches against the background of a ruined château. The witches (who were the only characters to speak with Scottish accents) were not supernatural creatures but were hags plundering corpses on the battlefield; they told the fortunes of Macbeth and Banquo by palmistry. In keeping with this diminution of the supernatural, Banquo's ghost in the banquet scene was Macbeth's own immense shadow, and Macbeth's second encounter with the witches was conceived as Macbeth's dream. In fact, the entire production, though evocative of World War I in

certain details, was somewhat dreamlike and expressionistic, with aluminum screens forming labyrinthine sets.

Three years later, in 1936, Orson Welles, working with
the WPA (Works Progress Administration) Negro Theatre,
presented in New York a black *Macbeth*. Jack Carter (who
had played Crown in *Porgy and Bess*) played Macbeth,
Edna Thomas played Lady Macbeth, and Canada Lee
played Banquo. (Carter and Thomas, being light-skinned
blacks, had to darken themselves for the parts.) Virgil
Thomson provided orchestrations of nineteenth-century
waltzes for court scenes, and African drummers provided
other music. This *Macbeth*, set in Haiti early in the nineteenth century (Napoleonic uniforms, with lots of gold
braid), began by showing a jungle, through which sounded
drums and the chants of voodoo celebrants. Welles deleted
the first two scenes, and began by showing Macbeth and
Banquo encountering the voodoo practitioners, including a
male Hecate. At the end of the scene, Hecate proclaimed,
"Peace! The charm's wound up." And at the end of the play,
after Malcolm was hailed as king, Hecate again appeared
and repeated the line, thus implying that Malcolm would
become (or might become) another Macbeth. The play was
a great hit, both in Harlem and later on tour, though some
white journalists complained that the verse was not delivered in the usual declamatory style then expected in productions of Shakespeare. Welles's script, thought for decades to
have been lost, turned up in 1974, and in 1977 Woodie King,
Jr., staged it at New York City's New Federal Theatre, with
Lex Monson as Macbeth and Esther Rolle (of the television
series *Good Times*) as Lady Macbeth, but the revival did not
prove exciting. Welles's version has been published in
Orson Welles on Shakespeare (1990), ed. Richard France.

There have, of course, been many productions of *Macbeth*
since Welles did his black *Macbeth* in 1936. Among the
most famous are a *Macbeth* directed by John Gielgud in
1952 (Gielgud pointedly rejected all suggestions of Scottish
history); a *Macbeth* directed by Glen Byam Shaw in 1955,
with Laurence Olivier in the title role, using sets that evoked
medieval architecture but were at the same time expressionistic; a *Macbeth* directed by Joan Littlewood in 1957, using

modern dress (Littlewood in her program note said she wanted "to wipe away the dust of three hundred years" and to strip away the interpretations of the "nineteenth-century sentimentalists," so she gave her Macbeth and Lady Macbeth no tragic dignity); a *Macbeth* directed by Trevor Nunn at Stratford-upon-Avon in 1976, with Ian McKellen as Macbeth and Judi Dench as Lady Macbeth, in which the Christian background was emphasized, for example by having the saintly Duncan dressed in white, and by having Malcolm and Macduff converse before a cross. But no *Macbeth* in the theater seems to have established itself as the great production of our age.

Three film versions and a BBC television version, however, are of interest. Orson Welles's film, shot in 1947 and released in the following year, cast Welles as Macbeth, Jeanette Nolan as Lady Macbeth, and Roddy McDowall played Malcolm. Welles cut the text fairly heavily, introduced some novel business (in the sleepwalking scene, this Macbeth awakens Lady Macbeth with a kiss), and added a character, the Holy Father, some of whose lines were invented by Welles while others were salvaged from characters whom Welles cut. The underlying idea seems to be that Macbeth is a doomed figure, not so much a man who made a wrong decision but a man whose fate has been long decided. To this end, expressionistic shots (rough stone walls, figures looming in the foreground, minute figures in the distance) offer images of Macbeth's tormented mind. Welles was trying to make a film version of *Macbeth*—a cinematic work, rather than a mere film recording of the play—but inevitably a viewer who knows the play is disturbed by the liberties taken with the text, and is also disturbed by the extremely poor sound track, which makes many speeches unintelligible.

The sense of Macbeth as a powerful warrior, missed by Welles, is strongly present in Akira Kurosawa's *Throne of Blood* (1957, in Japanese entitled *The Castle of the Spider's Web*). Kurosawa, using conventions of the Noh drama and the samurai movie, gives his characters Japanese names, and freely changes the story, so that his film is not so much *Macbeth* as a spinoff of Shakespeare's play, and perhaps that is why it is so much more satisfactory than most movies (or productions?) of Shakespeare's plays. That is, unlike an English-language film or production of the play, Kurosawa's work does not claim to be Shakespeare in plot, in character, scene, or even in any of its language. Without worrying about fidelity to the original, we can easily enjoy it for itself.

The most recent film of *Macbeth*, Roman Polanski's version (released in 1971), has been criticized as being excessively bloody; but Polanski might well plead that since Shakespeare's play includes the stage direction, "*Enter Macduff with Macbeth's head,*" blood might just as well flow abundantly in a film. Still, it is evident that Polanski (who shows us such sights as Macbeth repeatedly plunging a dagger into Duncan, and an arrow striking Seyton between the eyes) is influenced not only by Shakespeare but by Antonin Artaud's Theater of Cruelty. Many viewers find such stuff hard to take; only a few viewers—persons highly familiar with Shakespeare's play—find Polanski's tinkering with the ending equally hard to take, but for them Polanski is engaged in yet further violence. At the end of this film, as Malcolm is being crowned, his younger brother, Donalbain, rides off to listen to the witches. The implication is that he will conspire against the king, just as Macbeth had conspired against King Duncan, and so the play ends not with Shakespeare's suggestions of union ("loves," "friends"), fertility ("planted newly"), piety ("by the grace of Grace"), and order ("measure, time, and place"), but with a suggestion of unending treachery. Almost equally unusual, and more interesting, is the casting of a relatively young Macbeth (Jon Finch) and Lady Macbeth (Francesca Annis), emphasizing their sexuality and presumably also emphasizing the contrast between a fair exterior and an ugly interior. What is most lacking in the film, however, is a sense that Macbeth is a heroic figure, a man who has a moral sense—even if he wars against it.

The BBC television version (1982), directed by Jack Gold, features Nicol Williamson as Macbeth and Jane Lapotaire as Lady Macbeth. Williamson gasps and groans and grunts, squeaks and squeals and squirms, so that he is sometimes almost unintelligible. Ms. Lapotaire in the scene where she says, "Come, you spirits / That tend on mortal thoughts, unsex me here" (1.5.41–42), writhes orgasmically on a fur-strewn bed. Despite this abundant activity, the production is relatively static, especially in group scenes, where characters tend to stand stiffly together. Two small points: First, Seyton, a thoroughly vicious fellow in this version, is the third murderer, and after Banquo has been killed and Fleance has escaped, Seyton stabs the other two murderers (3.3) and is the leader in the slaughter—in a particularly savage scene—of Lady Macduff and the children (4.2). Second, the ending of this televised version is somewhat ambiguous. Malcolm is hailed as king, but the last shot is of Fleance, and the scene conveys the implication that Fleance may, like Macbeth, usurp the throne.

Bibliographic Note: For an edition of the play, with extensive annotations concerning productions, see John Wilders's *Macbeth: Shakespeare in Production* (2004).

A very large book, a medium-size book, and two very small books have been devoted to productions of *Macbeth*. They are, in that order, Marvin Rosenberg, *The Masks of Macbeth* (1978); Dennis Bartholomeusz, *Macbeth and the Players* (1969); Gordon Williams, *Macbeth: Text and Performance* (1985); and Bernice W. Kliman, *Macbeth* [Shakespeare in Performance] (1992). Rosenberg and Bartholomeusz cover numerous productions, old and new; Williams concentrates on a few recent productions, including Polanski's film; Kliman's small book gives remarkable full accounts of selected productions, including Polanski's film, Welles's WPA production, and the BBC television version. For further reviews of productions from the middle of the last century to the present, consult *Shakespeare Survey* (an annual publication) and *Shakespeare Quarterly*. For a survey of twentieth-century developments in staging Shakespeare's plays, see J. L. Styan, *The Shakespeare Revolution* (1977).

More specialized studies include Kalman Burnim, *David Garrick, Director* (1961); Arthur Colby Sprague, *Shakespearian Players and Performances* (1954, on William Macready as Macbeth and Sarah Siddons as Lady Macbeth); Alan Hughes, *Henry Irving, Shakespearean* (1981); John Houseman, *Run-Through* (1972, on Welles's black *Mac-*

beth); Jack J. Jorgens, *Shakespeare on Film* (1977). An article by Carol J. Carlisle in *Shakespeare Survey* 16 (1983) is devoted to Helen Faucit's mid-nineteenth-century Lady Macbeth but includes also information about Sarah Siddons's interpretation of the role.

Suggested References

The number of possible references is vast and grows alarmingly. (The *Shakespeare Quarterly* devotes one issue each year to a list of the previous year's work, and *Shakespeare Survey*—an annual publication—includes a substantial review of biographical, critical, and textual studies, as well as a survey of performances.) The vast bibliography is best approached through James Harner, *The World Shakespeare Bibliography on CD-Rom: 1900–Present.* The first release, in 1996, included more than 12,000 annotated items from 1990–93, plus references to several thousand book reviews, productions, films, and audio recordings. The plan is to update the publication annually, moving forward one year and backward three years. Thus, the second issue (1997), with 24,700 entries, and another 35,000 or so references to reviews, newspaper pieces, and so on, covered 1987–94.

Though no works are indispensable, those listed below have been found especially helpful. The arrangement is as follows:

1. Shakespeare's Times
2. Shakespeare's Life
3. Shakespeare's Theater
4. Shakespeare on Stage and Screen
5. Miscellaneous Reference Works
6. Shakespeare's Plays: General Studies
7. The Comedies
8. The Romances
9. The Tragedies
10. The Histories
11. *The Tragedy of Macbeth*

The titles in the first five sections are accompanied by brief explanatory annotations.

1. Shakespeare's Times

Andrews, John F., ed. *William Shakespeare: His World, His Work, His Influence,* 3 vols. (1985). Sixty articles, dealing not only with such subjects as "The State," "The Church," "Law," "Science, Magic, and Folklore," but also with the plays and poems themselves and Shakespeare's influence (e.g., translations, films, reputation)

Byrne, Muriel St. Clare. *Elizabethan Life in Town and Country* (8th ed., 1970). Chapters on manners, beliefs, education, etc., with illustrations.

Dollimore, John, and Alan Sinfield, eds. *Political Shakespeare: New Essays in Cultural Materialism* (1985). Essays on such topics as the subordination of women and colonialism, presented in connection with some of Shakespeare's plays.

Greenblatt, Stephen. *Representing the English Renaissance* (1988). New Historicist essays, especially on connections between political and aesthetic matters, statecraft and stagecraft.

Joseph, B. L. *Shakespeare's Eden: the Commonwealth of England 1558–1629* (1971). An account of the social, political, economic, and cultural life of England.

Kernan, Alvin. *Shakespeare, the King's Playwright: Theater in the Stuart Court 1603–1613* (1995). The social setting and the politics of the court of James I, in relation to *Hamlet, Measure for Measure, Macbeth, King Lear, Antony and Cleopatra, Coriolanus,* and *The Tempest.*

Montrose, Louis. *The Purpose of Playing: Shakespeare and the Cultural Politics of the Elizabethan Theatre* (1996). A poststructuralist view, discussing the professional theater "within the ideological and material frameworks of Elizabethan culture and society," with an extended analysis of *A Midsummer Night's Dream.*

Mullaney, Steven. *The Place of the Stage: License, Play, and Power in Renaissance England* (1988). New Historicist analysis, arguing that popular drama became a cultural institution "only by . . . taking up a place on the margins of society."

Schoenbaum, S. *Shakespeare: The Globe and the World*

(1979). A readable, abundantly illustrated introductory book on the world of the Elizabethans.

Shakespeare's England, 2 vols. (1916). A large collection of scholarly essays on a wide variety of topics, e.g., astrology, costume, gardening, horsemanship, with special attention to Shakespeare's references to these topics.

2. Shakespeare's Life

Andrews, John F., ed. *William Shakespeare: His World, His Work, His Influence,* 3 vols. (1985). See the description above.

Bentley, Gerald E. *Shakespeare: A Biographical Handbook* (1961). The facts about Shakespeare, with virtually no conjecture intermingled.

Chambers, E. K. *William Shakespeare: A Study of Facts and Problems,* 2 vols. (1930). The fullest collection of data.

Fraser, Russell. *Young Shakespeare* (1988). A highly readable account that simultaneously considers Shakespeare's life and Shakespeare's art.

————. *Shakespeare: The Later Years* (1992).

Schoenbaum, S. *Shakespeare's Lives* (1970). A review of the evidence and an examination of many biographies, including those of Baconians and other heretics.

————. *William Shakespeare: A Compact Documentary Life* (1977). An abbreviated version, in a smaller format, of the next title. The compact version reproduces some fifty documents in reduced form. A readable presentation of all that the documents tell us about Shakespeare.

————. *William Shakespeare: A Documentary Life* (1975). A large-format book setting forth the biography with facsimiles of more than two hundred documents, and with transcriptions and commentaries.

3. Shakespeare's Theater

Astington, John H., ed. *The Development of Shakespeare's Theater* (1992). Eight specialized essays on theatrical companies, playing spaces, and performance.

Beckerman, Bernard. *Shakespeare at the Globe, 1599–1609* (1962). On the playhouse and on Elizabethan dramaturgy, acting, and staging.

Bentley, Gerald E. *The Profession of Dramatist in Shakespeare's Time* (1971). An account of the dramatist's status in the Elizabethan period.

———. *The Profession of Player in Shakespeare's Time, 1590–1642* (1984). An account of the status of members of London companies (sharers, hired men, apprentices, managers) and a discussion of conditions when they toured.

Berry, Herbert. *Shakespeare's Playhouses* (1987). Usefully emphasizes how little we know about the construction of Elizabethan theaters.

Brown, John Russell. *Shakespeare's Plays in Performance* (1966). A speculative and practical analysis relevant to all of the plays, but with emphasis on *The Merchant of Venice, Richard II, Hamlet, Romeo and Juliet,* and *Twelfth Night.*

———. *William Shakespeare: Writing for Performance* (1996). A discussion aimed at helping readers to develop theatrically conscious habits of reading.

Chambers, E. K. *The Elizabethan Stage,* 4 vols. (1945). A major reference work on theaters, theatrical companies, and staging at court.

Cook, Ann Jennalie. *The Privileged Playgoers of Shakespeare's London, 1576–1642* (1981). Sees Shakespeare's audience as wealthier, more middle-class, and more intellectual than Harbage (below) does.

Dessen, Alan C. *Elizabethan Drama and the Viewer's Eye* (1977). On how certain scenes may have looked to spectators in an Elizabethan theater.

Gurr, Andrew. *Playgoing in Shakespeare's London* (1987). Something of a middle ground between Cook (above) and Harbage (below).

———. *The Shakespearean Stage, 1579–1642* (2nd ed., 1980). On the acting companies, the actors, the playhouses, the stages, and the audiences.

Harbage, Alfred. *Shakespeare's Audience* (1941). A study of the size and nature of the theatrical public, emphasizing the representativeness of its working class and middle-class audience.

Hodges, C. Walter. *The Globe Restored* (1968). A conjectural restoration, with lucid drawings.

Hosley, Richard. "The Playhouses," in *The Revels History of Drama in English*, vol. 3, general editors Clifford Leech and T. W. Craik (1975). An essay of a hundred pages on the physical aspects of the playhouses.

Howard, Jane E. "Crossdressing, the Theatre, and Gender Struggle in Early Modern England," *Shakespeare Quarterly* 39 (1988): 418–40. Judicious comments on the effects of boys playing female roles.

Orrell, John. *The Human Stage: English Theatre Design, 1567–1640* (1988). Argues that the public, private, and court playhouses are less indebted to popular structures (e.g., innyards and bear-baiting pits) than to banqueting halls and to Renaissance conceptions of Roman amphitheaters.

Slater, Ann Pasternak. *Shakespeare the Director* (1982). An analysis of theatrical effects (e.g., kissing, kneeling) in stage directions and dialogue.

Styan, J. L. *Shakespeare's Stagecraft* (1967). An introduction to Shakespeare's visual and aural stagecraft, with chapters on such topics as acting conventions, stage groupings, and speech.

Thompson, Peter. *Shakespeare's Professional Career* (1992). An examination of patronage and related theatrical conditions.

———. *Shakespeare's Theatre* (1983). A discussion of how plays were staged in Shakespeare's time.

4. Shakespeare on Stage and Screen

Bate, Jonathan, and Russell Jackson, eds. *Shakespeare: An Illustrated Stage History* (1996). Highly readable essays on stage productions from the Renaissance to the present.

Berry, Ralph. *Changing Styles in Shakespeare* (1981). Discusses productions of six plays (*Coriolanus*, *Hamlet*, *Henry V*, *Measure for Measure*, *The Tempest*, and *Twelfth Night*) on the English stage, chiefly 1950–1980.

————. *On Directing Shakespeare: Interviews with Contemporary Directors* (1989). An enlarged edition of a book first published in 1977, this version includes the seven interviews from the early 1970s and adds five interviews conducted in 1988.

Brockbank, Philip, ed. *Players of Shakespeare: Essays in Shakespearean Performance* (1985). Comments by twelve actors, reporting their experiences with roles. See also the entry for Russell Jackson (below).

Bulman, J. C., and H. R. Coursen, eds. *Shakespeare on Television* (1988). An anthology of general and theoretical essays, essays on individual productions, and shorter reviews, with a bibliography and a videography listing cassettes that may be rented.

Coursen, H. P. *Watching Shakespeare on Television* (1993). Analyses not only of TV versions but also of films and videotapes of stage presentations that are shown on television.

Davies, Anthony, and Stanley Wells, eds. *Shakespeare and the Moving Image: The Plays on Film and Television* (1994). General essays (e.g., on the comedies) as well as essays devoted entirely to *Hamlet*, *King Lear*, and *Macbeth*.

Dawson, Anthony B. *Watching Shakespeare: A Playgoer's Guide* (1988). About half of the plays are discussed, chiefly in terms of decisions that actors and directors make in putting the works onto the stage.

Dessen, Alan. *Elizabethan Stage Conventions and Modern Interpretations* (1984). On interpreting conventions such as the representation of light and darkness and stage violence (duels, battles).

Donaldson, Peter. *Shakespearean Films/Shakespearean Directors* (1990). Postmodernist analyses, drawing on Freudianism, Feminism, Deconstruction, and Queer Theory.

Jackson, Russell, and Robert Smallwood, eds. *Players of Shakespeare 2: Further Essays in Shakespearean Performance by Players with the Royal Shakespeare Company* (1988). Fourteen actors discuss their roles in productions between 1982 and 1987.

————. *Players of Shakespeare 3: Further Essays in Shake-

spearean Performance by Players with the Royal Shakespeare Company (1993). Comments by thirteen performers.

Jorgens, Jack. *Shakespeare on Film* (1977). Fairly detailed studies of eighteen films, preceded by an introductory chapter addressing such issues as music, and whether to "open" the play by including scenes of landscape.

Kennedy, Dennis. *Looking at Shakespeare: A Visual History of Twentieth-Century Performance* (1993). Lucid descriptions (with 170 photographs) of European, British, and American performances.

Leiter, Samuel L. *Shakespeare Around the Globe: A Guide to Notable Postwar Revivals* (1986). For each play there are about two pages of introductory comments, then discussions (about five hundred words per production) of ten or so productions, and finally bibliographic references.

McMurty, Jo. *Shakespeare Films in the Classroom* (1994). Useful evaluations of the chief films most likely to be shown in undergraduate courses.

Rothwell, Kenneth, and Annabelle Henkin Melzer. *Shakespeare on Screen: An International Filmography and Videography* (1990). A reference guide to several hundred films and videos produced between 1899 and 1989, including spinoffs such as musicals and dance versions.

Sprague, Arthur Colby. *Shakespeare and the Actors* (1944). Detailed discussions of stage business (gestures, etc.) over the years.

Willis, Susan. *The BBC Shakespeare Plays: Making the Televised Canon* (1991). A history of the series, with interviews and production diaries for some plays.

5. Miscellaneous Reference Works

Abbott, E. A. *A Shakespearean Grammar* (new edition, 1877). An examination of differences between Elizabethan and modern grammar.

Allen, Michael J. B., and Kenneth Muir, eds. *Shakespeare's Plays in Quarto* (1981). One volume containing facsimiles of the plays issued in small format before they were collected in the First Folio of 1623.

Bevington, David. *Shakespeare* (1978). A short guide to hundreds of important writings on the subject.

Blake, Norman. *Shakespeare's Language: An Introduction* (1983). On vocabulary, parts of speech, and word order.

Bullough, Geoffrey. *Narrative and Dramatic Sources of Shakespeare*, 8 vols. (1957–75). A collection of many of the books Shakespeare drew on, with judicious comments.

Campbell, Oscar James, and Edward G. Quinn, eds. *The Reader's Encyclopedia of Shakespeare* (1966). Old, but still the most useful single reference work on Shakespeare.

Cercignani, Fausto. *Shakespeare's Works and Elizabethan Pronunciation* (1981). Considered the best work on the topic, but remains controversial.

Dent, R. W. *Shakespeare's Proverbial Language: An Index* (1981). An index of proverbs, with an introduction concerning a form Shakespeare frequently drew on.

Greg, W. W. *The Shakespeare First Folio* (1955). A detailed yet readable history of the first collection (1623) of Shakespeare's plays.

Harner, James. *The World Shakespeare Bibliography.* See headnote to Suggested References.

Hosley, Richard. *Shakespeare's Holinshed* (1968). Valuable presentation of one of Shakespeare's major sources.

Kökeritz, Helge. *Shakespeare's Names* (1959). A guide to pronouncing some 1,800 names appearing in Shakespeare.

———. *Shakespeare's Pronunciation* (1953). Contains much information about puns and rhymes, but see Cercignani (above).

Muir, Kenneth. *The Sources of Shakespeare's Plays* (1978). An account of Shakespeare's use of his reading. It covers all the plays, in chronological order.

Miriam Joseph, Sister. *Shakespeare's Use of the Arts of Language* (1947). A study of Shakespeare's use of rhetorical devices, reprinted in part as *Rhetoric in Shakespeare's Time* (1962).

The Norton Facsimile: The First Folio of Shakespeare's Plays (1968). A handsome and accurate facsimile of the first collection (1623) of Shakespeare's plays, with a valuable introduction by Charlton Hinman.

Onions, C. T. *A Shakespeare Glossary*, rev. and enlarged by

R. D. Eagleson (1986). Definitions of words (or senses of words) now obsolete.

Partridge, Eric. *Shakespeare's Bawdy*, rev. ed. (1955). Relatively brief dictionary of bawdy words; useful, but see Williams, below.

Shakespeare Quarterly. See headnote to Suggested References.

Shakespeare Survey. See headnote to Suggested References.

Spevack, Marvin. *The Harvard Concordance to Shakespeare* (1973). An index to Shakespeare's words.

Vickers, Brian. *Appropriating Shakespeare: Contemporary Critical Quarrels* (1993). A survey—chiefly hostile—of recent schools of criticism.

Wells, Stanley, ed. *Shakespeare: A Bibliographical Guide* (new edition, 1990). Nineteen chapters (some devoted to single plays, others devoted to groups of related plays) on recent scholarship on the life and all of the works.

Williams, Gordon. *A Dictionary of Sexual Language and Imagery in Shakespearean and Stuart Literature*, 3 vols. (1994). Extended discussions of words and passages; much fuller than Partridge, cited above.

6. Shakespeare's Plays: General Studies

Bamber, Linda. *Comic Women, Tragic Men: A Study of Gender and Genre in Shakespeare* (1982).

Barnet, Sylvan. *A Short Guide to Shakespeare* (1974).

Callaghan, Dympna, Lorraine Helms, and Jyotsna Singh. *The Weyward Sisters: Shakespeare and Feminist Politics* (1994).

Clemen, Wolfgang H. *The Development of Shakespeare's Imagery* (1951).

Cook, Ann Jennalie. *Making a Match: Courtship in Shakespeare and His Society* (1991).

Dollimore, Jonathan, and Alan Sinfield. *Political Shakespeare: New Essays in Cultural Materialism* (1985).

Dusinberre, Juliet. *Shakespeare and the Nature of Women* (1975).

Granville-Barker, Harley. *Prefaces to Shakespeare*, 2 vols. (1946–47; volume 1 contains essays on *Hamlet, King*

Lear, Merchant of Venice, Antony and Cleopatra, and *Cymbeline*; volume 2 contains essays on *Othello, Coriolanus, Julius Caesar, Romeo and Juliet, Love's Labor's Lost*).

———. *More Prefaces to Shakespeare* (1974; essays on *Twelfth Night, A Midsummer Night's Dream, The Winter's Tale, Macbeth*).

Harbage, Alfred. *William Shakespeare: A Reader's Guide* (1963).

Howard, Jean E. *Shakespeare's Art of Orchestration: Stage Technique and Audience Response* (1984).

Jones, Emrys. *Scenic Form in Shakespeare* (1971).

Lenz, Carolyn Ruth Swift, Gayle Greene, and Carol Thomas Neely, eds. *The Woman's Part: Feminist Criticism of Shakespeare* (1980).

Novy, Marianne. *Love's Argument: Gender Relations in Shakespeare* (1984).

Rose, Mark. *Shakespearean Design* (1972).

Scragg, Leah. *Discovering Shakespeare's Meaning* (1994).

———. *Shakespeare's "Mouldy Tales": Recurrent Plot Motifs in Shakespearean Drama* (1992).

Traub, Valerie. *Desire and Anxiety: Circulations of Sexuality in Shakespearean Drama* (1992).

Traversi, D. A. *An Approach to Shakespeare,* 2 vols. (3rd rev. ed, 1968–69).

Vickers, Brian. *The Artistry of Shakespeare's Prose* (1968).

Wells, Stanley. *Shakespeare: A Dramatic Life* (1994).

Wright, George T. *Shakespeare's Metrical Art* (1988).

7. The Comedies

Barber, C. L. *Shakespeare's Festive Comedy* (1959; discusses *Love's Labor's Lost, A Midsummer Night's Dream, The Merchant of Venice, As You Like It, Twelfth Night*).

Barton, Anne. *The Names of Comedy* (1990).

Berry, Ralph. *Shakespeare's Comedy: Explorations in Form* (1972).

Bradbury, Malcolm, and David Palmer, eds. *Shakespearean Comedy* (1972).

Bryant, J. A., Jr. *Shakespeare and the Uses of Comedy* (1986).

Carroll, William. *The Metamorphoses of Shakespearean Comedy* (1985).

Champion, Larry S. *The Evolution of Shakespeare's Comedy* (1970).

Evans, Bertrand. *Shakespeare's Comedies* (1960).

Frye, Northrop. *Shakespearean Comedy and Romance* (1965).

Leggatt, Alexander. *Shakespeare's Comedy of Love* (1974).

Miola, Robert S. *Shakespeare and Classical Comedy: The Influence of Plautus and Terence* (1994).

Nevo, Ruth. *Comic Transformations in Shakespeare* (1980).

Ornstein, Robert. *Shakespeare's Comedies: From Roman Farce to Romantic Mystery* (1986).

Richman, David. *Laughter, Pain, and Wonder: Shakespeare's Comedies and the Audience in the Theater* (1990).

Salingar, Leo. *Shakespeare and the Traditions of Comedy* (1974).

Slights, Camille Wells. *Shakespeare's Comic Commonwealths* (1993).

Waller, Gary, ed. *Shakespeare's Comedies* (1991).

Westlund, Joseph. *Shakespeare's Reparative Comedies: A Psychoanalytic View of the Middle Plays* (1984).

Williamson, Marilyn. *The Patriarchy of Shakespeare's Comedies* (1986).

8. The Romances (*Pericles, Cymbeline, The Winter's Tale, The Tempest, The Two Noble Kinsmen*)

Adams, Robert M. *Shakespeare: The Four Romances* (1989).

Felperin, Howard. *Shakespearean Romance* (1972).

Frye, Northrop. *A Natural Perspective: The Development of Shakespearean Comedy and Romance* (1965).

Mowat, Barbara. *The Dramaturgy of Shakespeare's Romances* (1976).

Warren, Roger. *Staging Shakespeare's Late Plays* (1990).

Young, David. *The Heart's Forest: A Study of Shakespeare's Pastoral Plays* (1972).

9. The Tragedies

Bradley, A. C. *Shakespearean Tragedy* (1904).

Brooke, Nicholas. *Shakespeare's Early Tragedies* (1968).

Champion, Larry. *Shakespeare's Tragic Perspective* (1976).

Drakakis, John, ed. *Shakespearean Tragedy* (1992).

Evans, Bertrand. *Shakespeare's Tragic Practice* (1979).

Everett, Barbara. *Young Hamlet: Essays on Shakespeare's Tragedies* (1989).

Foakes, R. A. *Hamlet versus Lear: Cultural Politics and Shakespeare's Art* (1993).

Frye, Northrop. *Fools of Time: Studies in Shakespearean Tragedy* (1967).

Harbage, Alfred, ed. *Shakespeare: The Tragedies* (1964).

Mack, Maynard. *Everybody's Shakespeare: Reflections Chiefly on the Tragedies* (1993).

McAlindon, T. *Shakespeare's Tragic Cosmos* (1991).

Miola, Robert S. *Shakespeare and Classical Tragedy: The Influence of Seneca* (1992).

———. *Shakespeare's Rome* (1983).

Nevo, Ruth. *Tragic Form in Shakespeare* (1972).

Rackin, Phyllis. *Shakespeare's Tragedies* (1978).

Rose, Mark, ed. *Shakespeare's Early Tragedies: A Collection of Critical Essays* (1995).

Rosen, William. *Shakespeare and the Craft of Tragedy* (1960).

Snyder, Susan. *The Comic Matrix of Shakespeare's Tragedies* (1979).

Wofford, Susanne. *Shakespeare's Late Tragedies: A Collection of Critical Essays* (1996).

Young, David. *The Action to the Word: Structure and Style in Shakespearean Tragedy* (1990).

———. *Shakespeare's Middle Tragedies: A Collection of Critical Essays* (1993).

10. The Histories

Blanpied, John W. *Time and the Artist in Shakespeare's English Histories* (1983).

Campbell, Lily B. *Shakespeare's "Histories": Mirrors of Elizabethan Policy* (1947).

Champion, Larry S. *Perspective in Shakespeare's English Histories* (1980).

Hodgdon, Barbara. *The End Crowns All: Closure and Contradiction in Shakespeare's History* (1991).

Holderness, Graham. *Shakespeare Recycled: The Making of Historical Drama* (1992).

——, ed. *Shakespeare's History Plays: "Richard II" to "Henry V"* (1992).

Leggatt, Alexander. *Shakespeare's Political Drama: The History Plays and the Roman Plays* (1988).

Ornstein, Robert. *A Kingdom for a Stage: The Achievement of Shakespeare's History Plays* (1972).

Rackin, Phyllis. *Stages of History: Shakespeare's English Chronicles* (1990).

Saccio, Peter. *Shakespeare's English Kings: History, Chronicle, and Drama* (1977).

Tillyard, E. M. W. *Shakespeare's History Plays* (1944).

Velz, John W., ed. *Shakespeare's English Histories: A Quest for Form and Genre* (1996).

11. *Macbeth*

In addition to the items listed in Section 9, The Tragedies, and the items concerning stage productions listed in Section 4 above, consult the following:

Adelman, Janet. *Suffocating Mothers: Fantasies of Maternal Origin in Shakespeare's Plays, "Hamlet" to "The Tempest"* (1992).

Berger, Harry. "The Text Against Performance in Shakespeare: The Example of *Macbeth*." *The Power of Forms in the English Renaissance.* Ed. Stephen Greenblatt (1982), pp. 49–79.

Bradley, A. C. *Shakespearean Tragedy* (1904). Part of the material is reprinted above.

Braunmuller, A. R., ed. *Macbeth* (2008).

Brown, John Russell, ed. *Focus on "Macbeth"* (1982).

Drakakis, John, and Dale Townshend. *Macbeth: A Critical Reader* (2013).

Kahn, Coppélia. *Man's Estate: Masculine Identity in Shakespeare* (1981).

Kimbrough, Robert. "Macbeth: The Prisoner of Gender." *Shakespeare Studies* 16 (1983): 175–90.

Kliman, Bernice W., ed. *Shakespeare in Performance: "Macbeth."* (1995).

Leggatt, Alexander, ed. *William Shakespeare's "Macbeth": A Sourcebook* (2006).

Long, Michael. *Macbeth* (1989).

Mack, Maynard. "The Jacobean Shakespeare: Some Observations on the Construction of the Tragedies." *Stratford-upon-Avon Studies 1: Jacobean Theatre* (1960); reprinted in the Signet Classics edition of *Othello.*

Marson, Janyce, ed. *Macbeth* (2008) [critical essays].

Miola, Robert S., ed. *Macbeth: Authoritative Text, Sources and Contexts, Criticism* (2004).

Muir, Kenneth, ed. *Shakespeare Survey* 19 (1966).

Orgel, Stephen. "Macbeth and the Antic Round," *Shakespeare Survey* 52 (1999): 143–53.

Shakespeare Survey 57 (2004).

Sinfield, Alan. *Faultlines: Cultural Materialism and the Politics of Dissident Reading* (1992); part of the chapter on *Macbeth* is reprinted above.

——, ed. *Macbeth* (1992; twelve recent essays).

Tredell, Nicolas. *Shakespeare's "Macbeth": A Reader's Guide to Essential Criticism* (2006).

Turner, John. *Macbeth* (1992).

Walker, Roy. *The Time Is Free* (1949).

Wheeler, Thomas. *"Macbeth": An Annotated Bibliography* (1990).